In *Better Than We Dreamed*,  on a global journey from Chicago in ы and the warring Middle East, then nerica and finally Russia during the (weaves together lively narrative with Elaine's own thoughts and writings.

There is a cost to missions, and Elaine came face to face with that. She had to marry her love for the people with the risk factor. All along the way, God matured her heart and grew her vision, orchestrating every aspect of her life to coalesce perfectly for His purposes.

RICK DENHAM
President of Ministério Fiel (Brazil), International Director of 9Marks, and International Liaison for Desiring God

Open Simona Gorton's debut biography at your own risk. You won't put it down. Prepare to be caught up in a fascinating journey, inspired by sacrificial service, warmly encouraged by the zealous devotion of a loving helper, delightfully absorbed in the epic life of Elaine Townsend. Gorton's comprehensive work will thrill you with the power of the Word of God, in the language of the people, to transform hearts and lives with the gospel of Jesus Christ throughout the world.

DOUGLAS BOND
Author, leader of Church history tours, and director of the Oxford Creative Writing Master Class

Those familiar with the work of global mission know what a remarkable man Cameron Townsend was, and the remarkable impact he made resulting in the world wide work of Wycliffe Bible Translators. But behind every remarkable man…! Elaine Townsend certainly was a remarkable woman. Her exceptional gifts were evident early in life and those gifts were unreservedly committed to the glory of God for the whole of her life. This is important mission history, but it is far more than that. Every reader will be challenged to fresh steps of faith and commitment.

PETER MAIDEN
International Director Emeritus, Operation Mobilisation

It's easy for those of us in the Bible translation movement to credit William Cameron Townsend, but I am reminded frequently of the contributions and sacrifices of his faithful wife, Elaine. In *Better Than We Dreamed* Simona Gorton rightly places Elaine Townsend among the pantheon of women who stand as heroes. This moving biography chronicles the life of one of the most impactful figures in modern missions and challenges readers to be like her: eager to see God's Word spread, faithful in pursuing the work, and humble before the sovereign God who accomplished it.

Bob Creson
President and CEO, Wycliffe Bible Translators USA

There are far too many untold stories of the godly women who serve alongside of their husbands. This book offers a corrective. Here we have the story of Elaine Townsend, the woman behind the man behind Wycliffe Bible Translators. This delightfully written and meticulously researched narrative traces her footsteps around the globe, recalling her life of devotion to Cameron and her indefatigable zeal in proclaiming the mission of God to the world. May her earnestness and joy be an encouragement to all.

Stephen J. Nichols
President, Reformation Bible College,
Chief Academic Officer, Ligonier Ministries

This is the wonderful story of a woman who, together with her husband, was determined to fulfill the will of God for her life. In one poignant episode, at a time in life when they should have been considering a well-deserved retirement, her husband Cameron sensed the Lord leading them to the USSR at the height of the Cold War. Elaine's response was 'if that's what God wants you to do, that's what I want to do too'. A life of obedience to God that is a challenge to us all.

Neil Wardrope
CLC International

To read this story of Elaine Townsend is to step into the stream of a life lived on the move. Elaine's life determination and grit are evident throughout.

Sue and I had the pleasure of knowing Elaine while working closely with her the last decades of her life. On an almost daily basis we would encounter and be instructed through her thinking and her prayers. Elaine was always referencing the global viewpoint, the bigger picture. While not perfect, she was a Christ follower constantly learning through questions and applying Scriptural teaching to her personal journey with the Lord.

We count it a special privilege to have worked in with her in Kingdom building endeavors. We commend this book to the next generation to take hold of the promises of God as Elaine so plainly did.

JIM AND SUE AKOVENKO
Jim is VP of Mission Culture and Community for the Seed Company;
former president/CEO of JAARS, Inc., missionary to Indonesia,
and SIL Eastern Regional Director

Mary and I and our little boys arrived in Mexico in 1978 as missionaries. Our first missionary adventures and challenges began in the State of Oaxaca where we encountered 19 pure languages and over 50 dialects—and dozens and dozens of Wycliffe Bible translators attempting the humanly impossible task of translating the Bible into each of those tongues. After 40 years on the mission field I have never ceased to marvel at the dedication, brilliance, creativity, and sacrifice of the Wycliffe family of translators.

I highly recommend the story of Elaine Townsend's life. When one thinks of Wycliffe's story, one immediately associates it with Cameron Townsend. But as one reads *Better Than We Dreamed*, it is evident that without Elaine serving and sacrificing side by side with her husband, Wycliffe would not be what it is today. Tens and tens of thousands will one day—on that Great Day—rise up and call her blessed.

ELLIOTT TEPPER
WEC Missionary,
International Director of Betel International

Elaine Townsend, wife of the founder of Wycliffe Bible Translators, lived an eventful and inspiring life in service to her Lord and ours. Simona Gorton's biography captures her unique personality and her love for the Savior in a delightful way. While this book will be an encouragement for women, young and old alike, men would be wise to read it as well.

KEITH MATHISON
Professor of Systematic Theology, Reformation Bible College

BETTER
THAN WE DREAMED

THE STORY OF ELAINE TOWNSEND
AND THE FAITHFULNESS OF A GOD
WHO COLORED OUTSIDE ALL HER LINES.

SIMONA GORTON

Scripture quotations, unless otherwise indicated, are from *The Holy Bible, English Standard Version*, copyright © 2001 by Crossway Bibles, a publishing ministry of Good News Publishers. Used by permission. All rights reserved. ESV Text Edition: 2011.

Scripture quotations marked TLB are taken from *The Living Bible*, Kenneth N. Taylor, Wheaton: Tyndale House, 1997, © 1971 by Tyndale House Publishers, Inc. Used by permission. All rights reserved.

Copyright © Simona Gorton 2018

paperback ISBN 978-1-5271-0266-8
epub ISBN 978-1-5271-0315-3
mobi ISBN 978-1-5271-0316-0

Published in 2018
by
Christian Focus Publications Ltd,
Geanies House, Fearn,
Ross-shire, IV20 1TW, Scotland.
www.christianfocus.com

Cover design by MOOSE77

Printed by Bell and Bain, Glasgow.

CONTENTS

PREFACE   9

TIMELINE   12

SEASON 1

1. A PLACE IN TIME   17

2. HERALD OF THINGS TO COME   29

3. EASTERN SUNRISE, WESTERN GLORY   37

4. 'MOST PROMISING YOUNG PROTESTANT'   45

5. CHARTING PATTERNS OF THE HEART   53

6. CLAIMING A PATH   61

7. A LESSENING   71

8. 'BEST JOB IN THE OUTFIT!'   77

9. SPURRING ON AND POINTING UPWARD   85

SEASON 2

10. 'STRENGTHENING THE TROOPS'   97

11. AN UNEXPECTED DEVELOPMENT   107

12. CHANGE AND THE ART OF LEARNING   115

13. 'THE UNFOLDING OF YOUR WORD GIVES LIGHT'   123

14. PITCHING CAMP   131

15. SHINING FORTH THE GOSPEL   139

16. ALWAYS ADVENTURE   149

17. JOY IN THE JOURNEY   159

18. OPENING THE CASTLE DOORS   167

19. A CHART FOR THEIR PILGRIMAGE   179

20. FAMILY AS GOSPEL APOLOGETIC   187

21. A WOMAN OF ONE THING   197

22. 'SHE BROUGHT MAKEUP TO THE JUNGLE'   205

SEASON 3

23. THE RUSSIAN FRONTIER   209

24. 'REJOICE WITH US!'   219

25. THE GOD WHO ACTS   231

26. AND YET HE LEADS ON   239

27. JUST AS HE PROMISED   249

SEASON 4

28. WOUNDS OF LOVE   257

29. CONTINUING PURSUIT   263

30. 'SUCH AN INTERESTING PERSON!'   267

31. 'NOT JUST SOMEHOW, BUT TRIUMPHANTLY'   275

32. 'A GRAND RECRUITER AND A GRAND FRIEND'   283

33. GLIMPSES OF THE PORT   291

34. AFTER THE LAST MISSION   295

BIBLIOGRAPHY   299

PREFACE

As I climbed into the astonishing life of Elaine Townsend, I found myself captivated by the picture of a woman whose insatiable craving for God, delight in people, and vivacity of life challenged all modern notions of stodgy missionary women. Elaine herself would have been glad of this.

***

How was it possible that an accomplished teacher and social star of a Chicagoan could relocate to South America, braving the jungle wilds and making a home complete with chocolate fudge? Her story is one of lively grace overflowing a cup that spilled down the sides, drenched a life, a home, and seeped its way into hundreds of lives along the way. To enter her story is to be drawn into the drama of events that transpire when a Christ-follower trusts her faithful God.

The tale of Elaine's life is not without its twists and turns, yet in every area of surrender and loss, God brought increase. The day she understood unconditional grace, her world was rocked, and this encounter reoriented her life, beginning the process of redesign. Her fears proved unfounded as she spent a lifetime discovering the rich love of a God who had captured her affections.

Elaine Townsend was a remarkably gifted woman, but the more I came to know her, the more I realized that the point was not as much the talents she brought to the table, but the fact that God instilled in her the gifts to accomplish His purposes for her life. As Oswald Chambers so ably put it, 'The idea is not that we do work for God, but that we are so loyal to Him that He can do His work through us.'[1] Far from lessening motivation, this opened up a more earnest desire in Elaine to give, to do, and to pour out for the glory of the One whom she loved.

***

The opportunity to capture the memory of all this living was quite unexpected, and it held its own share of adventuring in Peruvian jungle, wading through thousands of airmail letters, interviewing former friends and missionaries across the States and internationally, and forming relationships with her remaining family. 'I can almost hear her say, "Go ahead, capture my life in words—I dare you!"' someone said to me during an interview, '—and then comes that wonderful laugh.'

Many, many stories will remain untold for lack of space, and this book represents but one life among many of those who learned to buy groceries in a different language, make a home of nothing, and counted all as loss for the surpassing worth of knowing Christ. In searching out men and women of the faith, we ourselves become liable to captivation by the same devotion, the same single-hearted pursuit of God, and the same willingness to follow where He leads, regardless of risk or mundanity. One prominent international apologist for the Christian faith wrote this of his early life:

> As I read about these inspiring lives, the old adage became true for me: 'Fire begets fire.' The standards these Christians set by their examples raised the bar for me. Though I later learned, as I grew in my faith, that these saintly lives weren't as perfect as their biographers made them out to be, the basic truths were undoubtedly in place, and their examples stoked my consciousness as to what the Christian life could be.[2]

It has been my object to bring alive the days and years of Elaine Townsend for a new generation of women, some of whom may live overseas, many of whom will be married or preparing as young women

---

1   Oswald Chambers, *My Utmost for His Highest*, (Uhrichsville, Ohio: Barbour Publishing, 1963) Dec. 18.

2   Ravi Zacharias, *Walking from East to West*, (Grand Rapids, Michigan: Zondervan, 2010), p. 117.

for the rest of their lives, but all of whom serve the same King and run the same race.

I pray that you, as a reader, will feel Elaine's eagerness for the Word, her earnestness of mission, her excitement in the everyday things of life, and that you will be encouraged toward faithfulness and joy in the rhythm of your own calling.

Therefore, my beloved brothers,
be steadfast, immovable, always abounding in the work of the Lord,
knowing that in the Lord your labor is not in vain.[3]

Simona Gorton,
São José dos Campos, Brazil
December 3, 2016

Author Note: This book has been organized by the 'seasons' of Elaine's life and calling: early life and preparation (focus on Chicago and Mexico); married life and mission (focus on Peru and Colombia); travels and later ministry with an aging Cameron (focus on Russia); and further adventuring and missions of an aging Elaine (focus on North Carolina). There exists, as Aimee Byrd put it, a 'beauty of belonging to the right hour or season, as well as fulfilling our proper role in creation…'[4]

Learning contentment and growing through the flow of these seasons is a lifelong pursuit, and Elaine succeeded in some aspects more than others, as any fallen woman. God ever multiplied her loaves and fishes and provided the strength and grace necessary for the joys and sacrifices unique to each.

In examining the resources at my disposal, I realized a broad sequence allowed a greater liberty to write more thematically within the chapters themselves and made the most sense of each individual component of such a colorful story. For reference, I have included a timeline to give a clearer picture of the sequence of events.

---

3   I Corinthians 15:58.

4   Aimee Byrd, *Housewife Theologian* (Phillipsburg, New Jersey: P&R Publishing, 2013) p. 42.

TIMELINE

- **1915 November 6:** Elaine Mielke is Born
- *(1918 Nov. 11: End of WWI)*
- **1919-1932:** School
- *(Oct. 1929-1940s: Great Depression)*
- *(1933 Jan 30: Hitler becomes chancellor of Germany)*
- **1934-1937:** Teacher's College
- **1936 June 19 to Sept. 3:** Trip Around the World (20 yrs)
- **1936:** Conversion
- **May 1936:** Single women allowed at Summer Institute of Linguistics (SIL)
- **1937+:** Spanish lessons, Mexican ministry, and further classes for disabled
- **1938-1942:** Night classes at Moody Bible Institute
- **1939-1942:** Teacher
- *(1939 Sept. 1: WWII begins with Germany's invasion of Poland)*
- *(1941 Dec.: Pearl Harbor)*
- **1941 October:** Cam issues a call to SIL colleagues to pray for fifty new workers in the coming year, doubling ranks
- **1942:** SIL Summer/Elaine joins Wycliffe

- **1942-1943:** Supervisor (26 yrs)
- **June 1943:** Mexico
- **1943-1944:** Teaching Todd Children in Tetelcingo
- **1944-1946:** Literacy Campaigns
- **Summer 1945:** Work helping make primers and teach teachers in Norman
- **Summer 1945:** Visiting family in Chicago + Cam asks for her hand
- *(1945 May 7: Germany Surrenders)*
- *(1945 August 14: Japan Surrenders)*
- **1945 October 6:** Cam and Elaine become engaged
- **1946 April 4:** Marriage (30 yrs)
- **1946-1963 April 20:** Peru
- **1946 Aug 27- Sept. 3:** Literacy Campaigns high in the Andes
- **1946 December 27:** Grace born in Lima
- **1947 February 25:** Plane Crash
- **1948 May 5:** Joy born in Mexico
- **1949 July:** Move into the tent house
- **1949 December 28:** Elainadel born in Yarinacocha
- **1952:** Home completed on the base
- **1953 January 20:** Billy born
- *(1956 Jan. 8: Five men killed in Ecuador)*
- **1963:** Shirley's death
- **1963-1969:** Colombia
- **1970-2007:** Waxhaw

- **October 1968, '69, '72, '72, '73, '73, '74, '75, '77, '78, '79:** Trips to Russia

- **1971:** Cam resigns from Wycliffe Bible Translation

- *(1974 Aug. 9: Nixon Resigns)*

- **Summer 1975:** Elaine goes to Vermont for 9-week Russian study

- **1982 April 23:** Cameron's death

- **2000:** Trip to Russia (85 yrs)

- **2005:** Attended first Bible dedication (90 yrs)

- **2007 July 14:** Death (91 yrs)

SEASON 1

1. A PLACE IN TIME

It seemed like a fairy tale of dreams suddenly dropped down to earth—
yet with a curious sense that it was no dream but a wonderful bit of
God's unfoldings… Such visions come of what God might make of
it [and] the only answer I get when I ask Him what it means is 'He
Himself knew what He would do.'

Lilias Trotter[1]

The afternoon stretched sultry as humid Chicago heat blended with
the colorful conversation carried on by the city. In one house among a
row, a little girl lay on her stomach on the wood floor, kicking a door
back and forth between her feet and reading a book. As soon as she
discovered the end of the story, she laid the book down and sat up.

Outside the screened doorway she could hear the metallic clatter
and grate of her father's printing machine—a background noise never
absent. Upstairs, footsteps meandered their way across the floor, and
voices could be heard. In short, everyone was busy. Time for leisure
did not regularly appear, but she was not about to let it go easily when
it did.

She stood up and walked to the next room where Daniel and Shirley
were playing. Or had been. Shirley now lay fast asleep on the floor,
and Daniel hastened to present the appearance of tidying the room as
he heard footsteps approaching. At the sight of his sister, all activity
ceased, and he sat back on his heels as she entered.

'What's up?' she whispered, so as not to wake Shirley.

---

1   Quoted by Miriam Rockness, *A Passion for the Impossible* (Grand Rapids, Michi-
     gan: Discovery House Publishers, 2003), p. 199.

He shrugged.

Elaine picked up one of Shirley's books and began to flip through it, then threw it down and crossed her arms, heaved a sigh, and turned on her back. A second later she sat up. 'Dan, how'd you like to make some money?'

'You *know* the teacher says not to say words like that!' he retorted impudently.

She rolled her eyes and turned on her back again, but kept watching him.

Curiosity won out, and Dan whispered back, 'Fine.'

Elaine had turned this idea over in her head for a good while, and now seemed the perfect time: no one to prevent the adventure, and Daniel old enough at last to be of use.

She darted out the door, followed by her brother and a frustrated 'What are you *doing*?'

At the front door she paused a second to listen and to consider if shoes were necessary to this expedition. The sidewalk was hot. She grabbed her own shoes—nodding at Daniel to do the same—and hopped around a bit while they took their time fitting on.

Finally they both stumbled through the door together, but then she remembered something. 'Stay here. And don't make one single noise,' she warned the cohort.

Racing back up the steps, she cracked the door, listened, then slipped inside. When she reappeared she handed a pewter cup to Dan and kept another for herself.

After silencing him yet again, she raced down the street. At the corner of the first intersection they slowed to a meander as both began to relish the novelty of going out on their own. For this was Chicago in all her bustle and glory—a queen among cities, epicenter of transpiring history.

A short while later, they reached a main intersection which Elaine judged would suit their purpose. 'Now,' she explained to Dan, 'try to look pathetic. Hold your cup out here. And don't let on that you had any breakfast today. Or lunch. If you co-operate we'll be able to get an ice cream afterwards!'

Turning away from her companion, she faced the streams of people flowing all around them, and began to recite an inspirational poem:

> I'm a poor little beggar girl
> My mother she is dead
> My father is a drunkard
> And won't give me no bread.
> I look out of the window
> To hear the organ play.
> God bless my dear mother,
> She gone far away.
> Ding-dong the castle bells…

After this first recital, Elaine slumped slowly down a light post and turned a sly face to her companion, mostly to check the state of his charade. He couldn't help himself, and winked.

The next recitation met with a fresh audience, since the crowds never slowed or stopped except to wait for a passing car. The coins began to pour in and before long, a bakery shop donated some bread. The encouragement provided for this act was substantial indeed, and neither child felt any urge to repent of their skill or sagacity. Until a neighbor happened to spot the pair and inquired of their mother, Lillie, if she knew the whereabouts of her children.

A CHICAGOAN SPEECH-MAKER

Elaine was the child of a German printer, the three-car garage behind their home housed the shop, with three presses each as big as a good-sized room. Paper salesmen and customers filled up the days, then after supper Lillie helped her husband run the Gordon hand-fed press till around midnight. In their lifetime, they produced more than three million gospel tracts.

Herman's aging mother, sister, and brother all lived with them, and his father also shortly before his death. Although the house was already full, it seems that Lillie, Herman's Norwegian wife, kept an open house and visitors were frequent. Epilepsy kept his brother from working, and many mouths stretched the money thin. One winter, Elaine wrote, 'we

Lillie Mielke with her daughters, Elaine (left) and Millie (circa 1918).

couldn't afford a warm winter coat for me [and] I had to wear grand-dad's heavy, military-looking coat to school. I was mortified. People weren't prompt in paying printing bills, which didn't help.'

One can only imagine the daily headlines shouting from Chicago's newspapers. Born into Al Capone's Chicago with the Roaring Twenties just around the corner and the Prohibition and the Women's Rights movements in full swing, Elaine walked in history-making footsteps all her life. Five days after her third birthday, Germany signed the armistice, ending the First World War.

'I think the very first thing I can remember is Dad pulling us all some two miles to Grace Church on the sled. I guess the cars weren't about to make it,' Elaine wrote to her mother once, years later. 'I can see you in the back of the sled with Milly and myself all bundled up good. Of course the bells on the sled and Dad's cheery singing added to the fun'. One winter 'the snow was so high it almost covered the car. People in Chicago were usually more friendly in a snow storm.'

Elaine's mother, like most mothers before and after her, recalled that 'she was the most beautiful baby I'd ever seen. She was so cuddly.' At two years old Elaine differed greatly from her older sister, Mildred. She loved music and as a toddler would quiet everyone around with a finger to her lips and make them listen. She also had a wild streak which showed itself increasingly as she grew. When she became angry, she heatedly declared 'I love the Tizer, I love the Tizer' (meaning Kaiser) as fast as she could.

Life with a large family became problematic around Christmastime, but Elaine started saving early in the year to buy each a gift. When the family's bank, just two blocks away, offered their customers a special Christmas savings account, eleven-year-old Elaine marched over and took advantage. That way, all those coins would have less chance of turning into ice-cream cones instead of presents. Every Saturday from that day till Christmas, she made a deposit of twenty-five cents, which she calculated should turn into thirteen whole dollars.

Walking home one day in January, she caught sight of an ad. in the window. In celebration of George Washington's birthday, the bank sponsored a contest for the person who could make the most words out of the letters in his name. For the next two weeks the family crowded around the dining room table on cold winter evenings, each with a dictionary, helping Elaine's list of words to grow. On February 22nd, Elaine proudly took her list of over 1,300 words to the bank and, unsurprisingly, was awarded ten dollars, which she promptly deposited into her Christmas savings account.

Elaine later wrote to her mother describing her impressions of early home life: 'The Lord certainly had a choice sweetheart prepared for Dad when he found you. What a team you have been down thru the years... I must mention... your untiring labor of love on behalf of getting the Word out in tract form. I know this has brought great joy to your heart and only eternity will reveal the blessing it has been to hundreds.' Herman gave away a large portion of the tracts he produced, and looking back, Elaine realized the sacrifice her parents made to provide piano and elocution lessons for their children. 'Rarely did they allow themselves any luxuries…'

The elocution teacher lived across the street, and took particular interest in her pupils. Around the time lessons began, Elaine was appointed to recite a short poem at the Ladies' Aide meeting, which ran sentimentally thus:

> Flowers on my shoulders,
> Slippers on my feet,
> I'm my mother's little darling,
> Don't you think I'm sweet?

Presumably, Mrs. Mielke intended this performance to display her daughter's progress and to bless all those in attendance, but neither aim was accomplished when Elaine stood up and brazenly recited:

> Ink, pink, penny wink,
> Oh how you do stink!

—pointing to the lovely wife of Pastor Schweitzer. At that moment, Lillie 'died a thousand deaths in Grace Church.'

Impertinence aside, Elaine excelled in these lessons, and this early training became especially significant years down the road. Before literacy training camps, radio broadcasts, meetings, and public speeches, early preparation enabled her, at twenty-one, to enter 157 churches with a remarkable presentation.

SIBLINGS AND SHENANIGANS

Elaine's childhood also featured a remarkable saga of sicknesses. At two weeks old she had a head cold, and a stomach sickness at nine months. She sprained her wrist three times before she was three, when she caught an influenza which affected her lungs, and scarlet fever which quarantined her for five weeks. Other episodes included a cracked elbow, measles, chicken pox twice, and falling down the stairs in her chair. Her father, a great lover of flowers, left a vase on her tray whenever she was sick.

Despite the prankster in her, Elaine later denied that she had ever pretended sickness as an excuse to miss school, which she loved from a young age. 'She once brought thirty-one children and two kindergarten teachers home to see the family's first baby chicks,' her mother wrote. She returned from another day at kindergarten and informed her mother that she was 'teacher's pet.' When asked how she knew, she replied, 'I asked her if I wasn't.' P.E. remained her least favorite subject through high school; she hated to change clothes, and was built rather heavily. This battle with weight ran in the family and Elaine never quite recovered from the self-consciousness it engendered.

From their youngest years, a sort of rivalry existed between the two oldest Mielke girls. Two years older than Elaine, Milly took naturally to most things while Elaine, in the words of Lillie, 'had to work hard for every accomplishment in life.' Her father's observation that 'the person with no nerve is kicked around—the person with nerve is admired and respected for having a back bone,' likely played a part in this habit, and she graduated from junior high at the head of her class.

No such competition existed between Elaine and Shirley, who was five years younger. The relationship between these two flourished, particularly after their individual encounters with Christ. Ten years after Elaine came Daniel (Bud). Mimicking her mother, Elaine put a beach ball under her shirt, paraded around the neighborhood, and proudly told everyone she too was pregnant—again, to her mother's consternation.

This propensity for larks was not original to Elaine, however, for Herman was 'a great tease,' and continually played jokes at the yearly church summer camp like slipping someone a rubber hot dog or cutting a hole in the bottom of a cup. Elaine soon refined skills such as tying boys' shoelaces together or rearranging their ties.

Once, after falling and breaking her arm, she intelligently remarked to her father, 'Don't spank me dad, for I just broke my arm; I minded you, I did not go down the hill on the tricycle but went down in a wagon—and if you do have to spank me for not minding you, please do not spank me on my arm.' In grade school, she spent an entire recess period trying on all the other girls' hats. 'I never did know which one was to blame for that awful kerosene treatment I endured to get rid of the lice.'

As a teenager, Elaine was pushing Shirley through the park on her wheelchair when she decided she had pushed enough and deserved a rest. So Shirley, somewhat able to walk at that point, began to push Elaine. Right then, a group of young men came along and a distraught Elaine implored Shirley to trade back. Nothing doing. Shirley walked right on, pushing her 'invalid' sister as the boys walked by.

Shirley's disability had resulted when she was seven, a terrible blow to hit the Mielke family. Shirley squirmed on the doctor's table while receiving a diphtheria vaccine, causing the needle to hit her spine, and a crippling arthritis began which slowly made its way through her body and nearly incapacitated her by the end of her shortened life. While symptoms evolved, the first months were doubtless bewildering and all-consuming to Elaine's already overworked parents. That year, Elaine, her mother, Milly, and Daniel enjoyed their annual retreat at Moody's Cedar Lake Campgrounds while Elaine's father stayed home in muggy Chicago, working long hours and caring for their newly-afflicted daughter who screamed in terror at the thought of attempting the stairs to her bedroom.

Herman revealed wistful dreams in his letters, 'Don't you wish we could sell our home and move to a place where we had lots of room and where we were near the woods and the river—and had pretty birds and squirrels—in a place where Shirley could go outside and play without getting run over by automobiles? Another day daddy is going to buy a home in the country with a big yard.'

But in seven years he would face another terrible reality. 'One time a check came in from a company for $600 which dad immediately took to our local bank. The next day the bank went under.' The year was 1929. Larger cities took the hardest hits in this national crisis. Conveniences grew scarce, and the activities of life were reduced to necessity.

The experience of these times formed habits that stayed with Elaine for the rest of her life. 'Although our family didn't have much of this earth's goods,' she wrote, 'they did have a strong faith in God.' Her

From left to right: Millie, Shirley and Elaine (circa 1924).

father once wrote to them at the yearly summer camp, 'I guess you will agree with me that every invention such as wall paper, rugs, autos, pianos, family furniture, although a blessing in life, yet I say they all occupy one's time and thoughts so much that people have no time to think of Jesus. This entire life is spent cleaning and polishing.'

TEACHING IN THE BLOOD

Lillie oversaw the four and five-year-olds' Sunday school at their church, and Elaine wrote later, 'Just to be near mother and be blessed by the way she made the Bible come alive with her special gift for storytelling was indeed something to be looked forward to.'

It was perhaps here that Elaine's lifelong affection for children and her passion for teaching found its beginnings as she saw her mother widen the eyes and brighten the cheeks of a class all circled up on the floor for her retelling of God's tale. Later, as a mother and a teacher, Elaine became known for her own creative ability to engage both children and Indians.

One particular boy demonstrated a preternatural ability to assess the lessons Lillie told. After relaying the story of Satan's temptation of Adam and Eve, Lillie closed by explaining how God drove them out of the garden because of their disobedience. All the children dispersed to their little tables to illustrate the story they had just heard. 'When it came David's turn to hold up his picture we were all amazed to see a crude car, with a man at the steering wheel and a man and lady in the back seat. He went on to explain that this was Jesus driving Adam and Eve out of the garden. We smothered our laughter until the boys and girls had sung their closing song. When the last little one had been clothed again in her winter things and waved goodbye, we had a good laugh and mother decided she would have to illustrate that story a little clearer next time.'

Lillie always dreamed of teaching, but as that goal faded due to tight finances, she did everything in her power to help her daughters fulfill that dream. Well-paying jobs were scarce during the depression, but teachers were always in demand. After graduating from high school, Elaine applied to the Chicago Normal College (now Chicago State

University) on the South Side, where Milly was in her third year. She passed the written exam easily, but the oral exam was a different story. Instead of the usual three-teacher examination, a certain Miss Jacobs appeared and asked one simple question: 'Are you Mildred Mielke's sister?' A few days later she received word that she had failed the oral exam, but several years passed before she understood why.

In 1933, the only job she could find was at a dime store a mile from home: the Five and Ten. The wage, fair for that time, was twelve dollars for sixty hours per week. After President Roosevelt intervened, it became fifteen dollars for forty-eight hours, ten of which went to the mortgage payment.

Here, one of Elaine's noted characteristics became evident: 'Of course I thought I had to be up-to-date and work in the three-inch heels that were all the vogue. Whenever we had a break we sales girls would go downstairs to the lounge and exchange shoes to get some relief.'

Without the technology available today, salesgirls presented a shop's most effective defense against theft. Elaine remembered pursuing at least one shoplifter, although she failed to catch her. More success was had with young boys, due entirely to the inspiration of the manager. 'Once caught with the goods, Mr. Pence would take them downstairs where the big furnace was located. After giving the lad a proper scolding he would start up the big furnace, which made a very scary noise. Then he would offer the boy a choice. He could either be thrown into the furnace or promise to go with Miss Mielke to Sunday school.' In this way, many a boy found himself forgoing a shiny pocketknife to escape the terrors of the flannel graph and the beautiful, but merciless Miss Mielke.

After two years, Elaine took the oral exam again and passed with flying colors—she had made the highest grade. For the next three years, Elaine rode the 'L'[1] an hour and a half to the Teacher's College, where she eventually became president of the student council. During her last year, Mr. Branom, the Social Science professor, called her aside and relayed the backstory to her first oral exam. Miss Jacobs was also

---

1   Chicago's elevated train.

the head of the drama club, it turned out, where Milly was a star. She always assigned Milly the part of the villain, for which she was particularly suited, but when Milly tired of it and put her foot down, Miss Jacobs became irate. When Elaine came along for her orals, she saw it as the perfect opportunity to get even with her sister.

BUILDING MERITS

As a young adult, Elaine increasingly involved herself in the activities of Grace Evangelical Church. In addition to playing the piano and teaching a Sunday school class, she helped with summer camps, midweek programs, Ladies' Aide meetings, church socials, and other events. She attended services every Sunday morning without fail, then returned at six in the evening for a young people's group, and the evening service that followed. Eventually, she was elected president of Christian Endeavor and spoke at meetings. Along with a handful of girls she sang on a Christian radio station and toured other churches.

'I read my Bible through every year because I was working for points; you know I wanted to get to heaven so badly,' she wrote later. '… we had our campground out in Naperville… and every year when the grounds opened and the evangelist came and gave an invitation, I was always the first one down because I wanted so badly to know that I could be sure of heaven but never got the assurance that I could really know. I knew that I wasn't living up to my own standards, much less God's standards, though I was trying very hard.'

She had no idea how much God might require for admittance to heaven, but she was going to get there no matter what.

2. HERALD OF THINGS TO COME

At twenty-one, Elaine became the envy of every young person in Chicago. The *Herald & Examiner* newspaper had sponsored a rather unusual contest, calling for Catholics, Jews, and Protestants across Chicago to select the young man or woman most avid in personal devotion and most active in their church or synagogue. Out of thousands, one Catholic, one Jew, and one Protestant would represent their respective religions on a tour of the world.

A thousand Protestant churches received ballots, and on Palm Sunday each voted. Predictably, Elaine won in her church, and she was the logical choice. Intelligent, pretty, sociable, articulate, and vivacious, she participated in church life like a bee in summer. This church on the corner of Kimball and Redwood had seen her grow from a baby to an accomplished young woman of twenty-one. Although she admitted surprise at their compliment to her, it could not have felt unjustified. Her small church of 250 could hold no chance against the many larger ones; but Elaine, widely noted for being 'a mischievous young lady,' also won in her denomination.

'The final decision was made at the Sherman Hotel on a rainy, dismal Monday night,' she recalled. This step of the contest couldn't help being the most intimidating as each young person entered the impressive façade of one of Chicago's historic landmark buildings. Ornate wood paneling, floor-to-ceiling engravings, golden, luxuriant light reflected off expensive chandeliers, and riotously colored carpet which seemingly extended for miles in every direction, increased the

29

surrealism of the moment for the sixty-four contestants nervously awaiting their interviews.

First up, Elaine was given fifteen minutes to convince a committee of pastors and heads of theological seminaries why she should be chosen. 'Strangely enough they didn't pick up the fact that I wasn't really a Christian,' she commented later. After she left, the committee decided to shorten the time to three minutes, and as a result, 'They didn't get to know anybody else nearly as well,' Elaine said, laughing. For four hours Elaine sat in agony, watching competitors go in and out of the examination room and waiting for the final decision. One disturbing young man sitting behind her urged everyone to leave, so sure was he of his own success. But there was a young woman from the Salvation Army whose sweet face particularly caught Elaine's eye, for if anyone was going to win, it would certainly be her.

At long last, Dr. Thomas Anderson (religious news editor for the newspaper) appeared with a piece of paper in his hand, and Elaine was sure it wasn't hers. Instead of immediately announcing the name, Dr. Anderson scintillated anticipation by describing the trip, and unfortunately he could describe everything in great detail. The party would sail from Montreal to the United Kingdom, then on to Northern Europe for the World Sunday School Convention in Oslo, Norway. After that, they would travel down through Europe to the Holy Land, and back again by sea to New York—a grand total of almost thirty cities, across fourteen countries, in seventy-eight days. The winner would keep faithful journals, take pictures (a novelty back then), and bring back their experience to share with all Chicago.

When at long last he read the name, Elaine wondered if she had heard right. Giddy with astonishment, she called home, then set out from the Sherman, only to find a flurry of rain outside. She had dressed to impress, and wasn't carrying an umbrella. A paper would do just as well, and she started to pick up a *Chicago Daily*, but thought better of it, and bought a *Herald & Examiner*. A few days later, this newspaper ran an article on her entitled 'Girl, 20, Wins Church Trip to Holy Land.' It read, *'At the end of the process, Miss Mielke's name was the first of a final group of five. Louise Jensen of the Salvation Army was second...'*

And so it was that Kitty Levy, the daughter of a prominent rabbi in Chicago, Bud Jennings, who was studying for the priesthood, and Elaine Mielke, who had no thoughts of religion other than the earning of her right to heaven, began preparations for their almost three-month journey. Chicago would see the world through their eyes.

A Dean of Women at the Teacher's College lent her $200 for clothing, and she needed no further encouragement. The image of Elaine that appeared in the *Herald*, ready to depart on the train for Montreal with Kitty, Bud, and Dr. Anderson is one of elegance and poise. 'It took me about five years to pay her back, however,' Elaine said.

On Friday, June 19th, the *Herald* ran another article with pretentious headlines: 'TOUR PLANS THRILL CHURCH HONOR YOUTHS, Trio will sail today from Montreal for Scotland.'

SAILING FOR THE WORLD

On that warm, bright day the group sailed away from Canada on a vessel which later earned the title of 'most bombed ship still afloat' for action in World War II. The world of 1936 stood on the brink of epic changes and events. Little did these laughing, adventuring twenty-somethings know that in almost every place they would walk, unveiling events were setting the stage for the rest of the century.

Always at ease among people, Elaine threw herself into the social life aboard ship. She formed new acquaintances, danced, and enjoyed conversation with many sorts of people. One can only imagine the contrast she felt as she left her depression-era home to join pleasure-seekers, students, immigrants, and people from many walks of life. During the trip she seemed to take on a new identity—one of fashion, importance, and the delights of the high life. It troubled her a little that all the best dancers and handsomest men aboard ship seemed, as she said, to be pastors.

'None of us knew the Lord,' Elaine said later, 'so you can imagine the hot arguments we had on the ship—each one thought they were right.' But she also recalled that this passage taught her to interact comfortably with a wide range of people. Eight days after leaving the continent of North America, the S.S. *Bedford* docked in Liverpool, where the *Herald*'s party spent the night before traveling the next morning to Edinburgh and touring the city.

That night turned out nearly as eventful as the day. At three o'clock, Elaine woke to find two big green eyes staring her in the face. 'Believe you me, I turned on the lights as fast as I could and woke Kitty up! However, she wasn't much help as she doesn't like cats either. I was so petrified I didn't dare get out of my bed, so I rang for the hotel manager. I could hardly make myself go to the door to open it when he did come for fear the black cat with the green eyes would jump at me. The hotel man just laughed and took the cat out. However, I had a terrible time trying to go back to sleep. When I finally did get to sleep I had a horrible dream about a man who had murdered a girl and was going to be hung. I believe I cried all night. What a night, what a night!'

Two days after their arrival, they set out for London on the 'Royal Scot' train which had featured in the 1933 World's Fair, and Elaine continued to fill her diary with comments about meals, outings, the horrible job of packing, the different sizes of silverware, and the abundance of sweets. Her remarks on the people lacked generosity, and provide a glimpse into the importance she placed on fashion and her observations of those unlike herself. 'The people of Scotland on the whole seemed very friendly. However, we did notice that they wore little makeup and had very red and coarse complexions. On the whole, the teeth of the people were very poor and the shoes they wore very similar to gun boats.'

A twelve-course dinner greeted them at their arrival in the Strand Palace Hotel, accompanied by an eight-piece orchestra. Later she wrote, 'We had planned to go for a walk in the evening but the good old London rain stopped us. Instead I am sitting here in the beautiful writing room listening to the stringed ensemble and writing in my diary. When I get through I have several cards to write, my hair to wash, and several clothes. Such is life without your mother with you!'

LONDON ET AL.

The England they entered that summer of 1936 was one in turmoil. Edward VIII faced a choice between his American divorcee girlfriend and the crown, which would fall to his brother, Albert George.

'It looked very much like rain as we hurried to Buckingham Palace,' Elaine wrote, 'and if it had rained the guards would not have changed. This means that instead of changing daily as they should they probably change once a week since it is always raining in London.' Westminster Abbey they saw under preparation for the coming coronation.

That evening, they met up with a companion from the boat, and 'went out parading' till the early hours. Dr. Anderson rarely acted the part of a chaperone, and on more than one occasion seemed to enjoy the nightlife a little overmuch.

After Windsor Castle, they traveled to Oxford City, of which Elaine wrote, 'It is not as hilly as Scotland nor as beautiful in my estimation, but nevertheless it still ranks very high. There are so many shades of green in the meadows.'

After breakfasting in bed and writing an article for the newspaper, Elaine visited the British Museum with a gentleman friend from the boat, which perhaps explains her painfully brief description: 'The Rosetta Stone was one of the main things in the Museum.' That afternoon they boarded a ship first class for Sweden, and Elaine recounted her social life in detail, generally based on her dancing partners.

Later, in reflecting on her trip, Elaine said, 'I'd never missed a Sunday school or church, but now, all of a sudden, Sunday would come around and seem like any other day. It just didn't seem right. We had three different faiths and Dr. Anderson didn't bother trying to find a service for each of us. The young Catholic man might have gone to Mass a couple of times, and I did get to church a few times, but nothing like I was used to. It wasn't the routine that my life was all based on.' But Elaine made the best of things, enjoying the warm weather, the plentiful Swedish cooking, and the deck games.

PLAYING HOOKY

Sweden, Norway, and Denmark lay just a skip across the North Sea, and a jump beyond them lay Russia. The first three countries captured their attention for the next week, but the last—Russia—was destined to capture Elaine's heart in years to come. Four months later, Joseph Stalin began his Great Purge in the Soviet Union.

The next day, at mid-afternoon, the *Patricia* disembarked her passengers in Gothenburg—Sweden's chief seaport, which lay along the Göta River estuary. American battleships greeted them—a welcome sight since the novelty of being a foreigner was quickly wearing off. From Gothenburg they caught a train to Norway for the International Sunday School Convention, where nearly fifty countries were represented.

The Pension Atlas did not entirely suit Elaine: 'This hotel certainly is old fashioned, no running water or anything. However, we do have feather beds in which to sleep. Our bedroom is larger than the dining room for the whole hotel.' Their stay was short-lived, however, for they relocated the next day. With its noble façade of stone running the length of an entire block, and a clock tower rising in the center, the Grand Hotel boasted first-class accommodations worthy of the *Herald's* guests. Doubtless, home seemed further away every day, and luxury a welcome feature of life.

The conference was sparsely attended by Elaine, who preferred to be among the people of the city and ride the streetcar with her free pass provided by the conference. This love for people would swell into a sincere theme of Elaine's missionary life, but even now she manifested a keen and genuine interest in the people of each country and a camaraderie with young people everywhere. The trip had barely begun, and already this Chicago girl had seen more of the world than all her friends and relatives put together.

They caught a train that night which crossed a ferry over the Baltic Sea to Copenhagen, Denmark, where the bicycle population was officially half that of the people. Late the next night they caught a train destined for Berlin, a place whose darkness deepened by the day.

Three years earlier, Hitler had become chancellor of Germany, and in the spring of that year he broke the Treaty of Versailles by sending troops into the Rhineland. A more insidious poison began its rampage, however, through his establishment of a state church which laid down boundaries in the spiritual realm and signaled the advent of persecution toward Christ-followers. Elaine, however, observed none of this during her stay in Germany for one signal reason: Berlin was preparing for its most magnificent act of propaganda to date.

GERMANY, 1936

After a glance at the hotel, a dash off to the church for a very formal Episcopalian service, and a meal, the party began sightseeing. The first street they entered was described by Elaine as 'a beautiful wide boulevard and probably the best known in Berlin, Unter den Linden.' Three years earlier, in a morbid, nocturnal scene, a torch-light procession had ended here in a massive bonfire of Jewish books. Elaine's oblivious travel journal continued, 'There are two people born every five minutes in Berlin, and prizes or gifts are still offered for families of six boys or six girls or more...larger for the boys as they can be used in the military service.' Hitler had also ordained it compulsory for all boys between ten and eighteen to take part in the paramilitary youth organization. The group also saw the Garrison church, where Hitler had inaugurated the new government on March 21st, 1933.

'Our guide spoke very favorably of all that Hitler has done and the present condition of the country,' she wrote. 'There is little unemployment in Germany compared to what it was. The population of Berlin is 4.5 million, two thirds being Protestants (Lutherans).'

Lastly, she mentioned the primary cultural happenings in Berlin at the time, and a visit to the Olympic Stadium: 'I forgot to mention that laborers and builders are at work all over even though it is Sunday. They are working day and night to have Berlin in shape for the Olympics... Everywhere we looked we saw symbols of the Olympics. Men and women wore pins with it on, boys and girls carried flags with the symbol on them, and almost every store had it in the window...'

Kitty's experiences as a Jew in Germany stood in marked contrast to the ostracized reception she would receive in the Holy Land. '… Kitty had a number of letters and money to give to professors and other Jewish men [friends of her father] in Germany trying to help them out. She was in her glory in Germany.'

That night Elaine saw the nightlife of Berlin: first the Broadcasting Tower, then the four most popular cafés with their orchestras and dancing. 'I felt as though this evening has been very profitable to us in seeing how these people really spend their leisure time,' she concluded judiciously.

The next evening saw them departing on a train for Lucerne, Switzerland, from which they would travel to Africa. On August 1, just eighteen days after Elaine left Germany for the Middle East, Adolf Hitler opened the 11th Olympic Games in Berlin.

3. EASTERN SUNRISE, WESTERN GLORY

God was not interested in success, but in obedience. If one obeyed God and was willing to suffer defeat and whatever else came one's way, God would show a kind of success that the world couldn't imagine. But this was the narrow path, and few would take it.

Eric Metaxas[1]

Passage on board the French S.S. *Providence* seemed rather quiet after their hectic days of sightseeing and night outings. On the way to Syria, they traveled around the toe of Italy, past Sicily, and stopped at Athens.[2] Here, they visited the Acropolis, with its tremendous view, Mars Hill, the Parthenon, the theater of Bacchus, and the Olympic stadium from the 1896 games.

The next day, Kitty, Elaine, and Bud collaborated in a report sent home to the *Herald*, describing their passage through the Dardanelles and past Gallipoli, both made famous in WWI. They reached Istanbul at sunset, and in their words, 'The majesty of the great bay on the shores of which lie the great Byzantine city, the glory of the evening sky, the welter of ships and many activities of the harbor set our minds aglow with anticipation.' Here, in this city of 500 mosques, they found the meeting of East and West.

---

1   Eric Metaxas, *Bonhoeffer: Pastor, Martyr, Prophet, Spy* (Nashville, Tennessee: Thomas Nelson, 2009), p. 363.

2   Six days previous, the Olympic torch had departed from Greece to arrive in Berlin twelve days later.

MIDDLING IN THE EAST

The next day they navigated the crowded oriental streets, visited mosques, and admired the religious devotion of this culture. On their way back to the ship in the evening they heard of the Turkish occupation of the Dardanelles, but they noticed no outward changes.

'The night came upon us,' Elaine wrote, 'followed by the morning breaking on the Mediterranean, blue and majestic. During the day, the coast of Turkey has been visible constantly on the left, while on the right, numerous Greek islands. The coast is rugged, and lies brown and dry under the sun, the heat of which has grown more intense daily as we have journeyed southward—a great contrast to the green mountains, fertile valley, and cool atmosphere of beautiful Scandinavia, Scotland, and England.'

The next morning, they set out 'in the company of a scrawny and exceedingly noisy little guide' to visit Rhodes, a Greek city which possessed a wealth of history. After a full day of visiting monuments and Turkish bazaars along the cobbled streets of the town, they set out for the ship in a small boat, but only after a heated discussion between its captain and their guide. The last portion of their journey led them to Beirut, following the route of Paul to Athens: 'past Cyprus and under Crete.'

Early in the morning, with the sun rising on the Lebanon mountains, they set foot in Syria, and were driven around Mt. Hermon's base, and across the desert to Damascus. 'That same evening,' Elaine continued, 'we went to the street called Straight, following the footsteps of Paul the Apostle to the house of Ananias; and from there passed through the gate and around the road to the place where, according to tradition, Paul escaped, let down over the walls in a basket by his friends.'

The next day they braved crowded streets and bazaars to visit Arabic shrines. Despite warnings about the current revolution, the group insisted on being taken to the area of Galilee. They could not enter Capernaum, but they dipped their hands along the shore of the Jordan, and returned to Damascus with a lack of incident, which caused Elaine to remark that the dangers 'were perhaps largely imaginary.'[3]

Guided by a Syrian nobleman, they visited a magnificent set of ruins first built by the Phoenicians in 1,000 b.c., then expanded into a series of temples by the Romans during the Christian era. They continued their tour by the light of a moon which caused the scene to glow with an unearthly beauty.

They returned to Jerusalem via Beirut and Haifa; but because of the unrest, their travel company refused to take them through Galilee and Samaria. Instead, they stopped at the Stella Maria hospices, situated atop the Carmelite range near the traditional site of Elijah's cave and operated by Carmelite monks. The hundred-mile journey along the Mediterranean coast disappointed no one.

'From our windows,' Elaine wrote that evening, 'we look out over the bay of Acre, famous in Roman and Crusader history, and the wider expanse of the blue Mediterranean glistening under the moon. Nearly 800 feet below us lies Haifa, wherein thousands of lights are shining like stars. On the other side of the bay, the city of Acre keeps watch. The brilliant appearance caused by the moon, the shining lights of the two cities, the sounds of the crickets, the frequent melody of the bells from the monastery, and the sound of the voices in the vespers in the churches of St. Elias combine to make this evening one to live forever. We go tomorrow highly expectant, knowing that we will be in the midst of the hills and in the valleys and on the plains made famous by Abraham and Moses, the great hosts of the prophets, Solomon and David, and Jesus of Nazareth.'

WALKING IN HISTORY

On the morrow, they took an armored train to Jerusalem, though no Arab brigands appeared. An Arab Christian guided them through the city's holy sites. They were prevented from visiting the Mount of Olives at moonlight. A curfew law allowed guards to shoot if no one responded to their call.

---

3   In April of that year, massive riots and protests had broken out in Palestine be-
     tween the Arabs and Jews, and hostilities had not yet abated. Few of the threats
     were as imaginary as Elaine optimistically commented.

Kitty drew great hostility everywhere she went. 'She suffered because she looked Jewish, and had a very Jewish nose,' Elaine commented. 'Almost every time we left the hotel the Arabs would spit at her or throw stones... She just wept, so confused. "Why, Elaine? What have I done? Why do they treat me like this?" She finally got so upset she stayed in the hotel all the time.'

The next day they visited the house of Caiaphas, the assumed site of the Last Supper; and, astride donkeys, the Pool of Siloam and Gethsemane on the Mount of Olives. Elaine described the view: 'From there we saw on the one side the ancient city lying on its eternal hills, on the other the wilderness of Judea stretched for miles... Between the wilderness and the mountains of Moab, the Jordan lay like a giant blue ribbon edged with green, and the vast expanse of the Dead Sea, 1,300 feet below sea level, glistened in the sun.'

The following morning found them at the Dome of the Rock, then outside the city to the valley of Hinnom, and back to Bethlehem by donkey. Then off by train across the Gaza desert, which made its miserable way into everyone's hair, eyes, noses, and mouths. They crossed the Suez Canal by ferry, and as they approached the safety of Egypt, the lights of Cairo began to glimmer along the horizon between the blackness of desert and sky. 'By the time we got to Africa,' Elaine confided to her journal, 'I was so homesick I couldn't wait to get home.'

Mohammad, a sheikh, accompanied them to the edge of the Sahara the next morning, and they spent the day at the pyramids and Sphinx. On camelback, they arrived at the base of the Pyramid Chezrah, and Elaine recalled the words of Napoleon to his troops in this spot centuries earlier: 'Gentlemen, at least forty centuries look down upon you.' The small party climbed Cheops, from which they looked 451 feet down to the sand, across the Sahara on one side and the green fields of the Nile on the other. They were told it took 100,000 slaves twenty years to complete the massive stone edifice. From there, they visited the oldest Christian church of Cairo, built in the fifth century by the Copts over the traditional house of the holy family during their flight from Bethlehem.

Their journey to Alexandria began by train at dawn the next morning, moving toward the Nile Delta. Gleaming roofs and minarets of cities gave way to fields of cotton and corn, punctuated by caravans of camels and donkeys laden for market.

In Alexandria they visited Pompey's Pillar, which had seen the martyrdom of early Christians, and the catacombs, where Origen and others had preached the gospel. Shortly afterward, they sailed for Marseilles on the coast of France. Customs cleared, they boarded a train to Avignon, a city very close to its original condition during the occupation of the Holy Roman See. As they traveled through the mountains and plains, they passed Nice, Monte Carlo, and Monaco.

Upon reaching Rome, they set out immediately for St. Peters, the catacombs, the Coliseum, and the forum; then the Vatican library, and the Cistine Chapel. The meeting of antiquity and modernity captivated them. But the highlight of their time—perhaps of the entire trip— came in the form of an audience with Pope Pius XI, obtained for them by a Cardinal in Chicago.

REFUSAL

It was a tense group which assembled in the audience room and awaited the entrance of this man, the head of the Roman Catholic church. The interview was intended to be private, but the number of people precluded this, and more than fifty formed a line to be inspected by the guard: heads must be covered, and bare arms wrapped in gauze. 'It was soon over,' Elaine wrote. 'The audience passed quickly and we descended the great staircase, aware of a milestone in our lives having been reached and passed.'

The measured, somewhat formulaic tone of this report home to Chicago fell far short of the actual events of that interview, which Elaine would recount elsewhere over the course of her life with great relish. 'What excitement there was as the heralds preceded him with trumpets and beautiful uniforms. At the appearance of the Pope everyone fell to their knees immediately—except me. Bud, the Catholic boy, kept pulling on my skirt saying, "Get down, Elaine! Get down or you will go to hell!"'

'Even though I wasn't a believer at the time,' Elaine said, 'I knew it wasn't right to bow down before any man, so I stood firm. However, I did have some rosaries with me from my Catholic friends and I was glad to have the blessing of the Pope for them. At the end, we all made a line to go by him and kiss his ring. When it came my turn, I put out my hand to shake his. He wasn't too happy, but he shook my hand. Now I jokingly ask my friends, "Would you like to shake the hand that shook the Pope's?"' She admitted that she felt a little akin to Daniel during that audience.

THE DENOUEMENT

The day was done, a climax had passed, and Paris—then home—lay ahead. Travels were nearly at an end, and with them 'the exciting days of trains, steamships, and distant and exotic cities.'

Paris sights included Notre-Dame along the Seine, the Eiffel Tower, the Louvre, Napoleon's Tomb, the Arc de Triomphe, and the gardens of the Tuilleries. 'Who can describe the streets of Paris?' Elaine wrote. 'Sidewalk cafés are everywhere, catering to people from all nations until far into the night. Few places offer such a variety of humankind... Tomorrow we entrain early in the morning for Cherbourg to embark on the great liner, the *Berengaria*.'

Of the seventy-eight days in their trip, thirty-eight of them had involved sea travel, and this last voyage lasted five days. When she landed in New York, having seen far more of the world than she ever expected, Elaine had no idea of the divine plots which lay just around the bend. Years later, she would speak fondly of this trip, but with positive triumph of the since-then: 'And now... I can see how God prepared me for a life of journeyings oft, and I love it.'

A COMING CURVE

During her last year of Teacher's College, Elaine recounted this international adventure to 150 churches, showing her black and white stills and movies 'which were quite a novelty in those days.' She took great enjoyment in this task, but as she looked back on the multitude of colors and textures of people and places, an episode stood out in her memory. During the Mediterranean leg of their travels, one of the judges for the competition, Mr. Mee, pulled her aside: 'You know Elaine, you really didn't win this trip.' By this time it was more than half over, and she thought, *How can that be?* 'Do you remember that little Salvation Army girl?' he asked.

'Yes, and I thought at the time that she would win.'

'Well, we called her in after we had interviewed everybody and asked her if she would be willing to play cards and dance and leave her uniform at home. "Oh no, I couldn't do that!" she replied. The *Herald* wanted somebody who would be a good social mixer and we thought you would fit the bill.'

'But you never asked me if I would do those things!'

'Oh, we knew you would—we could tell by looking at you.'

'I was crushed,' Elaine recalled later. 'He thought he was telling me something that would make me happy, but I found it terrible that I gave the impression that I would be worldly.'

This was highlighted by the news just one year after their return, that one of their traveling companions had died. Clearly intelligent, Kitty had graduated at seventeen from the University of Chicago with a degree in anthropology, and a bright future shimmered out in front of her. While on the trip around the world, however, she had contracted a fatal illness. Elaine chilled when she heard the news.

Another shock would soon strike deeper, completing the damage to her ego. This God of whom she knew so little, yet strained to please so faithfully, had set a radically different course for her life than she knew.

Elaine Mielke, 1933.

4. 'MOST PROMISING YOUNG PROTESTANT'

Why sayest thou, that thou art righteous by faith only?

Not that I am acceptable to God, on account of the worthiness of my faith; but because only the satisfaction, righteousness, and holiness of Christ, is my righteousness before God; and that I cannot receive and apply the same to myself any other way than by faith only.[1]

'Now for the exciting part... quite a thrilling story,' Elaine said (and one wonders how world travel fell short). 'One Sunday it was raining and Mother said, "Won't you go and pick up Shirley?"'

The church was a converted bowling alley on Fullerton and Central Park—the very idea was offensive to Elaine. 'I thought that you had to have robes and candles... That is where I had gone to bowl, but I couldn't see worshipping the Lord in a bowling alley.'[2] Grace-stripped gospel always smacks of form.

WHAT HAVE SQUIRREL-FUR COATS GOT TO DO WITH EPHESIANS?

While Elaine was gallivanting around Europe, her brother Daniel began attending the North Side Gospel Center, (NSGC), and although the family had faithfully attended church for years, he felt convicted under

---

1   *Heidelberg Catechism,* Lord's Day 23, Question 61.

2   Paul Rader, a man with a passion for the lost and hurting youth of Chicago, began this thriving center of evangelism and city outreach. Lance Latham, a founder of AWANA, and his wife Virginia, came to serve alongside him. Their passion for global missions and their heart to inspire youth radically impacted the NSGC and it became a thriving center of missionary support, community care, and solid scriptural teaching.

Lance Latham's preaching like never before. Shirley, too, would later point to this church as the means of her conversion, and together they became involved in this community of believers. Shirley still walked then, and the Center lay a mere two blocks from the Mielkes' house. But one day, as a heavy rain swept the city, Lillie made the request of her older daughter. 'I had no intention of going inside, however…' Elaine remembered.

Shirley didn't appear, and didn't appear. At last a pretty girl came out, wearing a beautiful gray squirrel coat. Elaine was commensurately impressed. She had assumed these people were 'poor church mice,' but this sight quickly changed her mind, and she decided to go in and observe the happenings.

Inside, she saw a crowd of young people, heard lively music, and sensed an atmosphere of joy. But what stood out most was their friendliness in welcoming her—so different from the cliques of her home church. Everyone stayed around and talked after meetings—the very reason she had to wait in the first place—and they treated her crippled sister well. It surprised her that Christian girls could wear furs and look nice despite their religion. She apparently thought of herself as a stylish, worldly-wise anomaly in the church.

When the girls invited Elaine to a hayride and harvest party she gladly accepted. At the harvest party, she received another invitation to Tuesday night Bible class. 'So I went,' she told afterward, 'and there were two ping pong tables of girls and some fellows in another room just devouring Leviticus of all things.'

All the girls in the group knew her from the publicity of the trip around the world, but Shirley and Dan had asked people at the Center to pray for her salvation. Of course Elaine, with her perfect church attendance and the title of foremost Protestant in Chicago, would have protested.

When Elaine suddenly appeared in her Bible study unannounced, Virginia wondered how she could present the gospel through the book of Leviticus. '… you were, I was told, a very sophisticated girl…' wrote Virginia, years later. She began to teach, and when Elaine asked questions about the offerings, she spoke about the Day of Atonement, presenting 'the shed blood of Christ as our only way to heaven.'

'I gave no invitation,' she told later, 'trusting the Word of the Gospel to use its own power to lead her to Christ. I was just a voice for the gospel. We talk so much about being soul winners, but we really have nothing more than love and a voice to give the Lord at such times.'

A SETTING STRAIGHT

The story of that evening could hardly be told better than by Elaine herself: 'Although Mrs. Latham was teaching from Leviticus, she included plenty of other Scripture for my sake, and in the midst of studying, led by the Holy Spirit, she very wisely made some statements that startled me, such as "You know girls, infant baptism has nothing to do with your salvation." I thought, why does she say that?'

'She went on to say, "Nor does confirmation." I thought of the lovely photos of all of the confirmation classes at our church decorating the basement walls. But when she said "Nor does giving your tithe or church membership assure your salvation," I had to speak up. "Oh, Mrs. Latham, I can't prove to you where you're wrong, but if you will come and talk to my Pastor Schweitzer, he could… show you where [it says] you have to have these things."'

Mrs. Latham—'Teach' as she was affectionately dubbed by the girls—held up her much worn Bible and said, 'Elaine, if I can prove to you that what I have been telling you is God's plan for salvation, would you believe it?'

'I knew the Bible was God's Word,' recalled Elaine, 'so I said, "Go ahead and try—show me one verse in the Bible that proves it."

'The first was John 1:12-13: *"But to all who did receive him, who believed in his name, he gave the right to become children of God, who were born, not of blood nor of the will of the flesh nor of the will of man, but of God."* Mrs. Latham turned to me and asked, "Elaine, where does it say that infant baptism, giving your tithe, perfect attendance, and all the rest of your good works will save you?"

'I read the verse and saw that it said, "as many as receive Him" and I said, "Well, it doesn't say it here. Give me another verse."

'She then had me turn to John 5:24 and read it out loud: *"Truly, truly, I say to you, whoever hears my word and believes him who sent me has eternal life. He does not come into judgment, but has passed from death to life."* "Now what tense is that verb, 'has'?"

'Well, it sounds like the present tense to me.'

'Yes, that's right. You can know here on earth whether you have salvation based on whether you believe that Jesus' work on the cross was sufficient or not.'

Elaine still wasn't satisfied. 'Okay, that one doesn't say anything about works, but give me another one.'

'Those twenty-four girls who later became my best friends didn't laugh at my ignorance but prayed for me instead…' Elaine said. 'They let Mrs. Latham spend the rest of the evening proving to me that I was wrong in thinking I could earn my salvation.'

The next verse Teach gave was Romans 4:4-5: *'Now to the one who works, his wages are not counted as a gift but as his due. And to the one who does not work but believes in him who justifies the ungodly, his faith is counted as righteousness.'*

Elaine had come to the Bible study that evening on a whim, but now she found herself wishing she hadn't. This was all most uncomfortable, and she felt as a man would who walks home one day only to discover that the street on which he has lived his entire life has vanished.

She became slightly irate: 'Do you really mean to say that works don't count for anything to get us to heaven?' It appeared that in all her years of faithfulness she had missed the key on which all the gospel turned. Was it possible? 'My first twenty-one years, I don't ever remember hearing the gospel of grace… I thought the only way to get there was by good works, so work I did.' Whenever the church doors opened, Elaine was sure to be there. During altar calls at camp, she was always the first one down. Admittedly, she didn't quite know how much was required, but she was reasonably certain a mansion awaited her. The thought that she could be secure in her assurance came as a bold of lightning in the dark.

'IT WAS THE WORD'

That night became a head-on collision: two routes to heaven, it seemed, with each invalidating the other. 'It was an awful struggle,' Elaine admitted. She found herself unable to reconcile the alternatives, but she began to recognize one thing, and this became the breaking point: *she was not good, and she could not satisfy a holy God.*

When Virginia asked her to read Ephesians 2:8-9, 'I couldn't believe my eyes,' Elaine said. *'For by grace you have been saved through faith. And this is not your own doing; it is the gift of God, not a result of works, so that no one may boast.'*

'Was I reading it right when it said, "not by works of righteousness"? … and here that was exactly what I was doing… Oh, it was like turning on a light!… I see it now! It is so clear, so wonderful—it's too good to be true. There's hope for me in heaven if I trust in Christ! … The whole world looked more beautiful as my heart overflowed with joy.'

Virginia described to Elaine later how 'your eyes just lit up and joy illuminated your face. You were a new creature in Christ, saved and justified forever.' At the point of desperation, in the realization of sin and justice, the Spirit broke through. The same Spirit whose power overshadowed the womb of a virgin, who descended in flames at Pentecost, now entered Elaine's heart and caused a rebirth.

Here in a former bowling alley during a Bible study on Leviticus, Elaine was jolted out of her established reality and thrown into a far wider one.

'It was the Word that got me,' she said later. And indeed, it could have been nothing less. The verses she read that day 'were indelibly pressed upon my mind,' and from then on she was captive. Her small perspective had changed, and it made *her* small. God had won out at last over all her worried, guilt-driven efforts.

Cal Hibbard, also a member of the NSGC and a man who would come to play an integral role in her life, commented, 'There [at the Center] the gospel of grace plus nothing was the keynote of the gospel message… and I know Elaine believed that deeply.' And so it was, just days before her twenty-second birthday on November 6th, that 'Elaine... realized that salvation was an accomplished fact—the finished work of Christ at Calvary.'

Gratitude would overflow throughout the rest of her life in prayer and praise. Handwritten journal entries speak clear of a shouting soul—'Thank you for rescuing me out of the darkness and gloom of Satan's kingdom and bringing me into your kingdom: *"He has delivered us from the domain of darkness and transferred us to the kingdom of his beloved Son...(Col. 1:13)"*... How thankful I am that you are my Savior from God's terrible anger against sin. Thank you for changing my old evil nature. Thank you that you are my *only hope* of glory and that you live *in me*! To think I am standing before you with nothing against me—all because of *your* work.'

HAVE YOU HEARD?

Gratitude leapt life into action that night. Not even waiting to pray with the group, Elaine ran home to the shop behind her home where Mr. Mielke was hard at work printing gospel tracts. 'Dad, stop the press!' she exclaimed. 'I have some wonderful news to share with you! Did you know you can be sure of your salvation while you're still here on this earth?'

'Sure I knew that,' he replied. 'Didn't you?'

'But Dad, you never told me!'

'Well, don't you listen to the messages? I see you go to church all the time—don't you listen? Aren't you hearing? Aren't you writing notes? I've seen you writing notes about the sermon, so I thought you knew the Lord.'

'I'm writing notes,' Elaine replied, 'but I've never gotten that message before. At our summer conference grounds you know I'm the first one at the altar and I've always wanted to know this for myself but no one ever told me that it was all the Lord's work. I went forward because I wanted this so desperately.'

'I don't think you must be listening,' Mr. Mielke said. 'You're the only one who's missed it.'

'No dad,' Elaine replied. 'I've been listening. On Sunday night I have to speak for Christian Endeavor; I want you to come and sit in the back and see if you think it is just me.'

Mr. Mielke came and sat in the back that evening while Elaine, after giving her message, presented a scenario: 'Suppose there was a young man here on the floor dying. What verses could you use to comfort him, to assure a believer he is going to heaven? What does the blood of the Lord Jesus mean to you?'

The young people began to snicker, and Mr. Mielke began to cry. 'He couldn't believe that all of us were missing this,' Elaine said. 'These were kids that I had grown up with from the cradle—we knew each other so very, very well, about twenty of us—and here was Dad, a deacon of the church, and he sat there and just wept.'[3]

Elaine stayed at Grace Evangelical for a few more years, but found increasingly that this congregation had abandoned the reality of its namesake.

Then she heard about the need of the Mexicans, and organized a mission with its own building to aid in their care. It was there that she heard about Wycliffe.

---

3   'Imagine!' she exclaimed later. 'And people are in churches like that all over and they think they're on their way. Eventually the pastor in that church took his life. So we need to pray for our pastors that they'd be true to the Word and make sure that it's not just church membership, or I'm born in America, or I'm white; that's not the way. I'm so thankful that somehow out of all those people God saw fit to make sure that I found the way…'

5. CHARTING PATTERNS OF THE HEART

...It is perfectly plain to anyone who wants to do a difficult and worthwhile thing that he's got to deny himself a thousand unimportant and probably a few hundred important things in order to do the thing that matters most.

Elisabeth Elliot[1]

Elaine returned from her gallivants across the globe just in time to begin her third year at Chicago Teacher's College. The next year she finished her major, took a special course for teaching disabled children, and became president of the Student Council.

After graduating at the top of her class of thirty-five students, Elaine was given the choice of any school in Chicago. Many were situated in lovely neighborhoods, with swimming pools and new facilities; but she chose a school in one of Chicago's roughest neighborhoods, one with much poverty and a high crime rate. For three years this school hadn't had a proper teacher, only substitutes, and Elaine remarked, 'I only found out how wild they were when I got there...' Elaine never gave a reason behind her choice, but this avenue of need, greater even than she knew, was not inconsistent with her increased eagerness to share the good news of the gospel since her conversion.

At twenty-four, Elaine became a teacher at Anderson Public School in the Damen and Division area of Chicago. 'It [was] a really wicked area,' she said later.

---

1   Elisabeth Elliot, *Trusting God in a Twisted World* (Old Tappan, New Jersey: Fleming Revel Company, 1989), p. 19.

'I was given a basement room, and I tell you, those first days of teaching school I'll never forget... Especially after having substitutes for two years they were really out of hand. The boys in the class were way bigger than I was because they hadn't been sent over to vocational school like they should have been, and their favorite pastime was to swing from the pipes hanging down in the room. So I was spending my time pulling these guys down from the pipes and I would go home at night weeping because I just couldn't make it. It took all my willpower to stay with the job. I thought, is this what my life's work is going to be?' My sister would say, 'Just think, every day you stick it out it's $6.50!' In those days, $6.50 meant an awful lot. For two weeks I did that, then those boys were sent to vocational study and it was heaven on earth.

PLOTTING

With the principal troublemakers gone, Elaine's attention turned to her other students. 'I was very zealous as a new Christian and I thought, *these are the days when whatever the child asks for you are supposed to provide. If I could only get those kids to ask, then if I were ever criticized I could say "They asked for it!"'* She thought up a plan.

During lunch time, the children would run along the windowsill and predictably peek in at their teacher. Every afternoon, there was Miss Mielke reading her Bible while she ate.

Finally, Alex, one of the more observant boys, approached her. 'Miss Mielke, you know they say we are slow readers but every time we look at you, you are reading the same book. Are you ever going to finish that book?'

'Alex, I'm never going to finish this book.'

'But why do you like it so much?'

'Listen,' Elaine told him, 'you go around and if all the boys and girls want to know why I like it so much and why I'm so interested, I'll tell you.'

'I had it made,' Elaine said. 'He was my press agent: *"You want to know what she's reading, don't ya?!"*'

Every afternoon from then on, the children gathered for Elaine to tell them a Bible story or teach them a hymn. '…they had been to the parochial schools and had been beaten so many times on their hands that they couldn't take it,' she recalled later. 'Those mentally challenged kids were mostly from broken homes and on Saturday afternoons they would go to see a doubleheader of gangster movies at the theaters—the only entertainment they had. On Monday morning they would come to school just physical wrecks, a bundle of nerves from the terrible pictures they had seen.

'I told them stories about the Lord and His love and they… always begged me to tell them more… I'll never forget giving them the story of Daniel with the flannel graph. So real was it to them that when I began to put Daniel down in the lions' den they just screamed "Oh, Miss Mielke, don't! *Don't!*" And then to tell them about the Lord's second coming…'

Eventually, Elaine began an after-school Bible class, and she and her brother Bud took some of the children to church on Sunday. They became friends, rather than merely pupils to her. She attended birthday parties in their homes, and they came to hers and met her parents. Their own parents were very grateful, she noted.

'Constantly they taught me lessons of faith… When they'd go out for recess or home for the night they'd say, "Miss Mielke, if we don't see you again, we'll see you *up there*…" I was impressed, and the Lord did a real work in my heart. I loved working with them and for years and years I received letters from them. When my Dad died… Wally, one of the most near normal (he's now married) saw it in the paper and called me to say how sorry he was—this was years after I had left.'

None of this came at the expense of their education, to which Elaine earnestly dedicated herself. After class she spent hours inventing games to help the children learn by intriguing their imaginations. Her object was always, *How can I get the same thought across in a new way?* This interest remained a lifelong passion.

ON THE CORNER OF CARPENTER AND HARRISON

Around that time Elaine began a mission for the local Mexican children, which she later called a 'highlight of my life.' Chicago contained dozens of ethnic groups, and presented as large a mission field as any.[2] On the corner of Carpenter and Harrison, near the historic Hull House (a hub of Chicago's immigration), lay an old, worn out storefront building. Elaine immediately set to work. Someone later commented that the place was so filthy it had to be scrubbed top to bottom before it could be used, and it gave out splinters like candy. All her time out of school she spent at this mission, and a large group began to gather. Around that time, she also began to attend night classes at Northwestern University.

There was one problem: Elaine didn't know Spanish. A friend of hers had been a missionary to Ecuador till her husband ran off with an Ecuadorian and she returned to the States. Elaine paid Ann to tutor her in Spanish at night, and enlisted her help to start a class for mothers while Elaine taught the younger children. At first she painstakingly wrote out every lesson in Spanish, but before long she began to speak it more fluently.

'Working with the Mexicans I saw how much God's Word... changed their lives,' she said later. 'And that's when I first began to realize how many people needed the Bible.' On the trip around the world, even before she herself had come to a full understanding of the truth, she had begun to wonder *who is going to teach all these people?* Now such thoughts came closer to home.

THE PRACTICALITY OF SINGLENESS

Life was good. In her season of singleness, Elaine took advantage of every opportunity before her. As a young single woman, she found herself in a unique position to serve those around her, and she would later find that many of the specific skills used over a lifetime of ministry were cultivated during this period. As Richard Cecil writes, 'Things are

---

2   About ten years later, Nate Saint would also work among these children of Chicago's South Side while attending Wheaton College.

Elaine in front of her 'dollhouse' in Mexico (circa 1943).

not to be done by the effort of the moment but by the preparation of past moments.'[3]

As far as she was concerned, the years to come would hold teaching, fellowship with family and a multitude of friends, and continued ministry among the Mexicans. 'God did gift her, but she also developed her gifts,' said one person of her. She made herself approachable and reached out to those on the fringes. She formed relationships with women of every age and sought counsel from wise older women— Virginia in particular. She volunteered as a mentor to young women at her church's summer camps, and several of these relationships lasted her life long. 'The single woman who turns away from regretting the absence of her own family,' writes John Piper, 'and gives herself to creating God's family in the church, will find the flowering of her womanhood in ways she never dreamed, and Christ will be uniquely honored because of it…'[4] Elaine demonstrated the remarkable truth of

---

3   http://www.backtothebible.org/devotions/respond-to-the-call *(Joy and Strength)*. Last accessed 1 June, 2018.

4   John Piper, 'The Ultimate Meaning of True Womanhood', last accessed 1 June, 2018, http://www.desiringgod.org/conference-messages/the-ulti-mate- meaning-of-true-womanhood

this statement during this season of her life. Her greatest honor was to be present where God was at work.

Speaking to a group of young women years later, she challenged them to seek out others who could benefit from their time and energy. 'Rather than simply saying you're available,' she said, '*seek out the need...* Offer to make a supper meal,' she suggested, 'or make part of a meal for unexpected guests. Perhaps someone isn't able to get away from home often—take them out; or watch a couple's children. Above all, pray for the needs you see around you,' she finished.

A TIME TO BECOME

A certain quietness of spirit still remained necessary to the cultivation of her inner person. Even her spiritual life took on a tint of busyness. During one seven-month stretch she spent every evening at the church. Her focus began to waver ever so slightly, not through willful divergence, but simply from neglect. In the woman who traveled the world, we saw an Elaine caught up in prosperity and glamour. Now she turned to people and to the liveliness of social life as refreshment and confirmation of her identity.

Throughout her life, this tendency to *do*, rather than to *become* haunted her, and at two notable points in her life she would come face to face with the spiritual barrenness and exhaustion this engendered. One of these came now, in the infancy of her relationship with Christ, while she remained heedless to the need for continual renewal in His presence.

Lance and Virginia Latham's spiritual mentorship and personal influence on Elaine cannot be overestimated. The teaching of her pastor Lance Latham laid a foundation for her fledgling faith. He and Virginia took an interest in this burgeoning young woman and encouraged her to further develop her giftedness.

The North Side Gospel Center quickly became a second family to Elaine. This church taught Elaine what true relationship looked like: how a group of believers could contribute to one another's growth and effectiveness for the kingdom. This period in her life later enabled her to play an influential role in strengthening ties of fellowship wherever she went.

Lance noted Elaine's impeccable attendance and heavy involvement at church, and though he approved of her eagerness, he realized that incessant work, even among believers, couldn't replace personal growth in grace. He also discerned the weakness this might sow in her spiritual life. Finally he told her, 'Elaine, don't think you have to come every night. You keep yourself too busy to cultivate your walk with Christ. Stay home and study for yourself. Meditate on the truths of the gospel—let them soak deep.'

'That was hard,' Elaine admitted, 'but very good training for the mission field, 'cause there you have to read everything for yourself.' This was the time for importing the Word so that later as a wife, a mother, and—later still—as an older woman, she could draw from rich stores to teach and encourage others. Should this not take place, she would have nothing to give. 'Unless a tree has borne blossoms in spring, you will vainly look for fruit on it in autumn,' Sir Walter Scott wrote so aptly.

PRESSING ON

Elaine found the Christian life to be unattainable without the animating power of the Spirit's work. The not-always-mountaintops loomed in the ordinary days when everything *but* her quiet time cried out for her attention and every pleasure *but* that of fellowship with Christ called out to be experienced. Even fellowship with other believers could act as a snare; a sort of equivalent to her previous social life, if it became the primary spring. Only time in His presence fueled growth and she began to deliberately put herself in the way of His Word, knowing the transforming presence of Christ.

Holiness, Elaine began to see, was not a name for starched collars and proper behavior as everyone generally supposed, but the opening up of new, rich worlds. Imitating Christ was not a gray, blank thing involving restraint and subversion of pleasure, but that which awakened a far deeper pleasure, better than she dreamed. Her sight had been transformed to see Christ as supremely desirable, fully satisfying. These realizations birthed in Elaine a passion to share this joy with others—a passion that would not diminish in the next five decades.

6. CLAIMING A PATH

... You have to learn that you cannot claim a path just because it is less intimidating. You must keep in mind that God does have an appointment with you, that there is a cost to serving Him... if you have not learned to pay the smaller prices of following Christ in your daily life, you will not be prepared to pay the ultimate price in God's calling.

Ravi Zacharias[1]

The hard, chill linoleum on which she sat offered no comfort, nor did the four small walls of the bathroom which loomed around her in the darkness. For weeks now the call had been nagging, but tonight she would have it out.

It had all started with that Ann girl. 'In 1942, the Second War was on and we were rationing sugar in the public schools,' Elaine explained. 'My school was in a Polish neighborhood, and the parents would come and tell how many children there were in the family and we'd tell them how much they could get. I found it hard to understand the little babushkas who came for their coupons, but I had a friend that could speak Polish.' The same Ann Williams who taught Elaine Spanish also happened to have Polish roots.

For several days the two women worked together; then one day Ann told Elaine about hearing 'the most wonderful speaker' talking about 'a brand new organization' at the Chicago Gospel Tabernacle the night before. The organization was Wycliffe Bible Translators, and

---

1   Ravi Zacharius, *Walking from East to West*, p. 199.

the speaker William Cameron Townsend. He had presented about the Summer Institute of Linguistics (SIL) in Norman, Oklahoma, which taught the skill of reducing oral languages to writing.

THE PERFECT PRICE TAG

Elaine hadn't even heard the name Wycliffe before, but Ann's excitement was contagious as she revealed her intention to take the course in Norman. 'Why don't you come with me?' Ann said. 'Just think, only $5.00 a week for room and board!' That got Elaine's attention.

Years later, when asked what drew her to that SIL course, she laughed. 'The price was right! All I could think of was the fact that I'd have money left over to buy a new car.' Mercenary? Perhaps. Providential?

'She'd always wanted a dormitory experience,' commented Cal Hibbard later. 'That's why she went… it wasn't for Bible translation!' Not able to afford Wheaton, Elaine had ridden an hour and a half each way on the train for Teacher's College. She was never able to experience college life fully, and felt rather cheated as a result. When this opportunity presented itself, plans to learn Spanish in Mexico were quickly set aside.

'I went just to have a good time,' she said. 'I was so stupid; I didn't know that you had to work hard on linguistics.' In those weeks, she embroidered a pillow with the names of her teachers and classmates: George Cowan, Ben Elson, and several others—men who would later become patriarchs in the mission's world. It turned out to be a wonderful summer.

Six years previous, Mr. Townsend had opened the summer camps to single women. Merely one year after Elaine took the course, this door would have been shut. As she explained later, 'In those days you didn't have to be interested in pioneer missions to take the course.' Beginning the next summer, only those with an interest in this field were accepted, and Elaine had no intention of being a missionary. Ministering to Mexicans in Chicago was different; that could be done on the side. The pioneering, international sort of mission was absolutely out of the question.

A COSTLY MISTAKE

In the fall of 1941 Cameron issued a challenge to all SIL colleagues to pray for fifty new workers who would double the ranks in the coming year. That next summer, Elaine unassumingly signed up for the SIL linguistics training camp in the state of Oklahoma. She recalled later, 'While I was there, they were praying for someone to teach the missionary children so the wives could help with the translation. I started figuring how many hours a week would be saved for Bible translation according to how many children were in the school, and how many years sooner the translation would be produced if someone met this need. When I figured it out, I thought, *"Whoever helps teach is going to help get these translations out so much faster!"* It was staggering to me, and I was all excited about it.'

Two in that class of 150 students that summer were teachers. During one break, Elaine leaned over to a friend—'Esther, I'm sure praying that you are going to answer this need.'

'Don't pray for me, Elaine! I hate teaching school.' Elaine was shocked. From that time on, she heard the question in her mind. What about me? And so the battle began.

By this time, Elaine's situation had changed considerably. When she returned to Chicago at the end of the summer, it wouldn't be to the basement room of Anderson Public School. Her energy in the classroom and talent for teaching had been recognized with a promotion to supervisor over the special-needs programs in 300 schools. The life of a supervisor was the good life indeed. In her own words, 'You go into one room in the morning and one in the afternoon, and the kids are angels during that time. The principal takes you out to lunch and you get a fabulous salary.' At twenty-six, Elaine became the youngest supervisor—and the first woman—ever appointed to this position by the Chicago school district. She had arrived at the top.

Needless to say, when she sensed the Lord calling her to the mission field, she assumed He hadn't been updated on the latest news. 'Oh, that would be impossible, Lord,' she prayed, 'You don't want me—I've already signed a contract with the Board of Education to be supervisor for 300 schools next year.'

She captured her attitude in a comment made years later, reflecting on this time, 'I was very happy, and very foolish. I thought, "I'll give you my money, Lord, but don't touch my life."' None of it made sense. It just wasn't logical. 'I'll tell you what I'll do, Lord,' she finally said. 'With my salary, I can support four missionaries. You know that you'd rather have four than one. Just let me stay home in Chicago.' Somehow, she never felt peace about this arrangement. 'He never assured me that He would prefer four over me. He didn't buy that one. For a year I was most miserable, knowing what the Lord wanted yet trying to offer my money instead of myself.'

SEEK FIRST THE KINGDOM

She never dreamed it like this. Somehow these divine communication wires had become mixed up, and it was her luck to get caught in the middle. Teaching in Mexico was not in her plans and no one would deny that it was completely irrational. Three fears she held, and if she went to the mission field they would certainly come true: she couldn't again have friends like she had in Chicago and 'I'd end up looking like the missionaries who came to church with bun-topped heads, thick glasses and run-down shoes.' But the hardest thought of all was that nearly every missionary she had met was single. She wasn't going, and that was certain.

Or was it? 'I'd hear missionary speakers and go home just torn apart inside and wondering where I fit in this program,' she said later. 'I'll never forget the night I couldn't stand the struggle any longer—I was determined to make the decision that night.'

That's what brought Elaine to the bathroom—the only room in the house with a lock on the door—to fight it out with God. She would not emerge till things were settled. She described those moments as 'a struggle to say yes to the Lord, that where He led me I would follow.' Later she would liken it to the wrestling of Jacob with the angel of the Lord, and when she did come out of that room in the early hours of the morning, something in her had died: a dream, the building of an image.

Yet something new had been birthed: a zeal for the glory of God. 'I remember the goose pimples as I said, "Well, Lord, if this is what you want, it is what I want too." And what a difference!' Elaine had been led to make the greatest, costliest abandonment—the abandonment of self. As David Platt writes, 'We can rest in casual, convenient, cozy, comfortable Christian lives as we cling to the safety and security this world offers... Or we can decide that Jesus is worth far more than this. We can recognize that he has created us, saved us, and called us for a much greater purpose than anything this world could ever offer us.'[2]

Elaine wasn't at all sure that things would turn out all right. 'I surrendered to God, believing I loved the Lord enough to stay single and to endure whatever else He asked me to do—but thinking I'd be so lonely.'

Few things about the new arrangements seemed ideal, and her friends thought her foolish for leaving her job. Her desires she placed on the altar; and in the midst of sacrifice, God undertook to fill her open hands. As one who knew Elaine in later life quipped, 'I love it when God chuckles! And then *later* He lets you know that He was chuckling.' Not one of her three fears would be realized.

That fall of '42, she wrote to Mr. and Mrs. Townsend, telling of her promotion to supervisor. 'I do praise the Lord for this promotion as it has given me many opportunities to witness of His saving and keeping power. My contacts have been mainly with principals. They often remark how fortunate I am to have this position when I'm so young, and that some day I'll probably be a principal. Then I have a chance to tell them that the Lord has called me to serve Him in Mexico.'

Mrs. Townsend wrote back encouragingly, describing the ways Elaine could use her gifts not only in teaching missionary children, but also helping with SIL's newest project of reading campaigns applying visual education among illiterate Indians. Elvira even asked for Elaine's input on experimental games.

Elaine's return letter beautifully demonstrates her quietness of heart, even a mounting excitement: 'Today as I am writing to you, I

---

2   David Platt, forward in John Piper, *Risk is Right*, (Wheaton, Illinois: Crossway, 2008), pp. 8-9.

am rejoicing anew, knowing that His place for me is Mexico. It will be a real privilege to teach the missionaries' children. Your plan of teaching… for six months and then doing work with the Indians for six months sounds very good to me.'

A LETTING GO

For the rest of her life, Elaine wondered what would have happened if she had not said yes to God's call, dropping everything to teach in Mexico. She would never fully know, but one thing was certain: '… you know what is best for me *at all times*,' she wrote in her journal.

But hers was not the only test of obedience. 'Although my Dad was in the business of printing gospel tracts it wasn't easy for him to let me go,' Elaine recalled later. 'My mother could see it, but not my dad. As I look back upon my life, I can see why it was so difficult for Dad to have me go. I had helped pay off the mortgage, aided in other financial ways, and was available to go on many errands. My older sister wasn't living at home and wasn't a Christian. My youngest sister was greatly crippled with arthritis so she couldn't help, and my brother was eighteen at the time. He was helping Dad in the print shop. So for Dad to say goodbye, he was losing his main source of help.' One can only imagine the brightness that Elaine's buoyant disposition lent to her father amidst years of difficulty, discouragement, and loss. But her parents' inability to set aside pragmatism and communicate words and affections of filial love would be a legacy that to some degree, Elaine inherited.

Elaine prayed, for her father in particular, and a few months before her departure she wrote to friends, 'How I do praise the Lord for the miracle He has performed in the hearts of my folks! They are constantly putting things away for when I go and they really seem to be happy. Of course I know that they feel it deeply, but their whole attitude is so entirely different from what it was when I first told them of the Lord's will for me.' Her father would write later that one of the hardest things he ever did was to transport Elaine's fifteen suitcases to the railway station and say goodbye.

'I'll never forget the train station,' Elaine said. 'About fifty of my Mexican friends came to see me off. They were there crying and hanging onto me and singing "God Be With You Until We Meet Again." It was a very moving situation and Mexicans are especially emotional. Then it came time to go. I got on the train, and Dad followed me on. He still wasn't going to give me up. My father isn't given to crying, but he cried so and said, "Elaine, don't go! Come and help me distribute tracts from my shop. I need you."

'I said, "Dad, somebody should do that, but not me. I've got to obey the Lord." Just then, the whistle blew, and along came the conductor— "*Everybody off! Everybody off!*"'

AWAKENING AND SETTING OUT

It was final. On June 18, 1943 Elaine boarded a train that left everything familiar and comfortable behind as it chugged its way into massive unknowns. 'If there were no ignorance about the future, there would be no risk,' writes John Piper. '… It is right to seek to make much of Christ by taking the risks of love. If our single, all-embracing passion is to make much of Christ in life and death, and if the life that magnifies him most is the life of costly love, then life is risk, and risk is right. To run from it is to waste your life…'[3]

There had been no safe way out of the dilemma. Taking off to Mexico was nothing if not a risk, but remaining as a director of Chicago schools posed another sort of loss. Trust was the pivot on which all problems turned to gain, for the life of a believer who bears fruit cannot exist apart from a heart that believes God is good. Elaine would say, 'The Lord guides us as we are in motion.'

Years later she challenged a group of young women, 'The biggest reason we hesitate in saying *yes* to the Lord is that we want to control our own lives… But when He directs there is a greater inner satisfaction, a sense of eternal rewards, a heavy leaning on Him. "… *Thou wilt show*

---

3   Piper, *Risk is Right*, pp. 18, 22, 17. 'Of course the motive for risk-taking is not heroism or adrenaline or glory'—but 'faith in the all-providing, all-ruling, all-satisfying Son of God, Jesus Christ… it's God who gets the praise because of his care. In this way risk reflects God's value, not our valor.'

me the path of life, in Thy presence is fullness of joy, at Thy right hand are pleasures forevermore.'"

Conflict swirled the globe as each day brought news of violent and pivotal events. The whole world, it seemed, was in a panic. Elaine left her homeland in the turmoil of war, yet set her heart to trust God when everything appeared to be turning out wrong. 'Thank you for your peace no matter what happens—something money can't buy.' She added in her later years. 'Thank you for reminding me that godliness with contentment is great gain...' The outcome of her battle to reconcile contentment with loss at this stage would endure with her for the rest of her life.

RISKING LOSS, GAINING REWARD

Three days after leaving Chicago, she and her friend Ethel Humbert arrived in Mexico City. Finding lodging became their first order of business, and although SIL owned a group house to rent in the city, even these sparse arrangements were considered too luxurious for these over-frugal girls. Instead, they took what Elaine described as 'this little dinky bedroom on the ground floor of a very cheap hotel.' Their windows opened onto a patio.

Before her departure, the North Side Gospel Center had thrown a shower for their popular Elaine Mielke, giving generously out of their little to provide for her needs on the mission field: blankets, tableware, silverware, camera, books, a typewriter, linens. On their first night in Mexico City, an intruder came on to the balcony and through the window, chloroformed Elaine and Ethel, and walked out with all their possessions except a few clothes. They awoke at noon the next day to discover a loss which could not possibly be replaced.

Yet even this came as a mercy. 'I was counting on all this stuff I had to keep me happy,' Elaine said later, 'but I could live without it. It made me realize how temporal these material possessions were.' God continued to work, clearing her sight, changing her appetites, and increasing her faith.

This emptying highlighted her own insufficiency, and she wrote to friends at home. 'I do praise the Lord that He has given His angels charge over me to keep me in all my ways'. Better things would come out of this than anything lost, for God continued to open up avenues of joy. As John Piper writes, 'Every loss we risk, in order to make much of Christ, God promises to restore a thousand-fold with his all-satisfying fellowship.'[4]

FINDING HOME

After the robbery, Elaine and Ethel moved to the mission's group home in Mexico City. 'The rich spiritual blessings and fellowship there shall long be remembered,' Elaine noted in letters home. Another literacy worker captured well the lively, focused spirit of the group, 'We have been having a wonderful time...and I am sure that the others feel as I do that there's no other place in the world we'd rather be right now. We have seen the Lord at work!'

Elaine found here 'a host of grand friends,' as she referred to them. She soon gained her own reputation. Adele Elson, one woman who knew her during that time, said, 'She was a gracious, wonderful lady, and quite talented. Everybody liked her, and she knew everybody by name. She was friendly, treated everyone alike and always included everybody...' Everything was a lark.

Throughout this daring change of life, Elaine never found reason to be ashamed of her confidence in God's purposes towards her. At the end of her life she wrote of this very thing, 'Thank you for your promise to me if I would leave father and mother, houses and lands in this life you said you'd give me a hundredfold and I'd inherit everlasting life. You have done that and more for me, Lord... I'm so glad I don't need to try pushing myself and making a name for myself; but rather my joy is in exalting you, Lord Jesus.'

---

4   Piper, *Risk is Right*, p. 40.

7. A LESSENING

A great necessity is a great opportunity. Nothing is really lost by a life
of sacrifice; everything is lost by failure to obey God's call… What we
do upon a great occasion will probably depend on what we already are;
what we are will be the result of previous years of self-discipline under
the grace of Christ, or the absence of it.

Henry Parry Liddon[1]

After meeting Cameron and his wife Elvira in Norman at the SIL
training camp, Elaine rejoined them on the field. This founder of the
fledgling Wycliffe Bible Translators and his wife lived in a little trailer
in the Aztec village of Tetelcingo Morelos, about sixty miles south of
Mexico City. Here they worked with the Indians on practical projects
like bringing water into the village, teaching the women to sew using
Singer machines, and raising vegetables in the town square. Cameron
also reduced the language to writing and developed primers. In these
days, their efforts toward literacy and cultural advancement were
warmly welcomed. Seven years earlier, when the Mexican President
Cárdenas visited their outpost, his great respect for their work had
birthed a deep friendship between him and Cameron Townsend which
lasted till the end of Cárdenas' life.

Nevertheless, Elaine certainly looked like she had lost her mind
when, after a couple months of intensive language study in Mexico
City, she arrived in the village to teach the missionaries' children and
found no classroom ready for her. 'The work was so new that there were

---

1   http://www.backtothebible.org/devotions/respond-to-the-call (Joy and Strength).
     Last accessed June 1st, 2018.

only three who were ready for school. I had a seventh and an eighth grader, and a first year high school student. The rest of the kids were too small. Our classroom was in the living room of the Todd home…'

RETURN TO THE CHALKBOARD

The students presented a marked contrast from her first class in the States, and teaching them was 'really more like play than work as the children [were] so eager to learn.' Years later, these former students would retain fond memories of their 'Miss Mielke' and the adventurous field trips she led.

Despite this, it proved a dismal prospect for this former director of 300 Chicago schools to dedicate the potential of an entire year to the education of three children. This altered situation could hardly fail to be disheartening, and Elaine admitted as much: 'Many times that first year I wished I were back in Chicago where I had an active ministry with the Mexican mission. Instead here I was, teaching three children. But wasn't the Lord good to have me stay there?' Her sphere of influence had painfully narrowed, yet she threw herself into the work wholeheartedly.

Elaine helped Elvira with the group's office work, and cultivated relationships with other missionaries. She also dedicated a good deal of time to the study of Spanish. Three times a week, she rode the bus to take Spanish lessons at the university. Seeing the need for a Sunday school, she prayed about it, then jumped in. 'One of the native boys, Refugio by name, and I went calling from hut to hut to invite the folks out. How grateful we were when the Lord sent forty-seven out for the first Sunday… more have been coming… Today being Saturday, I have the pleasure of going to the homes and inviting folks out for the service tonight and tomorrow. Oh how I love this part of my work!'

Invigorated by facing a full classroom once again, Elaine enchanted these students with her liveliness and care. 'The Lord continues to do the exceedingly abundant above that which we could ask or think. So far the highest attendance that we have had in Sunday school is seventy-nine. It is such a joy to teach my little darlings.' One is not a bit surprised by her cheery 'How the months do fly by!'

Elaine's conception of life had been proved wrong once again: 'All I ever thought about being a missionary was a life of loneliness and sacrifice. So stupid was I. When I went to the field, I took a box filled with books to fill the lonely hours I'd envisioned. I never got a chance to open them. Life became so fascinating and thrilling.'

Nevertheless, loneliness doubtless overtook her in occasional moments. Elisabeth Elliot, a missionary well acquainted with loss and hardship, wrote,

> Discipline very often involves loss, diminishment, 'fallings from us, vanishings.' Why? Because God wills our perfection in holiness, that is, our joy. But, we argue, why should diminishments be the prerequisite for joy? The answer to that lies within the great mystery that underlies creation: the principle of life out of death, exemplified for all time in the Incarnation… I am reminded that God is my Father still, that He does have a purpose for me, and that nothing, absolutely nothing, is useless in the fulfillment of that purpose if I'll trust Him for it and submit to the lessons… God's purpose for us is holiness—His own holiness which we are to share… [2]

TRIALS OF SINGLENESS

Elaine's trip around the world had given her a keen interest in other people and cultures. Her letters home to her family paint a lively occupation and colorful surroundings. To her sister, Shirley, she wrote about the unique culture that surrounded her: 'The streets and sidewalks here in Mexico are narrow and crowded. With all the people pushing us there are many men who stand on the sidewalk trying to sell little live puppies and cats. They hold them in their hands up around their heads. When Americans pass they just about put them in your face. More fun.'

Another cultural norm, combined with Elaine's natural charm and love for society, contrived to place her in a few awkward, and nearly dangerous, situations—'unusual experiences' as she called them. According to Elaine, one of the primary challenges faced by single missionary girls was the common assumption that they were in want of

2   Elisabeth Elliot, *Trusting God in a Twisted World*, p. 18.

husbands. 'It's just not in cultural patterns for a girl to go through life single,' she explained. 'And why else would you be leaving your home at all?' This created problems, along with the additional fact that the Indians valued weight as a sign of prosperity.

Writing home she told of a failed romantic endeavor on the part of an Indian. 'I had lunch with about 100 teachers of the state of Morelos last week and I certainly did enjoy their company. One was a young fellow who sat across from me and practiced the little English that he knew. This is the way the conversation ran on his part. "I love you Miss, I want you for my wife, you are very beautiful." I guess you will hardly blame me when I tell you that I laughed in his face. Almost all of the Mexican fellows know these few phrases and they practice them every chance they get. More fun.'

Elaine woke one night to hear the sound of bare feet, her door opening, and to feel a hand on her stomach. She screamed, and the intruder left. When she told the mayor, Don Martin, the next day he intimated that 'the señorita' was to blame, not Pancho. 'You talk with your eyes,' he told her, 'which is an encouragement to him.' After hearing of a similar occurrence from a friend, Elaine began wearing sunglasses when she went out.

Another day, a Mexican in police uniform sat next to her on the bus. When he learned that she was learning Spanish, he began to help her, and soon he had learned what time her bus returned. 'I was greatly surprised to find him at the bus station, wanting to return with me,' Elaine said. 'Well, he was a real—shall I say—pain in the neck? He just pursued me and pursued me. After several such trips, he called on me at the Todd home where I was teaching the children, bringing a box of candy and a bottle of liquor. He wanted me to go to the next town with him for a date.' When she refused the gift, he asked why, and she made up an excuse about a special friend in the States. 'Well, that shouldn't stop us,' he replied. 'I have a wife in Cuautla.'

When he saw that she was firm in her refusal, he threw the bottle against a brick wall, shattering it and frightening Elaine's young students. Elaine went to the Director, and he in turn informed the police station. The man did not return.

ALL THE NEWS OF LIVING

But life continued despite such disturbances, and in a letter to her family, Elaine wrote, 'Last week I went to a Flag Day celebration. It was great with the drums, bugles, bands, etc. It seems as though every one of the six bands were playing a different tune all at the same time. The more noise they could make the better they liked it.'

Soon she obtained a little adobe house of her own along one of the streets in that ancient town, just a short walk from the Townsends' trailer home. Making a home became one of her great delights. When the mayor of Tetelcingo happened in for a visit, he saw the bathroom and exclaimed, 'If this is what Señorita Elena's bathroom looks like, what must heaven be like!?'

Adele, who lived in Elaine's little house after she had left, briefly described the less-than-ideal circumstances and Elaine's success with them: 'I had a hat with a veil, and when I went to get it out one time, there it was—full of scorpions. They were caught in the veil… But the house was creative. She had put curtains up, flowers around, pictures on the walls. It was a nice cozy little place.'

In the midst of beautifying her home, Elaine wrote of her desire to have company and show her love in a practical way to those who had cared so well for her. To her, hospitality was the aide of gratitude; it showed honor, opened up relationships, strengthened community, encouraged friends, and shone forth the warmth of the gospel. She had learned hospitality from her mother, and from this time on it played a major role in her own life.

Sometimes deeper thoughts evaded her, and phone-style chitchat came through the mail to Shirley, 'Well snooks, there hasn't been anything real exciting here as yet, but I thought you'd like to know that I am still kicking.'

Elaine's joy in the work to which she had been called shows throughout her letters, 'I can't get over how very happy I am here. Of course I do miss you all dreadfully, but the Lord has given me real joy in knowing that I am where He wants me to be.' Soon, a new assignment would be given her, one for which God had emphatically gifted her.

TOO DEEP AN IMPRESSION

She wrote repeatedly of the passion which had led her to Mexico in the first place. 'The joy of seeing those heathen Indians receive Him as their Savior far surpasses all the comforts and pleasures of home. How are you planning to spend your life for your Redeemer? ... You consider spending your life in medicine, in science, in business, in teaching, in preaching, or in being a missionary. A Bible translator enjoys in part all these...Yet beyond all these, the translator leaves as the investment of his life, a permanent inheritance—the Bible. I know you will never regret taking this step for Him; for truly "there is joy, and peace, and blessing in the service of the King."' Late in 1949 she wrote,

> Now may I speak very plainly to you young folks back home? ... Usually there is just one big thing holding each person back from taking the precious gospel to those who sit in darkness. Often it is position, home, loved ones, fear of uncertainty, doubt as to whether the Lord will really provide. Oh young person, don't let any of these things which are so passing, keep you from obeying His last command and thus do a work that will last through all eternity! I know that you as well as I want to hear His 'Well done, thou good and faithful servant.'

Elaine's experiences in Mexico deepened her trust in the efficacy of the Word to change lives, and drew her to cling to her Savior ever more tightly. Her life echoed Jonathan Edwards' words: 'When we see the supreme beauty and glory of Christ, we see that he is worthy of our worship, our obedience, our very lives. This makes us follow him, despite all difficulties. We cannot forget him or exchange him for something else. He has made too deep an impression on us!'[3]

---

3   Jonathan Edwards, *The Experience That Counts*, (Grand Rapids, Michigan: Evangelical Press: 1991), p. 114.

8. 'BEST JOB IN THE OUTFIT!'

He, I know, is able to carry out His will, and His will is mine. It makes no matter where He places me, or how. That is rather for Him to consider than for me; for in the easiest position He must give me His grace, and in the most difficult His grace is sufficient. If God should place me in great perplexity, must He not give me much guidance; in positions of great difficulty much grace; in circumstances of great pressure and trial, much strength? No fear that His resources will be unequal to the emergency! And His resources are mine—for He is mine, and is with me and dwells in me.

Hudson Taylor[1]

When he and Elvira first wrote to Elaine about coming to Mexico, Cameron mentioned the great advantage her skills might lend to their fledgling reading campaigns. Now, after a year of observing her skill for engaging adults and children alike, and illiterate Indians, he became surer than ever that she possessed the ability and the flair to carry off such a project.

Few of the tribes engaged by SIL translators could boast any degree of literacy. This presented a challenge as linguists worked to compose a written language from oral. Mr. Todd, father to two of Elaine's pupils, had been applying the principles of visual education, and Cameron had begun work on a card game. Although several translators had developed primers for their language groups, not all were gifted with the spark needed to inspire natives who had never experienced a desire

---

1   Quoted in Howard Taylor, *Hudson Taylor's Spiritual Secret*, (Chicago, Illinois: Moody Press, 1955), pp. 165-6.

to read. At Cameron's request, Elaine now launched a year-long reading campaign for the Aztecs in Tetelcingo and several other language groups across Mexico.

Because Elaine could rely on the translator's own working knowledge of the local language, fluency in specific dialects wouldn't be necessary; only simple, conversational phrases, such as *How are you? What's your name? Do you have any children?* Although she would be teaching the Indians themselves, these campaigns were just as much for the purpose of teaching translators to teach, and to develop effective materials.

SALOONS, BABIES, AND LIZARDS

The first challenge facing Elaine was *where* to teach. 'The only place the men congregated was the town tavern,' recalled Elaine, adding humorously, 'I wondered how my home church would feel about my going to a saloon every night to teach these men.' In reports home she delicately wrote of a 'centrally located place, such as a store' where they held night school. The bartender was delighted at the increase in business, and Elaine had found a classroom. She noted the rapid progress of the men; but even here, ulterior motives were not entirely absent: 'The men came 'cause here were single girls teaching them to read.' One recalls Paul's remark, 'I have become all things to all people, that by all means I might save some. I do it all for the sake of the gospel, that I may share with them in its blessings.'[2]

Teaching the women, well, that was another story! From their earliest days they had been told of their own stone-headed stupidity, and what incentive did they have to read books? 'One of the biggest jobs in connection with a reading campaign is getting the Indians to have a desire to learn to read,' Elaine explained. 'I could never get one without a baby in their arms. I'd find the mothers sitting on a chair with a string wrapped around her big toe to rock the hammock with a baby in it, [carrying] another baby at the breast and making porridge with her hands. They couldn't stop working to learn to read.' But creative methods began to pay off, and Elaine wrote an engaging little excerpt for her church in Chicago, which captured the rhythm of her days:

---

2   I Corinthians 9:22-3.

Elaine with her pupils, circa 1945.

I'd like to take you with me on one of my daily routines of teaching...
As we approach the little adobe hut of Doña Juana, we can hear the
pleasant sound of the pat, pat, pat, of her hands as she shapes her
tortillas, which is their native bread. Mingled with this sound, we hear
a baby or two crying for attention. Since there are no door bells to ring,
or even a door upon which to knock, we pleasantly call, *'Buenos días,
Doña Juana,'* and with that our hostess graciously invites us to come
in. After offering us a little piece of wood to sit on, she hurries back to
her work. Then after playing with the babies a bit and trying to help
Doña Juana grind corn, we tell her that we have come to teach her
to read, and that we have brought with us some grand games to play.
The games are attractively colored and her interest is aroused. This is
perhaps the first time that Doña Juana has been asked to play a game
since she was married at the age of twelve. What fun we have playing
together, and how very pleased our pupil is as she sees that she is able
to recognize a few letters. We try to keep our classes short and to the
point, leaving the pupil before her interest dies down so she is really

glad to see us the next day. Thus we go from hut to hut, making friends with the natives and teaching the women how to read.

As relationships developed and trust increased, the reading campaign earned its own class time, and grew into a community activity. Years later she would write, 'I find that you should always start with your men folks first. If you start with children, it's children's play. If you start with the ladies, it's sissy stuff. If you get those men to play, then everybody else wants to do it.'

In one village, her class consisted of thirty-six rowdy children who had been taught to shout answers simultaneously. Elaine noted the many contrasts to her classrooms back in the States:

> Instead of having each child at his own desk, we have three children on a bench about three feet long, and all working at the same table. In order to have enough light in the classroom, we have two doors standing open. Instead of 'Mary's little lamb' following her to school, we usually have half a dozen of the neighborhood chickens attending classes. The chickens don't bother the boys and girls, (only the teacher), but the other day even the children were quite disturbed when a large lizard came to school, and ran up and down the aisles. The little girls jumped up on their benches and squealed with fright, while the boys as well as their teacher, pretended to be brave and tried to expel our uninvited guest. However, in spite of the many interruptions, I am very pleased with the progress of the children.

AND THE FRUIT RIPENS

In the mornings, Elaine held classes in the schoolhouse, and in the afternoons and evenings she taught the women to read, write, and sew. She saw great progress in the ability of the women as they responded to encouragement and gained confidence. 'I wish you could have been here a few weeks ago when the women sang from the hymn books for the first time,' she wrote. 'Truly, their faces just radiated with joy over this accomplishment which they had all their lives thought impossible. I think that they will be ready to begin reading the gospel of John in just another week or so.'

It was the hymns, rich with meaning and gospel clarity, which first captivated the hearts of the Indians. 'You know, they all wanted to be able to read the hymns,' Elaine remarked. 'And once they could read the hymns it was not too hard to give them the Word.'

Her experience in teaching underprivileged children in the roughest areas of Chicago had well equipped her to capture and retain the interest of distracted pupils. More than one Indian found himself learning to read from what seemed merely an entertaining game. From there, Elaine transitioned to primers prepared by the translators, and the Bible. She wrote with joy of people who 'worshipped the ant and the sun, and have thought that by their good works they would merit eternal life now reading for the first time that the price of their sin has been paid. They no longer need torture themselves, but can put their trust in the Lord Jesus and be freed from their constant fear.'

AN ENTREPRENEURIAL VENTURE

After Tetelcingo Elaine journeyed to other remote villages where SIL missionaries worked. Single girls were in short supply, so she whisked away Ester Juarez, a little Mexican maid in the kitchen of the mission. Together they traveled by train, bus, and mule into the remote hinterlands.

In the first of these small villages they met Doris and Marjorie, who had worked at learning and analyzing the language to develop an alphabet, create primers, and translate the New Testament for four years. Now here was Elaine, to kick-start the seed of literacy and foster an excitement in the Indians.

Elaine set right to work. After supper she said, 'All right, I have six weeks to teach this tribe to read, so let's plan our schedule for tomorrow.'

'Put down "water",' replied Doris.

'*Water?* What do you mean?'

Marjorie explained, 'It takes about an hour to go for it and the path is directly up hill, then down again an hour.'

'Can't we get the children to get the water? Don't you have money to pay these children?' Elaine was incredulous.

'We've asked the Indians time and again to go for us, but money means nothing to them. They only punch holes in it and wear it for a necklace, and they have so many coins around their necks now that another coin won't matter to them. There is no place to spend it here in town, and the kids would rather play than earn money.'

Well! That didn't sit too well with Elaine Mielke, particularly since the three-inch heels from her time at the five and dime store hadn't done as many favors for her feet as for her looks. She pondered a solution, unwilling to surrender her limited time, and remembering the efficiency so characteristic of the Townsends, particularly when it came to time management. Her ingenuity soon came into play, as well as her love for fashion. 'She brought a lot of costume jewelry with her to Mexico,' commented one woman, with a little shake of the head. 'I don't know when she thought she was going to use it all, but there it was!'

There it was indeed! Each of the three contributed pins, necklaces, bracelets, a flashlight, and a fountain pen, and soon fourteen items were mounted on a milk-carton board, sporting their value below in numbers of water buckets. A little meeting was held to inform the parents of the plan. Would their children work for these items? Oh, *would they!* Excitement ran high, and so the drama began.

The next morning, long before they had risen, the women found lines of children waiting their turn to bring water. There were only two buckets, but every concave item found itself enlisted, and soon the women had water enough for as many baths as they could have wished. At night they poured the extra down the mountain so the eager beavers could begin again in the morning.

FOR LACK OF A BRIDGE

'What did you say, Don Francisco?'

'The cyclone has destroyed all of the bridges and we won't be able to receive any mail for several weeks.'

'What a shame! We won't have any difficulty trying to leave the tribe in about seven more weeks will we? Surely by then the bridges will be reconstructed.'

'*Quien sabe?*'[3] came the not very encouraging reply.

'I had just arrived in Papalo to hold a reading campaign among the Cuicateco Indians,' Elaine wrote, 'when the cyclone, which lasted three days, struck. Reports came up the mountain that the Indians believed their gods had sent the cyclone to punish them for letting us—"the white witches," live in their village. So, of course, they wanted to appease their gods and the only way they could think of was to kill us. How precious was the assurance of His promise that all things work together for good as we faced possible death that Sunday in September. The Lord has told us to cast all our care upon Him, so having done this we went to sleep.'

The next day, they heard from neighboring villages where homes had been destroyed and people killed, but in Papalotepec,[4] all remained unharmed.

AN EDUCATOR'S EDUCATOR

In this village, Elaine managed an energetic schedule of classes from 10:00 am to 1:00 pm, 3:00 pm to 6:00 pm, and 7:00 pm to 10:00 pm. Despite their early concern over the complications of a tonal language, the class numbered fifty after the first week. Elaine and the two translators visited the women in their homes in the morning while they made tortillas, continued lessons in the classrooms during the afternoon, taught the group of men crowded into the store every night, and held Bible studies for the forty Cuicateco believers. 'I love my work more and more,' wrote Elaine, 'and it is such a thrill to see the Indians reading in their own language… the Lord has wonderfully undertaken…'

Her periodic report reflected the saturated peace of her heart: '"He doeth all things well." This is a promise that has come to me often during these last two weeks as we are shut off from all communication due to a flood and cyclone. I don't know when you will get this report as most of the folks say it might be six months before the trains are again going…'

---

3   '*Who knows?*'
4   'Butterfly mountain place.'

When the time came to leave, no bridge had materialized. Upon their arrival at the riverbank, they were greeted by a makeshift cable, and Elaine was elected to cross first, suspended above the rushing torrent by a small swing.

A CHERRY OF A JOB

Elaine frequently noted the joyful attitude of the translators. 'It was so interesting,' she wrote, 'to hear the girls who worked in these mountains where it was so cold say they had the best location… and those who worked in the difficult lower desert areas say, "Wasn't the Lord good to give us this place?" Each one the Lord placed so beautifully.' These women quickly became her role models of the heart. Just as she previously had valued the bustle and run of Chicago, now she was deeply impressed by their faith in the goodness of God and their spirit of gladness—a new measure of success.

In a short time, it became apparent that Elaine possessed unique skill for her new role. Peter Brouillette, a close friend in later years, said, 'She was an educator's educator from the get go. That stuff cannot be taught—that's a gift.' Many expressed surprise at the enthusiasm of the Indians for her approaches and the speed with which they became literate. Her style carried a certain magic, and with it she kept the Indians engaged for hours.

Elaine said of her reading campaigns, 'I often thought my job was like the cherry on the top of the ice cream sundae. The translators had done all the hard work… I had the joy of teaching them the Word.'

Predictably, that year of literacy work turned into two. Elaine moved out into a total of seventeen different language groups developing primers, games, techniques, and encouraging translators in their efforts. But behind all these advances was a higher ambition: 'Our goal is to see that every country gets God's Word in their own language.'

9. SPURRING ON AND POINTING UPWARD

> When I have learnt to love God better than my earthly dearest, I shall love my earthly dearest better than I do now… When first things are put first, second things are not suppressed but increased.
>
> C.S. Lewis[1]

Like Elaine, Cameron's wife, Elvira, also came from Chicago. Shortly after her engagement to Cameron, however, Elvira had begun to show signs of illness, and by the time Elaine came to live in Tetelcingo, things had reached a critical stage. Challenged by severe heart and mental trouble, she could do little more than minor household duties. Usually caring and earnest, she now fell prey to frequent and severe mood swings. These limitations, combined with Cameron's frequent absences, opened the door for a relationship between her and Elaine, who counted it a privilege to act as her companion.

But this relationship would be short-lived. In 1944, the Townsends traveled to the States in an attempt to strengthen Elvira's health. Cameron believed her to be improving, but she died on Christmas Eve, with her faithful husband by her side.

Elvira's road had been long and painful, but her heart sought the expansion of God's glory among the Indians and despite the mental battles she faced, this passion still shone through at times. One can be sure that many lessons were imparted to Elaine as a new missionary from the failing and debilitated wife of Wycliffe's visionary and founder. 'She

---

1   C.S. Lewis, *Letters of C.S. Lewis* (New York: Harcort Brace Jovanovich, 1966), p. 248.

was a wonderful correspondent and a very good Bible teacher,' Elaine remembered. 'She wrote a little book about Latin American courtesy and spoke Spanish flawlessly—beautifully. She was a very gracious person. I am so glad that I knew her.'

OBLIVIOUS CANDIDATE

Months after Elvira's death, conjectures circulated among the field workers. Many were certain that Cameron would not remain single for long—but who would be the lucky girl? Elaine recalled, 'About six months after Elvira's death, I overheard some of the single girls wondering if Cam would ever remarry.' Most liked the idea, and speculations abounded. Unbeknownst to her, five separate groups chose Elaine as the likely candidate. Unfortunately, she had decided some time ago that she would never marry a man more than ten years her senior, or anyone who had been married before. So that was settled.

Or was it? In this area, as in many others, God countermanded her dreams with something better.

'My first hint of a romantic interest brewing was one night on a stroll near the group house in Mexico City,' Elaine said. 'From the time I first met him in 1942, he'd been known to all of us as "Uncle Cam". He got this title when his niece, Evelyn Pike came to help care for Elvira. We followed suit calling him "uncle," as well and he liked it because it made for a much more friendly relationship. That evening, Cameron turned to me and said "Do you suppose you could leave off the *uncle* part?" It wasn't too hard to do. I tried it and found I liked it.'

DEVELOPMENTS

Lack of money and many watching eyes didn't preclude what Elaine termed a delightful romance, filled with many long walks and conversations. When Neil and Jane Nellis invited the pair over for dinner, Cameron spent the evening helping Elaine make curtains for her bathroom, even after an invitation from Neil to a game of chess.

In his characteristically strategic manner, Cam saw the possible advantages of all the planning and plotting which swirled around them. 'Incidentally, [Ethel Wallis] might try to push her idea about you and me and that would be lots of fun,' he wrote Elaine. 'Of course you should pay as much attention to the young fellows as to me, but if Ethel encouraged us sufficiently, we would be willing to take a stroll together, wouldn't we?' Elaine remembered the first time Cameron held her hand, 'and under a hat at that!'

Such creativity was certainly called for. The two were not yet ready to release news of a serious relationship till they became absolutely certain of God's leading.

EVEN IN LOVE

In Los Angeles during that spring of 1945, Cameron met MAF pilot Betty Greene, whom he cajoled into promising that she would pray about piloting a plane for SIL members stationed in the jungle. Cameron did not tell her, of course, that this particular plane was nonexistent at the time. By habit, he capitalized on the opportunities in front of him, then prayed and networked for the results, and this case was no different. He immediately wrote a pastor in Chicago asking if their church would fund the purchase of a plane for which he had 'secured' a pilot.

It was shortly after this that he heard Elaine was in Chicago for her grandmother's funeral. If a telephone call would be nice, he thought, a visit would be even better. Besides, it was probably very necessary that he visit the pastor in Chicago. He traveled by train, and at a station in Minneapolis he encountered the temptation of a telephone booth.

The next minute Elaine picked up, and as she answered, an impish idea sparked in Cameron's head. 'Temitztlasohtla meac.'

'Pardon?' Elaine replied in Spanish.

'Temitztlasohtla meac,' he repeated.

Not Spanish, she thought, but she had a hunch...

'The first time he told me he loved me was through long distance,' Elaine said. 'I had to pretty much guess that this was what he was saying because my Aztec wasn't that good. So I thanked him, not knowing whether that was what he was saying or not.'

After Elaine left for linguistic studies in Norman, Oklahoma, Cameron wrote,

Only twenty-nine hours have elapsed since you left us, but I find myself longing to be near you again. Your presence, however, has seemed to be hovering around. Everyone here has mentioned how they enjoyed you—how lovely you are... Well, girlie, I'm sure with you in prayer... Please take time off from work to enjoy the fellowship that abounds [in Norman]... give [Evie] and Ken my love, but keep an ocean full for yourself. [2]

'Follow after love, and desire spiritual gifts... Inasmuch as ye are zealous of spiritual gifts, seek that ye may excel to the edifying of the church' (I Cor. 14:1,12). How well you carried out the commands of those verses in the church of Tetelcingo! May God use you that way with a dozen tribes the next sixteen months and then give you as a special love gift to a one man tribe named

Your Cameron!

The next morning, Cameron added a short note: 'News over the radio tells of Japan's offer to surrender. Praise the Lord! That should bring us recruits and leaders. The next year or two will be busy ones, but with an unparalleled advance in pioneer missions...'

UNCERTAIN DAYS

From Mexico City Cameron wrote,

Dear Elaine,

You have been in my thoughts and prayers the past two days and today so much that you have almost been in my way. Que te parece?[3]... I love you so much that I want you to be happy and always in the center of God's will even if that means that you should have someone else for a husband (preferably one your own age). I really mean that, precious girl. My concept of love does not necessarily include having and holding... it is to see the loved one truly happy.

Selfishly, I hope and pray that some day God will show us that our lives should be united in His service. Until He does, though, is it right and fair to you for me to be talking, acting, and writing my

---

2   Evie, Cam's niece, and her husband Ken, who went on to become one of the world's foremost linguists.

3   *What do you think?!*

love to you? For me, it seems natural to do so, and I have had so many disappointments in the past that I could take it if God gave you to someone else and showed me that I should never marry. It's different, though, for you, and I want you to tell me frankly if you want me to act differently until God permits me to definitely ask you the big question. Surely He will reveal His will by next January and in the meantime, we'll be away from each other... much of the time...

... If you think that my letters should be just news and friendship until we know the Lord's will, I'll be careful to comply with your wishes. You know how people judge and criticize. They cannot know all the facts and so could not understand why I have fallen in love so soon after Elvira's death. Some would be caustic if they should learn of it and their criticisms would reflect on the work. I owe my first allegiance to the precious work He has entrusted to my leadership...

The source of this hesitation lay primarily in two considerations: their significant age difference, and his responsibilities as director, which would likely affect family life.

'If you were unknown to me, I could be perfectly happy living without a home as I am now,' wrote Cameron.

I've had a wonderful time. I feel free to go and come serving the Lord and belonging, as it were, to everybody. But when I think of you, I realize how much better my service would be if you were with me, and I ask Him, 'Please dear Lord, let me have her some day if it's Thy blessed will.' He hasn't said yes to me yet, but I have a feeling that after He has tested both of our hearts thoroughly, He will...

The risk of separation sobered both, and Cameron responded tenderly to Elaine's concerns:

We are becoming so attached to one another it would be a terrific blow if the Lord did not let us go through life together... Separations do cause heartaches... I cannot say that God has told me yet that He would have me marry again. Nevertheless, I've permitted myself to fall head over heels in love with you.

Darling, all I can say is that I am confident that God will show me His will in the next five months or will show you, or will show both of

us. How, though, can I be around you and not tell you of my love?…
And here I sit writing words as fraught with love as any… Where does
the logic of it all take us? … no more mention of love by word or letter
until God has said 'yes' to us! Can we do it? I admit that we should, but
are we able? I leave it up to you and will gladly fall in line with your
wishes, though it seems impossible.

THE ALTAR OF PATIENCE

The months grew agonizing. Letter after letter revealed Cameron
struggling with uncertainty regarding the future. They had set out to
spread the gospel, and foremost in their hearts was the desire that any
closer relationship would bring greater glory to their King. 'God will
guide,' he wrote. 'His will is best. I love it even when it seems hard at
the time. We don't need to understand the why and wherefore and
other details. If it is His will, that's enough.' This assurance would be
put to the test.

Elaine found her time with the Lord to grow sweeter in the process:
'How precious has been the fellowship I've had with Him these past
few days. This morning I read Philippians and there are several verses
that I know well which have taken on new life since you have come
into my life.' Her calling to strengthen this man of God certainly began
here in her willing submission to God's providence.

In leaving for the mission field, Elaine had offered up her fear of
lifelong singleness. Now she cultivated the patience to wait upon the
One who would do all things well, and engage in the work before her.
The tenacity which gave up desire and laid it at the feet of her Lord
drew Cameron irresistibly.

Elaine responded to one of Cameron's letters,

I appreciate your advice dear when you tell me to have dates with
young men, but please believe me honey when I say it is you I love and
I know I would never be happy with anyone else. Since I have been in
Mexico I know I haven't had many dates with young men but while
I was home I had my fling and no one can compare with Cameron
Townsend. I wanted ever so much to talk to you this morning face to
face but that seems so far away that I couldn't wait.

Whether they knew it or not, the yes had begun to wash over them like the rising tide—though it would take a few months yet to lift their ship.

A LANDSCAPE OF WAITING

During the next year, Cameron continued his travels and responsibilities as director of SIL and WBT. Elaine carried out reading campaigns in the remote villages of Mexico. Times together were rare and precious, and the development of their relationship took place primarily through letter. From Iquitos, Peru, came one letter from Cameron, 'As I write, a gorgeous tropical moon is looking at me through the window. It certainly is a beauty. If you were here and if there weren't so many mosquitoes, we could go for a stroll along the waterfront. Maybe there's enough breeze there to blow the mosquitoes away, but the first "if" persists and it is formidable.'

Clearly, Cameron used these communications to work through his own thoughts and emotions as he continued to earnestly seek God's leading. 'My adorable Elaine,' Cam wrote as June of 1945 began,

> ... Do we love Him more than all or anyone else? If so, His own blessed will is all that we want. Of all the girls I ever knew, I believe that you are the best suited for me and since the Lord has brought you across my path at this time, I can't help but reason that it is because He intended you for me. But whether that proves to be the case or not, I know this: He wants us to be willing to turn over to Him our dearest treasure on earth for Him to give back if He wishes, or to deny it to us. I have definitely turned you over to Him. To what better care could I entrust the object of my love. I'm so glad that you don't come between Him and me but rather draw me closer to Him and I hope and pray that the same holds true in your attitude toward me. Then, if He turns around and gives us to one another in His wonderful mercy, how flawless our joy will be and how confident we can be that He will use our united ministry!

From Saskatchewan he wrote,

You are in my mind more than ever, but the Lord gives no further light…If I were to insist, I rather think that the Lord would give you to me, but… His directive and not His permissive will is what we want, and that's what we shall have by His grace. You can't imagine, Elaine, how hard it is to write that when I WANT you so much, but how dreadful it would be for both of us if we got out of His directive will. Your beautiful attitude as expressed in your letters helps a lot, I tell you. God bless you, precious girlie.

Even as a veteran missionary, Cameron's letters overflowed with effusive affection which did not live up to common perceptions of dull missionary romance.

May our blessed Lord to whom we owe one another and everything else that we prize in this world enable us to keep our Savior first in all things—even in the ecstasy of love. Then we can be sure of His blessing in all things.

Another letter ran, 'I'm hopelessly in love. There's no doubt about that. By the grace of God, however, that love is going to remain sanctified to Him, though I can see that I'm going to need your constant help in this regard. He must always come first, even in this. By "sanctified" I mean subservient to Him—useful for Him. God bless you, my darling. I praise Him for you.'

He also appeared to possess a knack for interpreting Scripture. In a letter written from Lima, Peru in June of 1945, he wrote, 'Why are you constantly in my thoughts? It must be that in keeping with Phil. 4:8, my mind dwells upon the loveliest earthly object. Two letters came from you yesterday and were devoured before a very important engagement was taken care of. Wasn't that unbusinesslike! I must learn not to let you affect me that way.' It was quickly becoming evident that this single-minded missionary was a goner.

AT LAST, THE QUESTION

As the storms of war subsided, the waiting also drew to a close. Cameron at last became confident of what had been obvious to onlookers for months now. He wrote, asking her consent. She replied on a train to

Vera Cruz, on October 24th, in her typical systematic style (though she anticipated his impatience, and underlined the pertinent passage, which lay nearly halfway through the lengthy epistle):

> For years I have wondered if the Lord would ever bring across my life a companion whom I could love with all my heart, one whom I could admire because of his convictions and character, one whose interests were the same as mine, besides one who is thoughtful, understanding, loving, patient, one who loves children, is generous, hospitable, self-sacrificing, a dynamic personality, a leader, a pioneer in the Lord's work, one who practices what he preaches, a challenge [to me] spiritually, and a man of prayer. All of these qualities I have found in you dear, and so in answer to your question, 'Will you be mine as long as God spares our lives?' I can gladly say YES! I am looking forward to many happy years with you.
>
> Now about the problems which you thought I should consider carefully before answering, let me say this: I am sure the differences in our ages does not present any problem for the present, nor will it in the future. If for some reason the Lord would choose fit to have you bed-ridden for the last five or ten years of your life, I would count it a great privilege to take care of you. Just think, honey, of all the nurses who dedicate their lives to taking care of the sick just for the money they get out of it. Surely I could do the same for one I love so dearly. It will be a joy to help you bear some of the many responsibilities which are yours.
>
> As far as home is concerned, just to be near you will be enough. Though we probably won't be able to have a permanent home for many years, if ever, I think we shall enjoy making a temporary home wherever we are. I am thankful for your determination to always set an example to your colleagues and I am praying that I will be able to do the same. As far as being willing to undergo hardships, let me assure you that when I came to the mission field over two years ago, I came expecting to endure hardship as a soldier of Jesus Christ, and I shall still be happy to do so.
>
> I can't thank the Lord enough for bringing you into my life. It shall be a happy day in March when the preacher asks me, 'Do you take William Cameron Townsend to be your wedded husband?' and I can tell the whole wide world '*I DO!*'

In a humorous twist, this letter ran a considerable risk of being lost at the hands of a disinterested porter Elaine hired to post it. Her joy was evident to all around her, and one of the young missionaries just arriving at the mission center wrote, 'Elaine, I'll never forget when I arrived in from Jungle Camp… and with such a sparkle in your eye you said, "Beth, I'm engaged! Guess who?"'

A FRIENDLY SHOVE IN THE RIGHT DIRECTION

At Norman, in conversation with Dawson Trotman, founder of The Navigators, Cameron spoke glowingly of the faithfulness of God who had 'greatly blessed—providing us with a pilot, a plane, a doctor, and a wife for the director.'

Delighted, Trotman asked when a wedding would be. 'Well, the work in Peru requires a great deal to become fully established,' Cam replied with nonchalant self-control. 'In that light, I believe about two years would be prudent.'

'Two years!' Trotman exploded. 'Whatever *for?*' 'Why—' Cam was taken aback at his vehemence, but Trotman charged on.

'Don't be silly, Townsend! A wonderful girl like that? She would *make* the mission in Peru. It just doesn't make sense. It seems to me that anyone marrying a tremendous woman like Elaine would want to spend as many years of his life with her as he could! Who would want to wait?'

The date was set for March of 1946.

A REAL SHOCKER

In the months preceding the wedding, Elaine continued reading campaigns in three tribes, while Cameron directed Jungle Camp. Perhaps it was observed by the bride-to-be that the survival of all participants in this wilderness venture sufficiently demonstrated his abilities of coordination and planning. Cameron was fully entrusted with the details of wedding planning. That confidence was not misplaced: everything, *except one essential detail,* went off without a hitch.

Their announcement party was held in The Posada del Sol, a lovely hotel owned by a Mexican friend. Cameron's niece, Evelyn, prepared a large piñata, and when the names 'Cam and Elaine' came tumbling out to a general cheer Cameron exclaimed, 'Isn't it nice to make our friends so happy, and ourselves so *happy* doing it!'

In the end, no one could take credit for such a match but the paramour missionary himself. This didn't stop several from trying, however, and more than one friend was surprised that he or she had not played a more prominent role, recounting their match-making attempts.

SEASON 2

10. 'STRENGTHENING THE TROOPS'

A challenge to women… That all of your life—in whatever calling—be devoted to the glory of God… That the promises of Christ be trusted so fully that peace and joy and strength fill your soul to overflowing.

John Piper[1]

At the invitation of President Cárdenas and his wife, Cameron and Elaine's wedding ceremony took place on their lovely country estate in Pátzcuaro, Michoacán.[2] Elaine's family, as well as several friends, came from Chicago.

Friends from the mission, a hoard of Mexican friends, seven generals, and many prominent dignitaries and officials formed the guest list. Reports claimed that around a hundred chauffeured cars filled the patio outside the ornate home. The Cárdenas family spared no expense: a full orchestra played the dinner music, hundreds of flowers decorated the walls, and the cake was over three feet high—so tall they had to take out one of the windows to bring it into the room.

At the request of the bride and groom, General Cárdenas and Doña Amalia served as the *Padrino* and *Madrina*, or best man and matron of honor. The night before the wedding, Cameron spent hours walking with the General and took this opportunity to speak of the gospel.

---

1   John Piper, 'A Challenge to Women'. Last accessed 1st July 2018 https://www. desiringgod.org/articles/a-challenge-to-women

2   Years earlier, Cameron had earned the respect of the former president of Mexico through his mission to better the lives of the Indians. President Cárdenas, half-Indian himself, held a personal concern for the plight of the minority people groups in his country, on which Cam in his typical indomitable style had capitalized, thus forging a lasting friendship between the two of them and their families.

Cameron and Elaine, on their wedding day (April 1946).

Upon meeting President Cárdenas, it was said that Elaine's father stepped right up and placed a kiss on his cheek. 'Herman was a character!' said one. For years to come he spoke proudly of being 'the first and only white man ever to kiss General Cárdenas.' Always the prankster, he showed no regret for such cheekiness.

Despite the passionate addresses which had flowed almost daily from his pen during their separation, and the preparations 'to make sure that all of the Mexicans felt at home,' the groom failed to reserve a room in the one available hotel for the first honeymoon night. In the end, a friend gave up his reservation for the newlyweds.

FRUITFUL RELATIONSHIP

Without a doubt, Elaine walked into marriage with an expectation of hardship. Because of Cameron's extensive travels, a stationary home was doubtful, and his multiplying responsibilities made time together a precious commodity.

Shirley Brouillette, a close friend in later years, also observed, 'Her eyes were wide open and she made a decision—you know, love is a decision. As much as she loved children, she knew the chances of their having any were very, very slim. It was a very big sacrifice... And yet God really showed off, didn't He?'

On her wedding band Cameron had inscribed Ephesians 2:10, *'For we are his workmanship, created in Christ Jesus unto good works, which God hath before ordained that we should walk in them'*—a fitting legend of the life that lay before the two of them.

This lively Chicagoan teacher brought fresh vigor to his life, becoming 'the great encourager,' as one person put it. 'When Elaine came it was like the reinforcement of the troops.'

Even Cameron teased her about their age difference. After recounting an early-morning tennis match, he added '... I figure that if I'm going to be boyfriend to a young dynamo like you, I'd better get up before breakfast and work up some pep.' His sense of humor began to emerge, playfulness interspersed in his earnest letters.

Cam's affection was evident to everyone; he always brought something back from his travels for Elaine, even if it was only a wildflower. He wrote poems and delighted in creating pet names for her. 'My wonderful Alegria,' he christened her once; 'my marvelous partner,' 'my precious better half,' 'my beloved wifie.' One missive concluded in gushing, romantic Mexican style, 'Much, much, muchismimo amore a mi angel, Tu marido, Guillermo.'

Since cherry pie held a high and distinguished place in his heart, he lent it to Elaine as a nickname. She returned in her own style, beginning one letter, 'Hi Dill Pickles!' As an apparent afterthought she added, 'that doesn't sound as complimentary as I want it to but I am sure that you understand, knowing how much I love dill pickles.'

A UNIQUE HONEYMOON

Little did Elaine know what those first months would hold. After the first night, any semblance of a honeymoon evaded the couple. Several days were spent in Mexico City, where an abundance of people and activity surrounded them. 'The gang' decorated their room with toilet paper, tar-paper streamers, and little twin dolls cozied up in bed. The pair could hardly enter the room, which had taken a full day to decorate.

This mission group possessed all the beauty and hilarity of a vibrant community. An old mansion-style hotel had been divided into living spaces for a number of families, and affectionately dubbed 'The Kettle'. Many used this house as a stopping-off point before entering their jungle outpost, or as a station for refreshment after a long period in the bush. It became so packed that single men slept on mattresses in the storage room.

Children who lived there recalled the adventure of playing hide-and-go-seek amidst the curtained corners and divided spaces of the old building. Adults remembered close-knit fellowship. 'You lived together, ate together, and the kids fought and played together. You had to enjoy each other to get along and survive. Come any problem, we always had a prayer meeting, and every Sunday night people shared reports from their villages—that was the highlight, the cohesive part of keeping us all together.'

It was into this explosion of life that the Townsends arrived. Two women, Gloria and Ellen, produced a skit mimicking the director and his wife with affectionate good humor. 'You know Elaine always dressed so nice with her earrings and brooches and everything,' Gloria said. 'I dressed up like her, and Ellen was Uncle Cam. We looked at each other like we were in love and made fun of them. Someone "gave a report" after being in a tribe, and Uncle Cam would say, *"Can that be possible?"*… And as Elaine I'd say, "Look girls! I've lost *ten pounds!*" It's a wonder Uncle Cam didn't dismiss us right then!'

THE ADVENTURE CONTINUES

After much packing and setting in order, the newlyweds left this uproar and set out for Peru, trailed by a posse of new recruits. On the way, they stopped over in Caracas, Venezuela, where Cameron sensed an opening for SIL linguists and couldn't restrain himself. The visit included a conference with the president and cabinet members, and resulted in an invitation for SIL to start work in the country.

Cameron and Elaine arrived in Lima with no place to stay. Nineteen new recruits found themselves in a similar position, and since money was scarce among the new missionaries, the Townsends rented a house for the group using their wedding money. A month and a day after the wedding, the couple was in possession of a ten-bedroom house. A recent oil boom had made for slim accommodations in the city, and they were grateful for such specific provision. Donated sleeping bags and mattresses were soon strewn across the floor to complete the homey atmosphere.

Soon another circumstance dominated the landscape. Twenty of the missionaries came down with food poisoning, and Elaine was kept rather busy, being one of three who escaped.

SUITCASES AND POISE

It was not long before Elaine was granted the opportunity to use her teaching skills in an influential way. She wrote home to family in Chicago, '… The government has asked me to work on a large reading campaign in the Quechua and Aymara languages. They will be printing 50,000 primers. I am working on the making of the primers now, and in ten days I'll be going to Puno…'

Of course this did not halt the constant stream of visitors strategically lured by Cam wherever he went. Just over two weeks before her departure for Puno, Elaine hosted the General of the Peruvian Military Academy. Hours before she left, another distinguished guest turned up at the door of the massive house in Lima. 'I had a most wonderful visit with [the ambassador and his mother],' she wrote to Cam,

> The house didn't look too wonderful with my suitcases and materials all over the place. I showed them all of the games and gave the ambassador

Early SIL workers celebrating SIL's first aircraft - the Grumman Duck. *Elaine is second from the right (July 1946).*

one of the primers, which he asked me to autograph. He also wants to help me get a copyright on all of the material. What do you think about this? My suitcase with all of the stickers was on a chair and he noticed that he had stayed in some of the same hotels…They stayed for about an hour and were ever so kind and helpful…

Early in their relationship it appears that Cameron had spoken to Elaine about maintaining a certain poise in her interaction with others, which her sociable, lighthearted personality undermined at times. This he considered necessary if she was to undertake a position of influence among missionaries of her own age and the many officials with whom he frequently interacted. 'I guess I might as well confess that for a long time I have not exactly liked the idea of putting away my joking nature,' she wrote him in response.

Although I have tried to change and even prayed much about it, it was only because I wanted to please you dear, and I had not seen that it would be pleasing Him until just this morning. The verse that the

Lord spoke to my stubborn heart was Philippians 3:7 'But what things were gain to me, these I have counted loss for Christ.' I believe I had always counted this part of my personality a gain to me, and no doubt it was back home, but how plainly He has shown me that it is a loss for Christ. How my heart cries out to Him to change me into the type of vessel He can best use in the place He has called me to serve. And then as if in answer to my heart's cry I find the comfort that He alone can give in 4:13 'I can do all things through Christ who strengtheneth me.'

TOUCHING THE HEIGHTS

She was off to Puno! 'I have a heavy schedule ahead with a trip to Puno on the border of Bolivia and then to the jungle base,' she wrote. 'Puno is higher than La Paz, Bolivia and we thought that was too high for comfort. They say that it is very cold, not only on account of the high elevation but also because of the cold winds off Lake Titicaca.'

Before she left she suspected that she was pregnant, and Cameron's letters were filled with injunctions for her safety and rest. Extreme altitude and cold only increased the discomfort and stress of already full days, causing her difficulty in breathing and sleeping at nights. Yet still she harbored contentment: 'How good the Lord is to help me so and to let me do something I so enjoy,' she wrote.

In a September letter she described the assignment in more detail:

…it is more wonderful than I had hoped. There are fifty-six teachers here who have been very carefully selected as they are to be more or less supervisors in their own territories…These teachers are here for a six-month period, learning to teach children to read in their own language as well as acquiring new methods of agriculture, sanitation, etc. When they return, they will conduct classes in their own areas. This means that altogether they will reach well over 1,000 teachers. How I praise the Lord for this wonderful opportunity to help them as it will mean that thousands of children and adults will be learning to read in Quechua and Aymara, and will be prepared to read the Word in these two languages just as soon as [the translations] come off the press.

... I wish you could have seen the enthusiasm of the teachers throughout my whole stay. We could hardly get them to stop for their meals, and although the light at night is very poor, they would stay up all hours working on their materials.

In another letter she recalled their unique courtship, '... the moon is so beautiful tonight. I would love to be enjoying it with you dear. It reminds me of the walks we used to take down the airfield at the jungle camp. Remember? Tomorrow it will be five months. Soon it will be half a year. It hardly seems possible.'

On the last day of August, 1946 she wrote,

Good morning, Darling! As I was enjoying the Word last night I came upon the following verse which I would like to share with you. 'And let the beauty of the Lord our God be upon us; and establish thou the work of our hands upon us, yea, the work of our hands establish thou it (Psalms 90:17).' I believe that He is doing that very thing through us, but I long more and more that His beauty may shine forth from my life...[3]

Soon after Elaine's return, educational authorities requested literacy aids for the Quechua language. An American educator from the Embassy declared them one of the finest things he had seen done in the country.

DREAMS COME TRUE

In the months before Junior's arrival, Elaine stayed with the group in Lima and continued to work on literacy materials while Cameron scouted the jungle in hopes of finding a suitable site for a base. Current entertainment kept everyone amused: 'We are keeping a monkey for the Chama Indians and are to sell him if some tourist wants to buy him. Last night I had him on my shoulder and he wet me. Guess we'll have to put diapers on him! I'm not going to carry him any more.'

---

3   Elaine commented, 'I wish I had told Cameron many more times how much his messages meant to me. Billy and Ruth Graham are such great friends to one another, and this really impressed me... Ruth said that whenever Billy was home, they would kneel together and he would pray only for her needs and she would pray only for his needs. I didn't do that, and I wish I had.'

From Aguaytía, Peru, on September 1st, Cameron wrote his wife, '... Last night was the first time that I have dreamt of Junior. He had just been born and there was a lot of excitement around. My sister, Mary, was there and scolded me for not having been right on the spot when the baby arrived.' Little did he know that this dream would soon come all too close to reality.

On December 27, (four days before President Truman officially declared the end of WWII), while Cameron traipsed around the jungle, Grace Lillie Townsend made her appearance. When the labor began, Elaine assumed the pains were due to indigestion, and visited the hospital without a thought of the baby arriving two weeks early.

Upon his return, Cameron arranged a dedication ceremony for Grace at the Mexican Embassy, inviting around fifty friends. He and others prayed for this little girl, that she would grow in her love for the Lord and in her knowledge of His Word.

A few days later, the entire family departed for Mexico and Jungle Training Camp.

11. AN UNEXPECTED DEVELOPMENT

If you seek humility, try hard work; if you would know your nothingness, attempt some great thing for Jesus. If you would feel how utterly powerless you are apart from the living God, attempt especially the great work of proclaiming the unsearchable riches of Christ, and you will know, as you never knew before, what a weak unworthy thing you are.

Charles Spurgeon[1]

Jungle Camp was again in progress, and Cameron thought it important to welcome the new recruits. The three-month camp was unlike anything young Americans had ever experienced. It was one long test of survival. The students paddled heavily laden canoes through white-water rapids, hiked over rough mountain passes, hunted for food, constructed makeshift huts without tools, and learned how to treat snakebites and use penicillin, the newest drug on the market. And, of course, they did all this while continuing with their linguistics studies.[2] So he, along with Elaine and six-month-old baby Grace flew in an MAF plane to Chiapas, on the border of southern Mexico, near Guatemala. After three days with the forty young people, they planned a flight to Mexico City on the only plane available—a Piper Cruiser (or as the Indians called it, a 'pig plane').

The passenger seats had been removed for transporting pigs into the city, so Cameron and Elaine sat with their feet under the front seats,

1   Charles Spurgeon, Morning and Evening, (Wheaton, Illinois: Crossway, 2003), 2nd March.

2   Janet and Geoffe Benge, *Cameron Townsend*, p. 184

and Grace lay comfortably ensconced among clean cloth diapers in a Mexican cane basket. But Elaine found herself still struggling with the door as the plane began to cruise. 'We hadn't gone very far down the runway when I realized that this wasn't a normal takeoff; we were far too high too soon. I barely had time to express my concern to Cam when the pilot also realized things weren't right…'

Late the night before, after hours of drinking, the pilot had announced at his motel, 'There have been seven crashes in that valley the last couple of weeks. I'm going to be next.'

The tail of the plane hit the tops of the trees and nose-dived into the side of a ravine. The front seat collapsed on Elaine's feet and Cameron sustained injuries around his hip. The pilot failed to turn off the gas switch, and it was a wonder the plane didn't go up in flames. When the frightened group of Jungle Campers arrived at the scene, completely out of breath, most of the passengers were unconscious. But it seemed that someone had been there before them…

Elaine told one version, 'A Tzeltal Indian came running through the jungle when he heard the crash. Somehow he grabbed Grace out of my arms because I was still unconscious and ran off, thinking the plane was going to blow.'

But another clue lurks, handwritten by an observer on a long-buried picture taken at the scene: 'Baby Gracie was thrown out of the plane and an unknown Indian 'man' (angel) caught her.' No one was ever able to identify the man they had seen deliver her, nor did anyone see him again.

Jungle Camp placed a high emphasis on medical skills, and that year, for the first time, a doctor served as the director. The group made a makeshift stretcher out of tree limbs and army blankets and carried the three back to camp. Undoubtedly, several missionaries would tell in later years of how they rescued the director and his wife!

Cameron's mind immediately ran off toward the possibility of what this could mean. 'Something good is going to come out of this,' he wrote shortly afterwards, quoting Romans 8:28.

For several years now, he had tried to persuade the WBT board of the necessity of airplanes for missionaries. He was convinced airplanes could play a vital role in reaching hundreds of remote locations both efficiently and safely, but few shared this vision. Airplanes were a luxury at that time, and as everyone knew, missionaries didn't need luxuries. But too many jungle disasters, canoe wrecks, rapids, and other natural disasters conspired to take the lives of missionaries. Cameron only became more adamant: 'Our people can't go until they have the airplanes. We've got to have our own airplanes and our own pilots.'

UNLIKELY BEGINNINGS

As he lay on the ground waiting to be carried back to camp after the crash, Cameron began to realize the significance of this event: it could mean the turning point if others saw in it the need for a reliably staffed aviation program. 'Quick, someone get a camera!' he urged. That day, JAARS was born.[3]

Because of their critical condition, Dr. Culley judged it unwise to move Cameron, Elaine, or the pilot to a hospital. For two days and nights he worked around the clock on his three patients. Upon leaving Wheaton, Dr. Culley had packed his bags with sulfa drugs and penicillin, which doubtless saved his patients from the very real possibility of serious infection. The pilot sustained injuries to his face. Elaine's crushed left foot Dr. Culley suspended from the ceiling in a sling to provide some relief. For ten days they remained thus.

In typical fashion, Elaine commented, 'The clothes we had on were ruined. I had a beautiful red feather hat on that I was so tickled with, and it was completely mashed. Cam was wearing his wedding suit for some reason and it was also ruined.'

But more serious realities faced them. When they finally arrived in Mexico City, it was discovered that Elaine's arches were completely crushed, and her feet broken nearly beyond repair. 'I never thought I'd be able to walk again because when I looked at my foot the anklebone was exposed and it was hanging on by just a few tendons.' Cameron's own leg had been severely cut, and a metal plate was installed which he would carry for the rest of his life.

---

3   *Jungle Aviation and Radio Program*, now jokingly referenced as *Just About Any Required Service*.

For the next six months, Cameron and Elaine recovered on their backs—first in the hospital, then in a hotel, then at the Kettle. Baby Grace rotated between six different families, and Elaine commented that she probably didn't know who her real mother was, even though she was brought to visit them each day.

'Those were very, very hard times,' Elaine admitted. 'At that point I thought our ministry was over.' There they were, back in the Posada del Sol[4], the same hotel which had seen the announcement of their engagement, and all they could do was lie in bed.

'The nurses had to patiently rub and rub my leg to get the circulation going again. Some of the doctors said, "You'll never walk again if you don't stay off that foot!" while others said, "You'll never walk again if you *don't* use it." I was glad it wasn't my face though.'

When an Indian lad came to clean the Townsends' room, Uncle Cam asked him to read to them from the Scripture. 'You didn't say no to Uncle Cam,' as one missionary put it, but no one had yet informed this boy. Uncle Cam quieted his fears by responding that he was his boss's boss, so not to worry. From then on, when the boy came each morning he took time to read to Cam and Elaine, and eventually, the Spirit worked in his heart to save him.

After Elaine's cast finally came off it was excruciatingly painful. For the first time in half a year she began to walk again. Sixty years didn't erase the scarring from that injury, and from then on she endured significant pain in her feet and back. Many believed it was a miracle that she ever walked again.

Elaine remembered that time as one of the hardest experiences of her life, the one which tempted her to abandon the mission altogether. Towards the end of her life, she said, 'I think of that verse in Psalm 119:71 where it says, *"It is good for me that I've been afflicted, that I might learn thy statutes."* I wasn't so sure it was good for me. I really didn't want that verse for a while. How could it be good for me to go through more agony? Finally, I said, "All right Lord, if you think it's good for me, I'll believe it"—and that changed everything.'

---

4   During their stay the owner carried all the expenses.

Elaine and her children in the Peruvian jungle (circa 1955).

HOLIDAY BABY

During months of travel through the States, Mexico, and Peru, a second child was on her way. Not to be outdone by Grace, Joy Amalia made her appearance five days early, perfectly timed in conjunction with one of the biggest Mexican holidays: Cinco de Mayo. On Elaine's last trip to the doctor he commented, 'Just watch—Mrs. Townsend, she'll come to the hospital with her baby on the 5th, when no one will be here!'

Sure enough, Cameron had to scour the streets in search of a doctor as Joy began to make her appearance on May 5th. Elaine told her later, 'When Dad found your little feet were very cold, he spent hours rubbing them and holding them in one hand. From that very first day, you were special to Dad.'

Soon after Joy's birth, the family returned to the new SIL base deep in the Peruvian jungle. There, three years and two hours after the honeymoon baby, Elaine Adele (later combined to Elainadel) entered the world—renowned as the first baby to be born on the base. Three years after that, when Cameron was fifty-six, Billy completed the family.

Just when Elaine had resigned herself to permanent singleness, God set in her path the man of her dreams; and as if in amused response to the expectation of childlessness, she and Cameron were given four children tumbling over each other in their eagerness to arrive.

Later, Grace laughingly explained, 'Daddy told us that he prayed "God, please don't let my daughters be beautiful. I couldn't handle it!"

'I said "Daddy, why'd you have to include *that* prayer? You could have left that one out, couldn't you?"—cause we all knew that Daddy had a direct line to heaven!! But he was afraid that if we were beautiful we wouldn't seek the Lord, so it was more for protection of ourselves... he wanted us homely, and that kinda showed Daddy's sense of humor.'

SPILL SEASON

Joy's dedication service in Mexico City brought about a hilarious episode. Someone had hired a small orchestra, which played hot jazz while everyone gathered. At almost two years old, Grace made quite the impression with the musicians, insisting on a duet with the pianist, into which she put her full muscle. She then shook hands with everyone around the room, and hugged and kissed all the babies. One dignitary took her by the hands for a waltz. Regardless, the service itself went well, and Cameron presented the gospel clearly.

At first the children themselves weren't capable of much in the way of ministry: 'Right now [Joy] is taking all of the books out of the bookcase and bringing them to me one by one,' Elaine wrote her parents once. 'Grace is busy cutting paper....' The letter closed, 'Well, the bookcase is about empty now and breakfast is ready....'

One letter read, 'We were having quite a plague of frogs in the house for the last two months,' Elaine wrote. 'Joy is the brave one and picks them up and throws them out. She doesn't mind the live ones but she won't touch the dried up dead ones.' Obviously, the dead frogs were a job for someone else!

ENDURING EXUBERANCE

Cameron wanted to lead from the field, and in the first year of their marriage, this meant twenty-one moves in one year. They thought it would always be like that: wherever Daddy went, they'd all go. But once school started for the children, Elaine stayed behind with them in that house along the lake in the middle of Peru. 'I didn't realize how much of the time he'd be traveling,' Elaine recalled. 'I can remember when the kids were growing up there were months at a time when he would be gone… But they had a wonderful childhood in that lovely house in Yarina and I grew in many ways… If I hadn't married a man of his stature I wouldn't have had that to go through. But it was worth it.'

12. CHANGE AND THE ART OF LEARNING

Melancholy contracts and withers the heart, and renders it unfit to receive the impressions of grace. It magnifies and gives a false coloring to objects, and thus renders your burdens too heavy to bear. God's designs regarding you, and His methods of bringing about these designs, are infinitely wise.

Madame Guyon[1]

Gifted with a unique set of talents and strengths, Elaine chose to pour them into Cameron. 'I totally saw Mom coming alongside Dad to help him accomplish his calling,' their daughter Elainadel attested.

He truly was a visionary and she was an amazing helpmate. From small things, like remembering names, to big things like taking care of the finances, car, home repairs, and preparation for travel, she was right there taking the load off him so he could focus on the things he was called to do. They each took the assignments God had given them and delighted in serving Him and each other as a team… God used Mom in unique ways to build His character in Dad so that he was able to meet the challenges that came with his calling.

'I was the treasurer in the family,' Elaine said once. 'Cameron never knew if we had ten cents or two dollars—and it didn't make any difference to him either!' she laughed.

Her daughter, however, noted, 'I think she did it in a way that made him feel included and did not strip him of his manliness… she didn't

---

1   Madame Guyon, Public Domain.

tip the balance where she became the head of the home, even though she was making many of the decisions that most men make.'

ALONGSIDE

Elaine possessed a special sense of Cameron's calling to lead a varied group of dedicated, wholehearted, entrepreneurial kingdom workers. She didn't mind Cameron being in the forefront, but rather supported him in a multitude of ways surpassing the practical and obvious things he accomplished.

'I didn't dream of all the many different types of things I'd be called upon to do when I married Cam!' Elaine commented once. Film-making was no delightful task at the time when Cam decided Wycliffe should make a promotional film showing firsthand the needs and realities of the mission field. Irwin Moon traveled to the base deep in the Peruvian jungle and took hundreds of hours of footage. These were the days of reels, and when Cameron and Elaine arrived in the States with three young girls (all in diapers), 8,000 feet of film awaited them. To her parents, who were watching the girls, she described the tedious process:

> ...Our job is to cut this down to 1,600 feet and put sound on. We are now seeing the reels slowly, stopping the projector after each scene...I make a 3x5 card for each scene we think we might want to use with comments about them...When we have done this for all the reels, we have to cut the film, tack it on a board, and splice it together...always keeping in mind the story we are trying to get across...

They estimated that this project could be completed in three weeks, but *Oh For a Thousand Tongues* took five months of constant work. Despite the distinct lack of glamour, Elaine set her hand to the job. Cam wrote, 'Everyone agrees with me out here that Elaine's absolutely tops. We're indebted largely to her for the wonderful way the picture is turning out.'

In 1964, when Wycliffe lacked money to break even on costs for its pavilion at the World's Fair, Elaine traveled the States to speak and raise support. She thought back on touring churches to tell about her

Elaine in her kitchen in the Peruvian house.

trip around the world, and marveled at the contrast between a personal travelogue and the calling of sowing the gospel.

GOING WITH THE TERRITORY

Gloria Farah, who worked for Wycliffe in Bolivia, explained the state of affairs whenever the director came to town: 'He had so much for me to do I thought he'd wear me out and I wondered when he'd leave!' she joked. 'Until then there was nothing but a string of *"Can you... Can you... Can you..."*—to be taken as instructions, of course. This was met with a repeated "Yes, Uncle Cam... Yes, Uncle Cam... Yes, Uncle Cam." He would take a ten-minute siesta, then come out and wonder why everyone was tired!'

Plans changed constantly and Elaine caught on soon after their marriage. Uncertainty became the stuff of daily life, and she began to learn the art of purposed contentment without knowledge of what the next day would bring. Sometimes this meant sending copies of her letters to Cam to several different countries or cities—Guatemala, Ecuador, Mexico, and Lima, hoping one would find him. Sometimes this frustrated packing for travels. Sometimes this meant relocating to an entirely different country. Elaine began to exercise flexibility when she had no idea when Cam was getting back from a trip, where the family was going next, when they were leaving, how long they would be gone, or when they would get back.

Through all these changes, Elaine formed Cameron's tie to home, and she saw it as a critical part of her calling, no less than entertaining ambassadors, to keep his heart encouraged and lifted up. 'Dearest and best sweetheart of mine,' she wrote, 'It has been so very good of you to write every day. Every letter is a real thrill. I love you more and more all the time and can hardly wait to tell you so.' In another, 'I am looking forward to doing some moonlight canoeing when my sweetie pie gets back!'

HEART HELPMEET

To Elaine, Cameron was a man of God, a leader among men—one gifted with great responsibility and many abilities with which to meet it. She also saw a man who was flawed as all men, a man whose weaknesses she knew intimately; he needed her companionship, her prayers, her support, and her cheerfulness. Her respect was integral to her role as a helpmeet for him and his primary aide in every assignment. Elaine herself admitted, 'There were adjustments to make after we were married. It took me awhile to realize that I wasn't my own boss anymore.'

Friends close to them did not remember one instance in public when Elaine questioned Cam, indicating 'Oh here we go again,' or 'That's a crazy idea.' Elaine encouraged other women to disagree with their husbands only in private, and with attention to timing. Cal Hibbard, Cam's secretary—an indispensable part of the Townsend 'engine room' and a constant observer of their daily life—noted that disagreements were rare, and that when tension did exist it was not made public.

Elaine sought out practical ways to encourage his heart. 'She added to Uncle Cam,' observed another aptly. 'She was a strong woman with strong opinions and not lacking in capability, yet she wanted to be there 24/7 with him,' one friend said of her. 'She sacrificed her own gifts to help Cam,' Cal described her. 'She could have gone out on her own and been very influential doing reading and literacy for the government. But she didn't make that her emphasis; rather she helped behind the scenes, raised the kids, and helped Cam. It was never, ever about what Elaine Townsend could do.'

'Cameron was quiet and gentle and she was a take-charge person,' observed one woman. 'But when he had an idea or felt called to something he became almost assertive… and she was very affirming.' Through her words and actions, Elaine demonstrated admiration for how Cameron carried out his calling, and in so doing gave him one of the most precious gifts a wife can give her husband.

To a group of women, new missionary recruits, she counseled, 'Work on building each other up. Don't hesitate to compliment your mate. Write notes of appreciation to your husband.' Love your husband first and he'll be a king, Elaine realized, and the children will not go unaffected either… 'Ask the Lord to help you wake up happy. Put a smile on your face when going to bed and also when answering the phone. Make sure he comes home to a happy home with the table all set, and if you are late in getting the meal, quickly start frying onions and he'll think it's almost ready!'

Then, at times, she gave her opinion quite freely. 'Cam, you need to get a new coat! That thing is terrible!' she told him. Soon afterwards she left, and returned to find him wearing a rather expensive-looking wool coat. The girls loved it, and inquired further. He had bought it at the thrift store for about $3, and he wore that one ragged too.

THE ART OF LEARNING

In the last decade of Cameron's life, Elaine sometimes struggled to show patience. But Cameron could count her in, and together they learned to live out love, respect, and forgiveness.

Doubtless there was much to forgive. Cameron was absent a great deal, and Elaine frequently wrote about how deeply he was missed by all his family. 'These have been awfully hard days on me,' she wrote once, 'not feeling too well, much, much walking and shopping, plus parting with our children once again. I don't look forward to the three weeks alone until you get here but I know the Lord will help me. What would we do without Him?'

Bernie May, a man mentored by Cameron who would later become director of Wycliffe U.S.A., testified, 'Uncle Cam had a philosophy: he was a leader, a pioneer. But no one became a disciple of Uncle Cam as much as Elaine did. She learned from him.' Elaine spoke of Cameron among leaders who had been a source of strength in her life; she recalled his hours of prayer over the details of life, study of the Word, his faith and vision, fearlessness before presidents and humility before the poorest Indian. Cameron prayed for her often, and she gained encouragement from this knowledge.

The thing about Cameron, Elaine recognized, was that he actively drew her closer to her Lord. After his death, she wrote thanksgiving to God, 'for giving me such a loving, understanding husband whose sweet walk with You made me want to know You better too.' They had given their lives to the spread of the gospel, and the implications of this mission outside the home sometimes transcended its reach inside the home to a fault. Yet when Elaine spoke in later years of what God taught her, it was apparent that many of those lessons and realizations came through Cam. He modeled obedience, encouraged her in the Word, prayed with and for her, and infused their relationship with the healing love of God.

BECOMING A SAFE PLACE

Elaine assured him she would pray—and she did. She was the one to whom he opened the impossible when he expected everyone else to think him ridiculous. She provided a haven where he felt encouraged to reveal his heart, and his aspirations for the growth of the kingdom. His letters were filled with news of his meetings with dignitaries and heads of state, small daily blessings, steps of advance into countries, requests for remembrance before the throne, challenges faced, blessings of God's guidance—in short, countless doors both significant and small opening into his world, revealing it to her interested, committed gaze. She listened loyally, communicating excitement and admiration for who he was and for the distinct ways in which God had gifted him.

Cameron's confidence in her was demonstrated strikingly during a day of prayer at the Kettle one November. Cameron reminded the gathering that they had not because they asked not. Each person began to share what they would ask of the Lord in 1951, but when it came to Cameron's turn, he said he didn't feel he should mention his request except to his wife, as the rest would think he was crazy. Elaine said:

> You can imagine my amazement when he told me he was asking the Lord for a Catalina [airplane] for the work in South America. I knew that the Lord had answered other big requests for him, but I thought that this was one that was just too impossible. However, I did join him in prayer that if this was His will it would come to pass. Now, scarcely five months later, the plane is in our possession in a far more wonderful way than we could have ever dreamt of. What a wonderful God we have and how it does behoove us to ask more!

In 1949, three years after SIL's entry into Peru, Cameron wrote,

> Yesterday we worked out plans for our aviation work in the jungle with the chief of staff of the Peruvian Air Force. The Air Force is going to continue to give us all the gasoline and oil that we need, up to 1,750 gallons a month. They will also give us the services of their mechanics free of charge. We are to carry out mercy, emergency, and cultural flights for them from time to time without charge… They also continue to give us the use of their airports and hangars wherever they have them.

The woman God called to be Cameron Townsend's right hand would require a remarkable measure of courage, whole-hearted dedication to the cause of the Cross, and an outstanding liveliness to survive the safari of life ahead.

13. 'THE UNFOLDING OF YOUR WORD GIVES LIGHT'

I have found myself depending on the spiritual conversation of our home, the discussion of sermons, and the cocoon of ministry life as a crutch for my soul. In such times my soul emaciates; I become a spiritual anorexic... Do not feed your soul on the run. Do not substitute spiritual snacks for unhurried time before God in private prayer and devotion every day.

Catherine J. Stewart[1]

To Elaine, the Word was not lifeless, but a sharp and active treasure. 'It was the Word that got me. I couldn't live a day without it,' she said.[2] Her journals expressed deep contentment and joy in the presence of her Lord: 'Thank you that my greatest glory is that I belong to you... Thank you for your presence in me, guaranteeing that you'll give me all you have promised—guaranteeing that you'll bring me to yourself.' She echoed the Psalmist who over and over again identified God with His Word, placing value and worth on the Word because of its association with the very character of God: *'Oh God! You are my God, earnestly I seek you. My soul thirsts for you, my flesh faints for you in a dry and weary land where there is no water.*[3] *'I have said to the* LORD, *you are my Lord. I have no good apart from You... The* LORD *is my chosen portion and my cup, you hold my lot.'*[4]

---

1   Catherine J. Stewart, *Letters to Pastors' Wives: When Seminary Ends and Ministry Begins* (Phillipsburg, New Jersey: P&R Publishing, 2013), p. 26.

2   Lightbody, *2007 paper*.

3   Psalm 63:1.

4   Psalm 16: 2,5.

SLIDE OR STRATEGY

When life and kids and ministry crowded in and clambered for every second, time in His presence dwindled. Elaine discovered that the sense of spiritual life quickly dried away. 'I want to tell you ladies about an experience I had while on my first furlough,' Elaine began as she stood before a group of women preparing for overseas ministry.

'… in '46 we moved to the jungles of Peru where the Lord had called us to set up a base. You know, things got quite busy, and what with our three little girls born within three years and a day and Cam's role as director, I was kept quite occupied.' Several women nodded in sympathy and understanding.

'My time with the Lord began to slide, and of course everything that called for my attention seemed so important. I couldn't imagine letting anything slide, so I let my time in the Word go by the way, assuming, I think, that things would take care of themselves. After all, I had a committed missionary as a husband with whom I studied the Word when he was home; I went regularly to the services on the base, and I was doing the work of a missionary myself every day. What could be wrong with that?'

Elaine smiled, but her voice grew more earnest. 'Then we went to the States on furlough after four years on the field. I felt weary and worn down after those years on the field, and also discouraged about the work, though I loved doing it. We stopped over in Chicago to see my family, and to raise support at my home church, the North Side Gospel Center, where I first heard the beauty of grace. After service on Sunday, Doc Latham said, "Oh, Elaine is here! Come up, Elaine, and tell us what's going on in your work in Peru."

'It was then I realized how spiritually dry I had become. I pulled Cameron aside and said, "You go, honey. I have nothing to say," and I stayed back with the girls. I'll never forget that lesson. I never wanted to feel that empty and depleted again. Once I realized the problem, I knew the only way to fill my soul was with the Word. So I began to set aside a time each day for study.'

Shortly after this, Elaine heard Dawson Trotman speaking about the Navigators, and she began to study the Word more in depth, paraphrasing Scripture as she read and stretching her capacity to understand and process the written words. At several points, she kept a journal which included meditations on the Word, prayers, and thanksgiving, with various quotes and verses intermingled. For the rest of her life, she unashamedly encouraged young women to develop strategies for deepening their walk with the Lord: 'since the Bible is His clear message to us, a deeper study of that Book is a good place to start... *Don't let the urgent rob your time with the Lord.*'

NEVER VOID

'God's Word will not return to Him void,' Cameron once said. 'We stake everything on its power in the lives of those who feed upon it... The greatest missionary is the Bible in the mother tongue. It never needs a furlough and is never considered a foreigner.'[5]

Over and over she expressed praise to her King: 'Thank you for your precious Word that is so quick and powerful and sharp, discerning the thoughts and intents of my heart. Thank you for this powerful searchlight.' In another entry, '...my most treasured possession.'

In the back of her Bible, she listed a verse dedicated to each year, as well as the place she happened to be at the turn of that year. Such a habit reminded her of God's workings at that particular point in her life. Every lesson she ever thought she knew by heart, He taught her again and again. Not till she immersed herself in the words He spoke could she herself have anything worth saying, anything worth offering to a hurting world and to the souls of her hungry children. As an adult, Elaine wrote her mother, 'You taught me by your very life to put a high premium on my time alone with God in His Word and in prayer. You couldn't have given me a better gift—one which no one can ever take away from me.'

ENTICING HER CHILDREN

Day in and day out they observed her finding joy in the love of a good God when everything conspired against her—whether dirty dishes or deep sorrow. Sometimes her world was closed in by four walls, and

5   James and Marti Hefley, *Uncle Cam, 2nd edition* (Milford, Michigan: Mott Media, 1981), p. 182.

the inhabitants of the globe consisted foremost of the several small ragamuffins who frayed her world around the edges.

When 'going unto all nations' seemed overwhelming because of the surreal mess of living—in those moments, the 'going' meant simply waking up to live out grace for one more day. It meant speaking the gospel and acting a living apologetic before the eyes of her children. After all, these were her converts: a people group growing up into the gospel.

Elaine saw memorization as one pivotal aspect of this development. With her teacher's imagination, she crafted ways to engage her children during their younger years. 'Mom didn't just teach other people,' said Joy.

> She wanted us kids to understand God's Word too. One way she did this was at our family Bible reading at breakfast. She would misquote a verse to help us grasp what the verse was really saying—and to make sure we were paying attention. For instance, 'Children, obey your parents if you feel like it.' She would point out that God was not putting a condition on this command to obey, then she would say the verse correctly.

Elaine recalled a time when she was teaching them I Corinthians 15:58: 'Be steadfast, unmovable, sometimes abounding in the work of the Lord.'

'Oh, *Mother*, it doesn't say *that*!'

'Oh, doesn't it? What does it say?'

'Always!'

'Always? Really?'

'*Always!*'

Elaine used music to help her children memorize, and wrote verses out in her beautiful teacher's penmanship (which only appeared on the rare occasions when she slowed down), putting them around the kitchen so they could work on learning them while they washed dishes. Road trips were also a prime opportunity. 'Be sure each child has her own Bible,' Elaine encouraged a group of women, 'and be sure they're reading it. Don't hesitate to have them tell you what they're reading and how much they understand.'

Memorization forged lifetime riches from the Word. Yet it is true that Elaine didn't always effectively connect these links to real life as the children matured. There existed a tendency in that era, and Elaine was not exempt, to elevate performance over grace and fail to graduate children into conversations regarding hard or confusing things. On many occasions, 'the tensions of two seemingly opposite truths',[6] which teens so desperately need explained in their expanding world, was notably lacking. 'Maturing as any other children, we were continually asking, "How does the gospel speak to my questions?"'

'I CAN'T GET ENOUGH'

In the words of Gloria, a friend of Elaine and wife to a longtime missionary diplomat in Bolivia, 'What I've learned in the past doesn't allow for a fresh walk with the Lord… I need to experience *Him* rather than only what He gives and does… Before I ask Him for anything I just worship. I can't get enough of Jesus. It takes time with the Lord to grow into that.'

Elaine had observed her own mother's daily walk, and she wrote of how this impacted her: 'Not only is your joyful service to others one of your outstanding qualities for which I am so grateful as your daughter, but also your loving patience… I'm sure your secret along this line is your time spent with Him. How many, many times when I had occasion to go downstairs late at night when everyone else was in bed, would I find you, Mom, and your precious Bible.' Like her mother, Elaine treated the Word like bread from heaven to sustain her hungry soul, to bear her up in the midst of weariness.

Her own daughter, Grace, witnessed to the way her mother faithfully lived this out: 'She had a strong walk with the Lord… her quiet time— it was developing a relationship with her Best Friend.' She and her siblings recalled waking every morning and coming downstairs to the sight of their mother sitting in her office in the early hours, poring over her Bible, pen in hand, making notes. Later in the morning, she took

6   as one Missionary kid put it.

time to study with the family's maid, Clara, at a corner table in the kitchen.

She set a time, not like choosing the hour of execution, but executing the tyranny of the hours. Instead of moving this time around, she worked around it. She made it the figurative 'winding of her clock,' the rhythm of her hours and her days. Elaine sought Christ to the uncomfortable extent that ensured she would be a different person ten, twenty, and fifty years down the road—a person more awestruck with Christ, a person pouring out every day that His name might be glorified in those around her.

Such disciplined habit didn't come easily, and in one letter we find a record of the journey,

> I've had a wonderful answer to prayer recently. For a long time I've wanted to be more regular in my quiet time with the Lord and I also wanted to have it early in the day since once the day gets started it is almost impossible to get alone. So I asked the Lord to wake me up at 6:15 every day. It is wonderful the way He has answered! Now I am able to spend thirty to forty-five minutes in the Word and prayer before the day begins, and what a difference it makes for the entire day. Truly my heart is full of praise for this answer. Rejoice with me!

6 A.M. AT THE HANGAR

Along with her own personal engagement in the Word, Elaine placed great importance on group fellowship. She took every opportunity to encourage those around her in deeper ways, whether in person, over the phone, or by letter, sharing things the Lord taught her. Her daughter said, 'I can remember waking up before 6 a.m. in Yarina and finding my mother already dressed and looking so fresh, happy, and pretty with a flower in her hair like it was just the best thing in the world to be dressed up and heading out the door for prayer meeting at the hangar. She just looked smashing.'

These women weren't the only ones affected by this ministry: 'Each week we wrote a challenge in our own words to the effect— "Whatever it takes to make me more conformed to Your image, to make self die,

I'd be willing, Lord." A Mr. Adams, overhearing, was so impressed he just wept. The next day, he had a heart attack and he was down in bed for months, but he would always remember that challenge and say, "Did you ever hear anything so beautiful?"'

TRAINING OF THE HEART

Elaine lingered her whole lifelong on this truth—that those things which captivate one's heart will take captive one's time as well. Excuses slay devotion, as they deny the lifeblood of the Word and prayer to the believer. Two sentences she wrote beautifully encapsulate her pursuit: 'My predominant thought constitutes my present action. Keep my mind stayed upon His loveliness, His tender care for me, His desire to perfect that which concerns me.'

Elaine's deep affection for the Word was plain to all. As one woman exclaimed, 'Her love for the Bible—oh my! Tremendous!' She surrounded herself with this life-giving torrent day in and day out, and no other single source can account for the tremendous energy which so marked her life.

14. PITCHING CAMP

Each of [the gypsum crystals] sprang out of some atom of a growing point round which clusters crystalize, this endless beauty of form. If we may but be a crystallizing point from which God can work, it matters nothing—how insignificant that starting point... 'He calleth those things that were not as though they were.'

Lilias Trotter[1]

'I'm in a mess myself right now,' wrote Elaine from the group house in Lima. 'The four of us are living in one room and trying to pack our things as well, so you can imagine how crowded it is. Besides, Cam tells me that we will have less floor space in our tent than we have in this one room so I am wondering how we will manage, especially since we will have to squeeze one more in it in December. I'll let you know how we make out.'

Ten days later, she wrote cheerily from the jungle, 'We have much to do yet in getting settled but it is lots of fun and much more comfortable than I had supposed it could be. As I write this I am looking out over a beautiful, quiet lake and a gorgeous sunrise.'

HOME, L-SHAPED

When God called Cameron to establish an outpost on the shores of Lake Yarinacocha, few had ventured into these remote areas of Peru—except perhaps specimen hunters for the Smithsonian. Yarinacocha was the end of the world. Six miles of rutted, clay-caked road lay between

---

1   Quoted in Miriam Rockness, *A Passion for the Impossible* (Grand Rapids, Michigan: Discovery House Publishers, 2003), p. 291.

them and Pucallpa, which was itself remote, inhospitable, and unsafe. Their nearest neighbors were the Shipibo Indians, known for their practice of flattening the heads of their babies by tying boards to their skull after birth and tightening it for the next six weeks (to prevent them looking like monkeys). Sporting a simple airstrip and a machete-whacked trail through the dense vines and trees, this hot, steamy place could not have felt less homey.

Back in Lima some months before, Cameron had stumbled upon the *perfect* building material for a new house: army tents, surplus from

The Townsends' Peruvian home for fourteen years, from 1949 to 1963.

the war. Upon their arrival in the jungle they ripped them apart and sewed the canvas, thick as an elephant's hide, into one giant whole using an enormous needle.

With such beginnings, this home could not help its singularity. As Elaine forbearingly put it, 'Our tent house in Peru was *interesting*.' By this time, the Townsend family included two little girls, who loved the new arrangements. Mosquito netting formed walls, and the girls slept on a platform surrounding a tree that grew up through the middle. Nails placed in the tree acted as convenient hooks. The entire construction was in an 'L' shape, with handmade furniture from Pucallpa. Elaine creatively arranged the books, supplies, a radio, and a mending box. Curtains divided a nursery, bedroom, office/sitting room.

'Our table looks out over the beautiful lake,' she wrote her family. 'Then, under a shelter of palm leaves, we have our kitchen and work room. The whole thing is on one wooden platform. The Starks are letting us use their refrigerator until they need it. All we had to do was pay the shipping expense across the Andes. It hasn't arrived as yet, but it will be a wonderful help as it is very hot here.'

This place welcomed Cameron home from long trips, and Elaine never apologized to guests for the circumstances. All living and entertaining happened in this shelter in the middle of newly cleared virgin jungle. Their company remembered a gracious, loving hostess, always looking to encourage and to love those who came through her doors (or, more accurately, tent flap). Joy remarked, 'I do *love* the picture of Mom looking radiant, sitting outside of this tent house, looking like a million dollars with her snazzy necklace, which, on closer look was most likely made of monkey teeth.'

PICTURE TO HOME

One humid afternoon, amid the hilarity and giggles of two chubby, dressed-up little girls, a picture was snapped. Eventually it made its way to the desk of Mr. Crowell, a businessman in the States, who looked past the faces of the girls and gasped in horror at the contraption behind them. Several weeks afterward, mail arrived at Yarinacocha bearing a $2,500 check 'for the building of the Townsends' proper home.'

When they moved in, Elaine again set her hand to make a home; and for the next year she went through a season of setting it up for the rhythms of their life. 'She was very gifted in decorating with what she had,' said Joy. This gift extended outside as well. 'I loved our cup-of-gold arches and our brilliant bougainvillea growing to the third floor.'

In those days when you traveled—especially overseas—everything went in metal trunks. In our living room in Peru Mother lined up three large trunks and covered them with afghans (Shirley, her crippled sister, crocheted a lot of afghans). She leaned them up against the wall, and that was our couch in the living room. A slanted board came out from the wall for the backrest to these trunks that we sat on, and it was great!

You made our homes so charming! … I loved it that you sewed beautiful beads around the edge of our cranberry Christmas tablecloth. It made us feel so incredibly special and honored that you placed importance on something like that—that to you it was valuable to decorate our home and make it beautiful…

Grace, Joy, Elainadel, and Billy's bedroom was a large affair, and as they grew older Elaine sectioned off the room with bamboo slats about six feet tall so each room had its own door. Elaine made Grace a pink ruffled room on the third floor with a floor-to-ceiling screen window overlooking the lake. As a birthday surprise for Joy, she fixed up a blue bedroom facing the back of the house where the aluminum ceiling sloped almost to the floor.

Creating an environment of attractiveness didn't necessitate all the comforts of a Western life, buying expensive accessories, and crafting just the right look. 'It was homey and always felt comfortable,' recalled Cam's secretary, Cal Hibbard.

What, then, was the essence of home? *Did it need to be beautiful?* For missionaries in particular, these questions were critical, as home was often their only stable retreat. A family's home signified its haven—the heart of its identity. Care dedicated to making that home not only livable, but *inviting*, grounded its occupants in ways which may have remained hidden, yet which could not be substituted.

It was Elaine's privilege to craft the lively, attractive atmosphere which welcomed her husband from long trips, drew her own heart to reside at home, and gave her children stability amid their discovery of the world.

EVERYWHERE-HOME

Elaine also possessed the rare ability to create a sense of home amid the family's frequent travels. Wherever they went she carried along a few things from home to set out, like a family picture, a tablecloth, or a doily, establishing a sense of place and belonging. Thus their travels became a continuum of normal life.

While her four children grew up, the family moved ninety-six times. Often, Cameron would fly from coast to coast, while Elaine drove across. She made the most of the time learning Scripture, singing, and playing games with them. The children loved those weeks.

Her daughter Elainadel remembered, 'She always made home wherever we were. One time, when I was fourteen, I went out to an Indian village to be a partner for a single gal. When I opened my duffle bag, right in the top Mom had put a lace doily, a picture of the family, and a throw rug. I put that rug down on my dirt floor and the picture on my bamboo shelf and it felt like home. I sensed her constant love and prayers even though I was very isolated and couldn't communicate very often.'

JUNGLE TO WINDSWEPT WILDERNESS

After seventeen years in Peru, the Townsends moved to Colombia and occupied an apartment building in the capital city of Bogotá. After the wide expanse of jungle and free-roaming space at Yarinacocha, this greatly cramped the children. 'Here they were, raised in the jungle, at perfect liberty, they knew everybody, every tree and path,' Elaine remembered. 'Now we were on the third floor of a group house with not a tree in sight [where they] didn't know a soul, with school work to be done by correspondence... The children didn't complain and I admired them so much for it.' While in Bogotá, the family somehow managed to keep pet ducks, and the children walked them around, garnering strange looks from passersby.

Of course the children were not the only ones who faced challenges. Elaine's feet and back suffered from the climb to their living quarters, and her children remembered the clop-clop, clop-clop of her feet as she took long flights of stairs with the same foot. But they never remembered her complaining… During this time there was also terrorist activity in the city, adding an element of danger to their daily lives. Bombs went off at night, the windows shook, and local papers were none too encouraging.

In Lomalinda, in contrast to the lush verdure and bustling activity of Yarina, there were no buildings here and very few trees. Rolling hills surrounded, and volcanic ground lay beneath. Home became a mobile home that Cameron bought and reconditioned, then drove down on the winding, treacherous mountain roads.

Grace left that summer to attend college in the States, and Joy the spring following. Elaine's newly widowed mother came down from Chicago to help teach the missionary children, and life became quite cramped. She only added, however, to the cheery atmosphere in that makeshift trailer and could often be found down on her knees playing with junior guests. Many noted her abilities with children as she held the first preschool class just outside the door of the trailer under a shelter.

Even Elaine admitted that things got rather uncomfortable when they used the oven in the daytime and kept the space closed off from hoards of mosquitoes in the evening. The wind was so strong that it blew the soup out of their bowls on one occasion. Elaine was imperturbable, and continued entertaining friends and officials. 'She never complained, never apologized,' witnessed one person. 'She was always gracious. It was what God had given them and they worked with it.' Eventually, a man from the States came down to build a screened porch and add two bedrooms on the little single-wide caravan.

Their local friends were greatly impacted by Elaine's perseverance. They too were just beginning their lives in this foreign country, their families and ministries; and the way this veteran missionary opened up a home in that impossible trailer, where one described her like a queen holding court, entertaining Colombian visitors and neighbors who flocked to her door, left a lasting impression.

Uncle Cal, Cam's personal secretary and close family friend, said later, 'I've often marveled at Elaine being willing to "pull up stakes," leave their lovely home at Yarina, and move to Colombia for five years, never to return to Yarina except for occasional visits. Not being a woman I can't imagine how difficult that was, but apparently she was convinced that it was God's assignment for them, so off she went with the four kids. That took a lot of grace. I don't know what conversations she might have had with Cameron regarding the move. Doubtless there were serious moments when they really felt they should go.'

A GUATEMALAN RUG IN RUSSIA

During an extended stay at a hotel on their first trip to Russia, Elaine renovated their room. In a letter to her then-grown children in the fall of '68, she wrote, 'Today the maid here at our hotel commented on how homey our room looks. I have our little Mexican scarfs on the dressers, the fur rug on the couch, a Guatemalan weaving on one of the chairs and the picture of our wonderful family on the wall. It really is quite cozy.' The concierge even brought tourists to visit their room. Elaine also set her hand to their house trailer during a later trip to the USSR. On the ship to Russia, they had been given a magazine with beautiful botanical pictures which she cut out and used to decorate the fronts of cabinets. She enlisted cheery curtains, fresh potholders, and even wallpaper. This was no camping expedition!

Her daughters captured it well: 'She was a Chicago gal who happily and beautifully adjusted to life in Mexican Indian villages and the jungle of Peru. She made our lives such a *grand* adventure. She was happy. She sang to us… She read to us. She laughed. She made places look pretty.' 'Mom made Dad a happy man; she made him beautiful homes wherever we were, and was an excellent team-mate with her warm hospitality.'

15. SHINING FORTH THE GOSPEL

The surest method of arriving at a knowledge of God's eternal purposes about us is to be found in the right use of the present moment. God's will does not come to us in the whole, but in fragments, and generally in small fragments. It is our business to piece it together, and to live it into one orderly vocation.

F.W. Faber[1]

'Mama! I'm thirsty!'
'Is there something to eat?'
'May I read my book when we get inside? You got it off the airplane, right Mom?'

Such was the symphony of needs that mingled with the dust and sticky air to welcome Elaine home on that hot afternoon.

Marta hung back. For an hour she had waited, and finally the truck arrived. Now here she was, and Marta couldn't go back without speaking to her.

WHAT TO REPLY?

Since early dawn, tensions had run high. Cameron was in the States, leaving the rest of the family to travel back to the base. The plane departed for Lima several times, but weather prevented the full crossing. It all made for an exhausting day. Elaine turned to pick up a suitcase. Then she saw her—a shriveled up old lady, slightly heavy, her dark hair straggling down around her shoulders. She walked with a stoop as one accustomed to work. Elaine's eyes caught on her hands—they were

1   F.W. Faber, Public Domain.

thick and knobby with irritated pink elevations dotting the skin; some had already turned an ashy white.

'*Ha estado en la clínica?*'[2] she asked, a little startled, and wondered what she could do to help this leprous woman. She was unprepared for the answer.

'*Are you Señora Townsend?*'

'*Yes.*'

'*I haven't come for the clinic. I've come to ask if you can teach me to read.*'

Billy's feet could be heard pounding up the steps, and the girls clambered for first place in the hammock.

What was she to do? Elaine thought of the piles awaiting her in the house… piles of letters to read, piles of letters to answer, piles of suitcases to unpack, piles of hot, hungry, tired children…

The answer formed itself in her mind: '*I'm so sorry, I can't give you an answer right now. Could you come back tomorrow?*'

Then she remembered the three small children who had awaited her in Mexico years before. The incredulity: was this all? And the waiting on the Lord—to bring some sort of gain from the havoc He seemed to be playing with her life—with her *conception* of life…

'So,' Elaine said, 'When I got there to the house with four kids and all our baggage, who met me at the gate but Marta, the Indian lady. She wanted a lesson right then, so before I did anything else I pulled out the primer and gave her the first lesson.'

A LEPER AT THE DINING ROOM TABLE

Except when tropical storms threatened, Doña Marta came by canoe across the lake three times a week. During this time she was also supporting herself and raising two grand-daughters. She and Elaine sat at the circular table in the dining room looking over the lake and pored over language primers. Afterward, the family wiped off the plastic tablecloth and set plates for a meal.

When a Peruvian educator arrived at the house, Elaine thought about postponing the lesson, but decided against it. What Marta

2   '*Have you been to the clinic?*'

prayed that day brought tears to the eyes of all who heard: 'Lord, I can't thank you enough for having Mrs. Townsend leave her home and guests for me in order that I might know You. I just lived like an animal before she came. Nobody cared if I lived or died.'

'My, but she was eager to learn!' Elaine said. In three months, Doña Marta was reading, although her failing eyes made it difficult. Elaine bought her a large print Bible and a magnifying glass, and for hours she sat and read by candlelight. What she found in the Word began to change her. Not only did she come to know the redeeming glory of the gospel, but this assertion of God into her life bore fruit. On their way through the New Testament, she and Elaine came to the command *Love your enemies, do good to those who spitefully use you.* Marta stopped.

'Is it God saying that?'

'Yes.'

'How could I do that?'

'What are you thinking about, Doña Marta?'

'Since I've become a Christian, my neighbors are jealous that I'm not afraid of the evil spirits. When I go out at night to meetings, they put their animals in my garden to dig up my carrots and lettuce and produce. When I come back and see this, I open up the gates and let my animals eat their food. But the Lord said, "Do good to your enemies," so I can't do that anymore.'

From then on, revenge cycles ended with Marta. 'Her simple, wonderful faith taught me many lessons in obedience,' Elaine said. '"If the Lord says to do it, who are we not to do it?" she'd ask.'

Marta also demonstrated a passion to share with others the world which was opening on her view. Elaine wrote Cam, 'The last time [Marta] came she brought with her a lady about my age who has five children and just recently accepted the Lord and now is eager to learn to read.'

One Tuesday, Elaine had guests from Lima when Doña Marta arrived. Three of the four traveled by plane to Tournavista, but limited space forced the fourth to stay behind, and to her, Marta told a radiant testimony.

She told her how she had been a vile woman, smoking constantly, drinking heavily, and living like an animal. She was hopeless and desperate. Someone suggested that she visit the linguists on the base, and it was there that one of the nurses led her to the Lord. When Marta expressed a desire to read, Beth told her to wait a few days, for Mrs. Townsend was arriving shortly and would be glad to teach her. That was when Elaine met her at the gate. Now, her joy could not be contained. When sickness brought her low for months and nearly took her life, though she was too weak to read, she found comfort in repeating Psalm 23.

When the rest of the group returned from Tournavista, their companion related with amazement the faith she had witnessed in a humble Mestizo lady.

THE DIFFERENCE

Life among primitive Indians provided countless opportunities for ministry just outside the front door, but it also brought challenges. 'We love to see these Indians come to visit us, for each visit means one more contact for Him,' Elaine wrote. 'On the other hand, the natural man would like to run when you see them coming...' Sanitation was nearly nonexistent. Often, Indians carrying tuberculosis would spit in the yard where the children played every day.

Many marveled at Elaine's care for these people. She was patient and friendly; she invited all into her home, cooking and waiting on them. When asked once what made her respect indigenous people, she replied,

> Before they come to the Lord... they live miserable lives... But once they come to know the Lord you can tell the difference. The gospel brings a change in every part of life: the children are cleaner, the husbands treat their wives with respect, they want education, and the community becomes vastly different in every way. Going down the rivers in the canoe you can tell which communities are Christian. Some are swept clean and have flowers. Others have no care at all and drunkards are common...

You've probably seen pictures of them with their Bibles and hymn books wrapped in cloth—so happy to have the Scripture for themselves. And now they themselves are supporting other missionaries—it's wonderful! They really have a heart for the Lord. They're willing to walk hours and hours to get to church, rain or shine, it means so much to them… and they're willing to pay the price.

LELIA

Another Indian woman from a staunchly Catholic family in Cuzco, and the wife of a prominent Peruvian educator, also encountered Elaine's gospel witness. One day, as Elaine prepared to take her siesta after lunch, she felt the Lord prompting her to invite Lelia over.

'Surely You don't want me to go now! It's hot out there. I'll do it at three o'clock, Lord,' she replied (apparently not remembering how that kind of exchange usually ended.) Sleep would not come. She could not rest till she had taken her umbrella and walked nearly a mile to Lelia's house, where she tapped on the door and invited her for tea.

Unlike Elaine in her twenties, Lelia had no record of a good life. She wanted to clean up her life before becoming a Christian, but Elaine urged her otherwise. As the two women spoke, Elaine emphasized the beauty of grace in a way reminiscent of her own encounter with Christ. That day, Mrs. Morote Best was gloriously saved. 'She got up radiant— just radiant,' remembered Elaine. The next day she returned, bringing her Quechua maid (an unheard of thing for such a high-ranking lady to do). Anna, too, came to know the Lord.

Later, someone sitting next to Lelia's husband on a flight heard him describe an unaccountable difference in his wife: 'I don't know what happened at Mrs. Townsend's house but there's been a most wonderful change in her life. She's more beautiful—just radiant—but not only that, she's a better wife, a better mother, a better housekeeper—in every way this has changed her life so completely.'

From Peru, the Morotes moved to China, where Lelia continued to follow the Lord. 'She grew because she had the Word in her own language,' Elaine said, adding,

… the Lord is making His promise in Isaiah 58:10 very precious to me these days. It says *'And if thou draw out thy soul to the hungry and satisfy the afflicted soul, then shall thy light rise in obscurity and thy darkness be as the noonday.'* Isn't that a wonderful promise? I don't know when I've seen a hungrier soul than Lelia. She is hiding the Word in her heart as fast as she knows how.

RISK: TAKEN

As she and Cameron readied for bed one evening, Elaine pulled off her shoe and stopped still.

Quietly she called, 'Cameron, come over here.'

One look at her toe and he wanted to call the doctor. But it was Saturday, when the doctor took a break from his regular commotion of patients.

'The doctor needs his rest too, let's wait till Monday,' Elaine urged.

Cameron consented, though the sight of his wife's white, porous toe alarmed him not a little. They prayed over it together, then turned in.

'There were many different jungle diseases it could have been,' Elaine said later. 'Cameron didn't say what he was thinking, and I didn't say what I was thinking. It seemed to be spreading quickly.'

During the Sunday morning rush of hair-brushing, shoe-finding, and record oatmeal-eating, to the tune of chipper tropical birds and crickets, Elaine saw a group passing by on the path in front of their house. Again, she called Cam over.

It was Doña Marta, a group of her grandchildren walking along beside and running on ahead. 'For that sight, this all will have been worth it,' she said to him, 'even if I do have leprosy.'

On Monday, when Elaine got out of bed, the toe had returned to its normal state, and it would be years before her own children learned of the incident.

Doña Marta promised to pray for Elaine every day, and she remained true to her word. Through her life, Elaine counted the prayers of that woman among the greatest treasures given her by a good God.

But Elaine was not the only one for whom Doña Marta came before the throne. She prayed that all her descendants would come to know the captivating love which had found her. God answered this indomitable faith, and children, grandchildren, and great grandchildren[3] were drawn into the family of God, including some who had mocked her faith. Several also became missionaries. According to her namesake granddaughter, 'She had a huge love for everybody—always with her arms wide open to receive you. She was always quoting Scripture, because Elaine helped her learn Psalms.'

STRATEGY ON THE BASE

For Elaine, opportunities for ministry came as a natural result of her husband's calling, and she sought to creatively invest in areas which would bear fruit in her home and near community. She did not always achieve a perfect balance in this regard, and her children sometimes felt the need for more focused family time than was possible with the constant flow of company that came through the Townsend home.

Among the daily busyness, Elaine encountered unexpected opportunities. Once she sent a box of Christmas cookies to the Catholic bishop in Pucallpa who had come over for Sunday dinner the week before and stayed four hours. He was Canadian, but had lived in China for fourteen years, three of which were in a communist concentration camp, with thirteen months in isolation. They read Scripture, sang hymns and showed evident goodwill. This was remarkable for a country in which Catholic and Protestant hostilities ran high, and Elaine noted to her family that he could be relocated if the news of his friendliness was broadcasted.

More than a few marriages took place in the Townsend front yard or living room. Many of the couples were new missionaries whose relatives and friends couldn't afford to travel to Peru, so Elaine stepped in. 'She was my mother for the day,' recalled one such bride. Elaine loved to take credit for these marriages performed on her turf, even if she had nothing to do with the initial germ of love—though more than a few times it was the romantic Cameron who claimed this role.

---

3   Now, more than a hundred.

A MINISTRY OF AVAILABILITY

Without question, Elaine was the ringleader for organizing events on the base. A tradition of having new members over for tea introduced young singles and couples to life in the jungle and made them feel welcomed. 'I have missed you popping in and saying it is exercise time,' one woman said, 'your wonderful Sunday dinners—a tradition we tried to keep up in other countries—your moral and tangible support, as well as physical help in packing when we had a family emergency.'

This ministry of availability which Elaine cultivated on the base once meant taking over a folding table and some chairs for a couple who had just moved in to their home and didn't have any furniture. Another time it meant opening up the third floor attic for a translator who desperately needed space and quiet. The quiet ended later when she allowed someone to build a boat in that same third story.

A new missionary at the time, Rebecca, told of a time just after the birth of her first child, when no one came to visit but Elaine, who dropped by with warm congratulations. When she saw the bare room, she left, and returned again with a pink rose. 'Elaine became a mom to me; I really needed that. She made me feel like "Our family is your family."'

FRUIT BEARING

Teaching Indian children was another experience altogether. 'One little boy—a second grader—went home with the prize for knowing 500 different kinds of birds, and his father said, "That's all you know? And you've been going to school? I can name a thousand!" Can you imagine? But their memories were so very good. It was such a privilege to teach them to read. Oh! They just read, read, read, once they came to know the Lord. Those were fun days.'

Elaine's skill in this area opened the door to a rather monumental task—that of creating primers for the Peruvian government to use in literacy campaigns. Every year the base held a teacher-training course for indigenous people who had been noted for particular ability by the leaders in their villages. Cameron described the camp: 'The Word of God is being taught in seventeen languages right here at the base…'

DOMESTIC MISSION

Instead of setting up a committee, she established a home. Instead of organizing programs, she invited families over for dinner. Perhaps she was tempted to be overwhelmed. Perhaps, if given a choice, not all of these things would have appeared on the priority list of that for which she seemed gifted or to which she felt particularly called. But the ministry of the home was one of the primary means God used to draw her into close fellowship with Himself, and He ordained treasure troves of blessing to be discovered along the path of obedience.

A note jotted in her journal encapsulates her spirit well, 'How can I know the will of God for my life? Grow in my dependence on Him. Be willing to submit without any reservation to the sovereignty of God. God has a plan for me and He'll put me in it.' Rather than holding to a preconceived idea of her talents, Elaine stepped in where help was needed most, following the immediate call of God.

A GRACIOUS PIONEER

On the hard days, and the busy days, and the cockroach-finding days, Elaine's ministry came down to obedience. She loved to refer to 'God's honor roll,' found in John 12:26—'If anyone serves me, he must follow me, and where I am there will my servant be also. If anyone serves me, the Father will honor him.'

A group of dignitaries, upon hearing Cameron tell Rachel Saint's testimony at an official dinner with the President of Ecuador, 'marveled at the terrific sacrifices that Rachel and the rest of our workers are willing to make.' In writing of the incident later Elaine said, 'I was glad to tell them that for us it wasn't a sacrifice, but rather pure joy. I told Mrs. Velasco of the excellent salary I had been receiving in Chicago and that although we didn't know now from month to month what our income would be, the joy we had from seeing the transformed lives of the Indians far surpassed the pleasure received from a good salary.'

'I'd much rather work this way than go back to education,' Elaine said. 'Every day is so full and so rewarding.' Exuberance spread to those whose lives she touched. 'She made life so pleasant and such fun,' attested Sanna Rossi, a close friend.[4] 'She goes all out—doesn't do things halfway. She's full of energy and sparkle. Everything she does, she does fast—talking and working.' Elaine sought God's glory and lived generously—'a gracious pioneer,' as one person called her.

---

4   Wife of Tropicana Founder.

16. ALWAYS ADVENTURE

An inconvenience is only an adventure wrongly considered; an adventure is an inconvenience rightly considered.

G.K. Chesterton[1]

Flying across the Andes with several small children plus several not-so-small suitcases consisted of almost pure ordeal. 'Greetings from Lima!' Elaine wrote after one such flight with Cameron, 'We had a good trip over the Andes, going to a height of 18,000 feet… It is really quite a picnic taking care of three babies on the plane, especially when there are only two oxygen tubes for five people and you have to keep them making the rounds.' Clearly, this was not *anyone's* piece of cake.

OXYGEN AND DIAPERING

Another time she wrote,

> It's very tricky, getting all four kids to breathe oxygen at the same time. It's also hard to get over the Andes when the rains are the heaviest. One time I had the four small children (Billy was just a baby at the time). We tried four times to get over the Andes. The fourth time, we got all the way across and were about to land when the weather broke and we had to go back to Lima. The kids were so disappointed.

---

1   G.K. Chesterson, 'On Running After One's Hat, All Things Considered', *In Defence of Sanity: The Best Essays of G.K. Chesterton* (San Fransisco, California: Ignatius Press, 2011), p. 24.

Early during her days on the field, Elaine showed an ability to turn her gaze away from inconveniences and make light of troubles. One of her daughters said later,

> I still remember the fabulous excitement of being woken up in what seemed to be the middle of the night to put on our prettiest dresses and black patent leather Sunday shoes and gathering up our dolls and our knitting to go to the 'airport' on the base. And Mom acting like we were the luckiest people in all the land to get to do this. Mom always made flying so much fun!

Life presented opportunities for great misfortune, but Elaine's ingenuity was unparalleled. Her calm grace in the midst of diverse situations was coupled with the energy she poured into creatively adapting whatever scenario faced her.

In one of her letters home from Mexico as a single girl she commented offhandedly, 'The doctor from the Latin-American hospital… made Sunday dinner for us, and it is from his Sunday dinner that I am now sick. Oh well, I'll be better by tomorrow.'

The Townsend family in the 'bubble' of a Catalina friendship airplane (1959).

Elaine turned daily living into an art form, priming those around her to look for gifts in an unusual life; and settling her children's hearts while lending an air of excitement to the inconveniences.

Her attitude changed the way her children viewed their circumstances. 'One of the earliest things I noticed about Mom was that she made our life an exciting adventure.'

Traveling with three cloth-diapered little ones would have coaxed a murmur out of many women. Elaine explained, 'When we were traveling, we'd always wash the diapers out in the motel room at night, then hang them in the windows of the car to dry. When it got hot, we'd roll the windows down and there would go the diapers!' White objects benevolently showered along the road like coins tossed by a victorious Roman emperor. 'If we'd only had Pampers, our lives would have been so much easier!' But Uncle Cal said of her, 'I never heard her complain about that or really about much else.'

When they grew older, each of the Townsend children had a regular space in the car and their chosen precious toys. 'As long as they had a few of their special things and their bedtime routine, they felt secure wherever they were,' Elaine said. 'One time we were packing up to leave a lovely lakeside resort where we had stayed with friends, and I was sure the children would hate leaving. I'll never forget Gracie settling into a corner of the back seat and saying, "Finally I feel at home. We're on the road again!"'

AND ALSO, THE DAILY

Living life joyfully required skill, practice, and intention—as with any art.

At one point, land disputes between Peru and Ecuador fomented turmoil, and Elaine wrote supporters asking them to pray for translators in Peru during a revolution. News of robberies and a murder in Pucallpa reached Yarinacocha. Men with their faces covered in mud were rumored to be coming towards the base. 'You can imagine how excited the girls were,' Elaine wrote to Cameron, who happened to be away at the time. They sang a hymn together, which calmed the girls down sufficiently to go to sleep, and no harm came their way.

Cam gave testimony to the peace and beauty of their home amidst the full days and inconvenience of a third world country:

Today is a beautiful day in the jungle. We have many supremely lovely days, especially when the heat is moderated by rain or breezes. As I write this, I can look from my office upstairs out over Lake Yarinacocha to the dense forests on the opposite shore and observe storm clouds rolling in. One of our planes has just landed and the wind-driven waves break over the floats with silvery spray.

Next to my office is one of our guest rooms now occupied by the Peruvian Professor who directs the Indian Teachers' Training Course and from it come the cries of the pet monkey he bought for his wife yesterday at a nearby Indian village. In my office sits a retired general of the U.S. Army who is visiting for a few days…

Elaine is downstairs getting time in between home duties, I hope, to help Mr. and Mrs. Wakelin on the Aguaruna primer as she has been helping other tribes, or on her correspondence. Yesterday she baked some of the best bread I ever put my teeth into and also delicious pie for the dinner we had for the General and Mr. and Mrs. Rolfe Dunbar of the Le Tourneau project who are also visiting us.

RAIN AND ENEMAS

Things were less lighthearted when little Joy almost died from an unexpected surprise. 'The other day as I was getting a diaper out of the closet for Joy I found a scorpion hidden away in the folds,' Elaine wrote to her family. 'How thankful I am that the Lord let me find it, as otherwise it probably would have stung Joy and very often these bites are fatal to babies. I know you will rejoice with us over His goodness.'

When someone was out of sorts, Elaine termed it 'feeling rather punk,' and this state of affairs could have disadvantages, particularly when Elaine got it in her head to give the children enemas all round. Administering enemas to small children required a definite sense of humor, and revealed Elaine's generous amount of pluck. Another veteran missionary, when asked about Elaine's sense of adventure said, 'Well, it was there or she would never have stayed on the field! Elaine was up to anything.'

Even when it came to tropical downpours, Elaine's determined sense of the comedy of life won out. 'Going back to the Grubers,' she told once, 'we got caught in a downpour and even our big banana leaves didn't bring any shelter. The rain really did add to our fun however, and instead of dampening our spirits made us happier than ever.'

Another time, while visiting friends in a remote jungle outpost, a torrent of rain caught up to them. How it did rain! The group of missionaries and Indians waited under a little thatch shelter and looked for things to entertain the Indians.

I took off my shoes and showed them my four boneless toes and they thought that was terrific. Each one of them had to flip them back and forth and then they wanted to know if Mrs. Cudney's were that way too, so she took off her shoe and showed them her normal feet. Then, since no one in the party had false teeth, I took out my partial lower plate and showed it to them. This, too, was an item of great interest.

ANOTHER FRONTIER

After spending seventeen years in Peru, Cam asked his family if they would be willing to start all over again in Colombia. In a letter to supporters on 1 May 1963, he wrote,

Dear fellow dreamers:

Eighteen years ago today I landed in Lima, Peru for the first time. Fourteen years ago [our Peruvian Base of Operations] was solid jungle. Now it has forty buildings for shops, classrooms, a clinic and other group services, besides sixty-eight private homes. 'This is the Lord's doing and it is marvelous in our eyes (Matt. 21:42).'

It had been a grand adventure, and one which continued to bear much fruit for years to come; but the prospects of beginning a new work in Colombia were bleak. This was among the most disheartening times Elaine would face in her life, though she barely intimated as much. One letter bears hints of the battle she waged, 'Pray for special strength for me as I'll be getting ready for the big move during May. The Lord is good to give us strength for each day's task.' She bravely signed off, 'In His joy, Elaine.'

1963 marked the year of transition. On July 25th, the Minister of Foreign Affairs in Peru, Vice-Admiral Edgardo Llosa, decorated Cameron and Elaine with the rank of Knight Commander for Distinguished Service. A few weeks later, at a large gathering in Lima, the Townsends said goodbye to their many Peruvian friends. The next day, Cameron and Elaine were decorated with another award: Peru's 'Teachers' Laurels'—*Palmas Magisteriales*—a prestigious educational decoration. From her limited strength and ability, God had granted much increase. She had gone from a supervisor of 300 schools to the teacher of three young children; and now to a nationally acclaimed literacy worker in Peru. Three days later, the family departed for Colombia by ship, arriving in this new field on August 19th. This too, Elaine took from His hand.

The testimony of her children speaks louder than anything: 'Mom enjoyed life. She wasn't afraid to move on to a new situation, even though that meant a lot of good-byes.' Another said,

> It was always presented to us as an adventure because she made it that way. It was never presented as a disappointment. I remember when we had to sell all our belongings to leave Peru, and that was a shock for us all. We had to sell our toys, we had to sell everything. She said we could each pick a toy, and a couple books, and that was it. But I don't remember grieving, or having self-pity. It was simply what we did, and every trip was exciting.

In the midst of uprooting she remained joyful; no one observed her pining over lost relationships or house or community—each one of which had been intentionally developed and cultivated over long years. Her determined gratitude, her peaceful courage, and her inimitable love punched rays of light through hardship.

ABOARD THE OX AND A BUS

As if the move itself was not enough, travel inside Colombia held its own novelty. Judy, a missionary who also served in Colombia, recounted a memorable journey with Elaine. Judy's husband had gone ahead into their tribe with their oldest son, but when the time came for her to join him with the rest of their four children and the family's belongings, the plane broke down, leaving her to find ground transportation from Lomalinda to Bogotá.

Around that time, the Townsends were leaving for the States on furlough. Cameron was traveling and would meet them later, and Grace and Joy were already studying in the States, leaving Elaine, Billy, and Elainadel. No procrastinator, Elaine quickly arranged a ride in 'the Ox,' as the missionaries had termed a Dodge power wagon. Off they went: Judy with her four children and all their family's belongings, Elaine with Elainadel and Billy, plus a cranky back.

Once in town, Elaine found a bus to drive them to Bogotá; but after everyone was loaded up, the driver informed them that he had taken on a load of pigs instead, and they would have to get off. Undaunted, Elaine walked over to a five-ton truck sitting on the other side of the street and bargained with the driver.

Unfortunately, the truck was already fully loaded, but Elaine knew how to use the 'pesítos' when needed. Soon all the children were climbing on top of the load for hours of driving over impossible road. Judy put ten-month-old Scott in an inner-tube, and Elaine sat up front with the driver, due to her bad back. Things could only get better.

'Billy got sick on the way and lost his luncheon and made it even less pleasant,' Judy remembered. 'We were headed for San Martin, a town about six hours away… We arrived there at dark, only to find that another couple had just come in from the field and were filling the guest house, so there was no room for us.' Elaine negotiated with another bus to pick them up again at the house—all the children, all the luggage. They reached the next town around midnight. Elaine stood up in the bus: 'Now we have all these sleeping children; would some of you gentlemen help us carry them inside to the hotel?' All the droopy children were brought inside, and off went the bus.

Judy recalled clearly what happened next: 'I had four little kids to get into bed and she had her two. Elaine gets out this beautiful doily from her suitcase and lays it across the dresser, then all the family pictures. For that night, this was home for us.'

Next morning, the trip would be easier, since they planned to catch a flight up to Bogotá. But due to bad weather over the mountains, all the flights were canceled. This was growing desperate, but Elaine was undaunted. Again, she went to the bus terminal and negotiated for a bus to pick the group up at the hotel.

During the day that followed, Elaine's back, so painful from its merciless jolting the day before, became unbearable. As they approached a small town on their ascent up the mountain, Elaine made her way to the front of the bus and 'said some lovely thing to the driver,' as Judy put it. '... next thing I knew, the bus slowed, the door opened, and she alighted onto the main street. Elaine walked through that town ahead of the bus like a queen, greeting storekeepers and pedestrians on every side, strolling like someone on a Sunday walk and just enjoying that little town so much! The driver crept along behind her with never a protest from the other passengers, and when she reached the end of the street, she climbed aboard and off we went again!'

When the travelers arrived at the group house on Calle 42, they were greeted by friends: 'How was your trip?'

'Oh, it was just *wonderful!*' Elaine replied without hesitation.

DISCOVERING HIS WILL

The smallest incident, along with the largest disturbances, can then be seen as His love at work, and nothing is irrelevant toward the accomplishment of His purposes.

During a particularly painful time when controversy threatened to undermine Wycliffe, even to shut down the mission entirely, Elaine referred to the multitude of promises in Scripture saying, 'The Lord must have known we would certainly need these passages of comfort some day.' Elaine called herself back to the source of her hope—the unshakeable trustworthiness of her faithful God.

Doris Anderson, a close friend who observed her during some of the hardest years of her life, said of her, 'I cannot remember ever hearing a complaint or criticism from Elaine's mouth. She exemplified contentment with whatever she was currently doing and courage to face whatever tomorrow might hold.'

'I think her greatest gift was always being happy,' commented her daughter, Joy. The heart of the gospel shone through the energy of gratitude. Elaine took practical efforts to set the tone of the home each day, like filling their home with music, smiling when answering the phone (particularly for her husband), and beginning each day with spoken praise. 'I find this joyful spirit is very contagious,' she observed.

She once told the story of the year when a bad back kept her in bed and Joy came down with bronchitis. 'We were both in the same bed while I tried to keep Joy up with her school work. As the hot, sticky days rolled into weeks, I became complaining. One day Joy suggested that we make a list of all the things we could praise the Lord for— thirty-seven items!' she said gleefully. 'Two days later, we were both up and praising the Lord.'

Joy remembered, 'You never acted like you wished I would just hurry up and get better so as to make your life simpler... Oh, that was a summer to remember! That house was so fresh and airy, with a big tree for climbing out back and gorgeous Shasta daisies in the front yard. We girls have adored Shasta daisies ever since!'

As Elaine said, 'There are many things that we aren't real sure about being the Lord's will, but we do know it is His will for us to give thanks in everything, for this is the will of God in Christ Jesus concerning each of us.'

17. JOY IN THE JOURNEY

One reason the Bible is so relentless in insisting on our joy is because of the goodness of God. The imperative to joy in us is based on the indicative of good in him. 'You shall *rejoice* in all *the good* that the Lord your God has given to you' (Deut. 26:11). Joy in the heart of the creature corresponds to goodness in the heart of the Creator. Joy is the fitting response in the receiver to the goodness of the Giver.

David Mathis[1]

'Put the pie in pioneering,' Cameron always quipped, but it was Elaine who implemented it. Indeed, the atmosphere of the base was certainly celebratory. Casual get-togethers and rollicking parties happened frequently. Every Friday night, families on the base gathered in 'the Auditorium' for games, skits, talent shows, recitals, and singing. Cameron emphasized the need for lighthearted fun and the camaraderie it encouraged. As one person put it, 'everything had to be celebrated.' On one occasion, Cameron played 'Do the Bunny Hop' over the loudspeaker on Sunday morning to alert the village that it was almost time for church.

ALLIGATOR-THEMED BIRTHDAYS AND JUNGLE DOWNPOURS

'Mom could throw a great party!' said one of her daughters. 'A *real* party had to include Mom at the piano dashing through "The Burning of Rome" while we chased around the chairs in the living room. Mom

---

1   David Mathis, 'Joy is Not Optional'. Last accessed September 18, 2018. https://www.desiringgod.org/articles/joy-is-not-optional

could think up all sorts of games for people to play even though they didn't speak the same language...'

Birthdays in particular heralded special times. 'Of course it was actually Dad who made our "thrones," but Mom joined in making us feel thoroughly celebrated,' Joy remembered. One of Billy's birthdays was commemorated by an alligator hunt. Four friends, plus the Townsend family, Chief Tariri, and a Shapra boy composed the party. They bundled up because of the cold, but the alligators seemed rather chill as well, and only their red eyes shone along the shore. After two hours, the hunters had only captured one about thirty inches long, so they returned for birthday cake, ice cream, and hot chocolate.

Christmas, the greatest of all celebrations, was greeted with excitement in the Townsend home. Throughout her life, this remained Elaine's favorite season, and with a little ingenuity and much liveliness, she threw herself into creating special times her children never forgot. 'Christmas at our house was simply magical! The Christmas "tree" Dad made with bubbly lights on our screen window (Elainadel and Bill used to bet on which light would bubble first)... Who would believe that a single string of wires fastened on our screen window could be so beautiful? ... The paper Christmas train that sat on the book shelf... Mom's little porcelain Christmas tree that sat on the table by the window... Our "magic" trunks, disguised most of the year as an ordinary living room couch, filled with all sorts of Christmas things...'

TRUMPETS AT DAWN

The children too began to exude this celebratory spirit. When they were young, Elaine wrote about their unique preparations for her birthday: 'The girls have big plans for tomorrow—Mommy's birthday. All the presents are wrapped and ready for breakfast. Perhaps you'd be interested in knowing just what those presents are. Well, they've gone through my dresser drawer and picked out the newest-looking slips, etc. and wrapped them for me. I do appreciate their loving thoughtfulness; they are trying hard to make it a happy day for Mommy and I'm sure it will be.'

If Elaine was tempted to amusement by this, she must have realized that they were serving her right back, since she had come up with the brilliant idea to hide toys they no longer played with— castaway gifts— and re-wrap them for the next Christmas. Perhaps they remembered more than she gave them credit!

Life wasn't one long, continuous string, and Elaine took time to add flourishes every now and again. Most of these episodes weren't anything magnificent—just a small savoring of life, and times to remember. 'We tried to keep a time for the family right after supper each night,' said Elaine, 'not only for our devotions but also for us to enjoy each other. How much fun you had with Daddy on the living room floor on all fours with you children trying to stay on his back at one time! And then those wonderful times when you would crawl into bed and I would read to you with the tropical rain beating against the roof.'

Jungle rain created a formidable din, but the children all grew to love it and looked back on the torrential tropical downpours with enchantment. 'Wasn't it awesome when Mom would go sign out the yellow jeep from the shed across from the Gammons' house and drive us to school?' recalled Joy. 'I'm telling you—I felt like the Queen of England herself was driving us in her royal chariot!'

However, life on the base could grow a little *too* celebratory at times: 'Billy is doing so well on his trumpet,' Elaine wrote Cameron once. 'I hope the neighbors don't mind when he starts in at 6:30 a.m.'

YELLOW FLOWERS ON THE BACKYARD CACTUS

Everyday events held a certain charm—like experiencing the coolness of a big city after the muggy heat of home or pajamas made all toasty-warm by a room heater. The grateful, fun-loving attitude of the Townsends opened their children's eyes to the undeserved gifts of their good God. Beauty didn't necessarily involve the bought and the brilliant—sometimes it was as small as a butterfly or as simple as crisp white sheets. Each of the children received Spanish Bibles with their names engraved on the front, and Cameron brought back pretty gifts for his girls from his travels.

The Townsends' pet boa.

When one of the children fell sick, a special meal tray appeared, made by Elaine and often bearing a cheery bouquet picked by Cameron—ever a lover of flowers and the courageous rose-grower of the jungle. Elaine also took time to read to the afflicted one. As Joy wrote, 'I never minded getting sick because the TLC you gave made me feel like a cherished princess.' No doubt this habit was responsible for a few mysterious sicknesses!

'Wasn't it fun putting flowers on the tips of our huge corner cactus in the front yard?' Joy also remembered. 'Mom and Dad gave us the freedom to do all kinds of things. Swimming every day was another one of those treats that you didn't worry about having to get permission for.'

While most parents would have worried about the very real dangers of snakes and piranhas and parasites, Elaine released her little adventurers to the rare freedom of romping on a base where adventures abounded.

AND THE BOAS

Sometimes the adventures just couldn't help themselves! For a couple years it was all the rage for school children on the base to own boas as pets. The snakes could be easily caught in the jungle or bought from the Indians, and were kept happy with daily installments of mice. They became the children's constant companions, going everywhere with them like friendly dogs.

When the snakes began to appear in school, the teacher put her foot down. *'Ok kids, you can bring your boas to school but they must be kept in your desks! You may take them out at recess.'* So into the desks they went, no doubt peeked at and affectionately fed from time to time. The Townsend children were no exception, but one morning their private boa disappeared—'it had bit Daddy.'

DONUTS AND OTHER USEFUL THINGS

Then there was Lima. Elaine took the girls to tea at a lovely hotel—a splendid event involving polished wood floors, beautiful flowers, white tablecloths, elegant servers, and curled balls of smooth butter. On other occasions she took them to a primitive stand in the shadow of an ornate building for anticuchos.[2]

To her children's great delight, Elaine possessed the skill of stand-hopping in this large city, and a certain beloved donut shop lived long in their deep regard. 'Mom was so fearless about getting around,' her daughters remembered.

In addition to feeding them donuts, Elaine also set aside time to teach her children skills like piano playing and typewriting. Grace learned to knit at four, and by the age of seven she had made Cameron a sweater which he wore threadbare. One of the children commented in retrospect, 'We never felt like we were working, we were just taught to be constructive.'

---

2   A popular and inexpensive Peruvian dish consisting of skewered slices of cow heart.

Joy spoke of how her mother's love for music nourished and encouraged her. For birthdays and Christmas, she gave the children their own records, and years later they remembered the hymns she sang constantly around the house: 'Possibly the gift I received from mom that has blessed me the most over the years has been the songs that she taught us.'

THE CREATIVITY OF LOYALTY

'It was primitive. But so was everything else at Yarina in those early days,' remarked one missionary who lived on the base. 'Everyone had to learn to live with what they could manage...' This base, hidden away in the massive jungles of Peru, met a wide array of challenges. 'No running water and lights [only] part of the time was a challenge, but it didn't feel like a sacrifice,' Elaine said of their tent home. Joy wrote, 'We had running water pumped up to our big house from the lake complete with tadpoles...'

'This was a special era,' commented Adele Elson, a missionary who served in Mexico at the same time Elaine was settling in Peru. 'That's because of the way Uncle Cam and Elaine made it—it was life. It was not hard, just normal. That's a lot of what Jungle Camp and SIL were about, and it created an atmosphere: "That's life! Just be thankful! It's good!"'

Elaine, Adele and their fellow missionaries during that era left home and parents, with little idea of when they'd return. Many married overseas in a day when travel took months, and contact was almost nonexistent. Adele laughed with her bright eyes, 'You'd have to make appointments two weeks in advance to do a radio call with the "over-n-out" type things.'[3]

Their attitude was captured well by the remark of one friend: 'Loyalty to mission and submission to authority characterized that generation, which produced staggering results for that age of missions. They found a way to do everything.' These men and women exercised remarkable

---

3   The real advantages of technology and communication pose a different kind of challenge to missionaries. Instead of the relatively one-time commitment of forsaking one's homeland and kin, missionaries today are continually torn between the dual worlds opened up by technology.

inventiveness. They used dynamite from the Bolivian mines to clear an airstrip, then rolled gigantic logs over it to flatten it; they made water tanks for their houses out of old airplane floats. Always, they assumed a solution existed and they threw every skill they possessed (and some they didn't) into furthering the mission to which God had called them.

Elaine once told of a visit paid by three men from an oil camp not far away. The men saw great joy at Yarinacocha, even though it lacked the modern conveniences of their own camp. Circumstances were similar: both groups consisted of Americans living in a foreign country with more or less the same educational background. Yet one was happy, the other not. One group saw money as their goal; the other sacrificed money and self to help others, 'and it was the Word of God that made the difference.'

18. OPENING THE CASTLE DOORS

We do not think of hospitality… as a central expression of Christian holiness and the glory of God. Paul corrects this notion. If we are not practicing hospitality, we are not loving, and when we do not love, we cease to be a living church.

Steve Wilkins[1]

When Elaine's career of hospitality debuted with eighteen new recruits on her honeymoon in Peru, she realized she had not only married Cameron, but Wycliffe as well. Every year from then on was filled to the brim with guests of every nationality. Newly-made Peruvian friends were invited to their makeshift quarters, even though the group lacked proper tableware of any kind. Their first guests from the Ministry of Education showed up, but they were dismayed when one cracked his fork trying to cut the meat. This broke the ice, of course, and Cameron, the eternal optimist, commented that at the very least they now knew the missionaries were not a bunch of wealthy Americans coming for gain.

'You were welcome no matter what,' said one. Elaine wasn't ashamed of what they didn't have and never apologized for what they offered, no matter how seemingly inadequate. 'Nothing seemed to rattle her. She never knew a stranger.'

After two weeks of settling into her newly-completed home, Elaine entertained around sixty people who were about to head back to their tribes in the jungle.

---

1 Steve Wilkins, *Face to Face: Meditations on Friendship and Hospitality* (Moscow, Idaho: Canon Press, 2002), p. 90.

MOTHER OF THE BASE

Both in Peru and Colombia, Elaine became the 'mother of the base.' Such an effort was not insignificant. These bases included several hundred people from diverse backgrounds and experiences all living together in a remote location and adjusting to a new language and culture, plus handfuls of lively children. Over the course of each year, Elaine purposed to have all the families of the base into their home.

Everywhere she went, even when traveling, Elaine helped newcomers adjust, developed relationships, organized social gatherings, and made everyone feel cared for. She devised ways to bless others and exercised her imagination in countless scenarios.

One woman described their warm welcome:

> Housing was scarce and Elaine invited us to move in on the privacy of their family, a real demonstration of her selflessness and graciousness. Our bedroom was upstairs, just across the hall from theirs, and she immediately ordered a carpenter to transform the entryway to our bathroom into a tiny kitchenette. It was like a honeymoon suite. We felt so loved, especially the day following the women's Bible study when she surprised me with a baby shower for our first. That was a three month span of time in our lives that we will never forget.

Elaine hosted, in the words of one person 'a table always big enough to include others.' 'Big enough' came to be an impressive term on that little base in the isolated Peruvian jungles. Elaine loved to count everything: how many letters she had written and how many she had yet to write; how many overnight guests in a month; how many people had been to dinner that week. These notes, recorded in letters, provide glimpses into the real magnitude of the undertaking she faced. One group came for lunch, but due to a downpour, Elaine offered to let them stay the night. 'That brings the total number of dinner guests for the month of April so far up to 124, and 27 different overnight ones,' she wrote, 'making an average of nine per night.'

One year, 900 guests came for dinner, including some 450 who stayed the night. That year, the Townsend children slept in their own rooms less than six nights.

The year Bill was born, she entertained 120 people for dinner in the space of six weeks—nearly the entire base. Admirable ambition; nonetheless his sister expressed the cost aptly in later years when she said, 'I'm afraid my heart cries out to that little baby boy!'

A rumor circled the base that every time Cameron came home from a trip Elaine had built another bedroom in the house to welcome him home, and people almost believed it! Yarina acted as the midway station for all—visitors, dignitaries, translators, and families going into their tribe or coming from an outpost in the jungle. Few days failed to bring an Indian 'clad' in native attire, a bountifully beaded chief, or a heavy, elegant duchess. A guest of the latter sort once gravely entrusted her jewels to Elaine for safekeeping in the lockbox she assumed Elaine possessed. Elaine put them in a drawer simply to ease the lady's mind.

Cameron habitually read the Word with his guests; and many noted how often Elaine looked for opportunities to turn the conversation toward the gospel with all its wonders, or to challenge people of all ages to read and memorize Scripture.

WINNING OPPOSITION

Many outposts in the Peruvian jungle remained isolated, including military camps and Catholic missions, and Elaine frequently sent packages of homemade bread, cookies, pickles, and produce with the pilots who stopped off at these settlements along their routes. 'We had many opportunities to show love and kindness to our Catholic neighbors,' Elaine wrote.

> One day, several nuns from the school in Pucallpa brought the graduating class out for a swim in our Lake Yarinacocha. When Cam saw the nuns sitting on the shore, he suggested I go down and invite them in for lemonade, which I did. I then asked if they would like a tour of our home. I saw how their eyes lit up, and I knew they were eager, but I was amazed to learn that the thing that impressed them most was the cockroach-proof paper lining the shelves in my kitchen cupboards. This bit of kindness opened up a wonderful friendship with Sister Marie, who had never owned a Bible of her own.

Years later, Sister Marie wrote Elaine a letter expressing gratitude for this kindness and telling the story of her journey to Protestantism. 'It was all because you were so good to us,' she said.

'I had no idea that just bringing them in for a cup of tea could do much good,' admitted Elaine.

CHIPPED CHINA STYLE

During an orientation class for women, Elaine advised, 'Always have something in the pantry that you can pull out for guests at a moment's notice.' At least one man remembered how wonderful he found pound cake, strawberries, and whipped cream (Elaine's go-to dessert) the first time he visited; and the second time, twenty years later. She gave of the best she had, but if it didn't happen to be up to standards, she was content to let it be.

'She always seemed so organized,' noticed one woman, 'with wisdom to deal with whatever came her way, and I admired that very much. I asked her one night, after a busy evening with official guests from Lima, how she entertained so effortlessly… "Oh, it's easy," was her reply. "All you need is enough dishes to set the table and a simple menu…" That encouraged me many times in later years.'

Allotting responsibilities was another of Elaine's secrets to simple, effective entertaining. 'Be open and willing to have someone help you, rather than just doing it all on your own,' she told a group of women. Several women on the base made themselves available to fill in for Elaine when the balance of company and children, making meals, and cleaning became too much. She frequently invited her guests to help, and she considered this part of her hostess role, putting guests at ease.

One woman's experience illustrated Elaine's relaxed style of hospitality: 'I was helping Elaine set up a banquet in the house at Yarina for three ambassadors and some officials from the Ministry of Education. We were working in the kitchen and she said, "Get my china out and just put it on the table; we'll arrange it later. It's in the first cupboard on the left in the dining room."

'I went into the dining room and looked in the first cupboard—no china, just a few chipped cups and plates. I looked in the second cupboard—no china. And in the third cupboard—no china. I returned. "Where did you say it was?"

"In the first cupboard."

'So I looked again—no china. I wandered back into the kitchen, "Sorry, Elaine. I can't find it."

'She looked at me, perplexed, went into the dining room, opened the first cupboard, and started bringing out the chipped pottery cups and plates. "That's my china," she said.

"But these are all chipped!"

"Oh, they'll be just fine. I figure that if people come to the jungle they should be ready to accept what we have."'

Commenting on this incident, one of the Townsend children said, 'They didn't stand on ceremony. It was more important to entertain and bring people into our home. That was the best we had and so that's what we used. To my Mom, that was all nothing—it was more important to have the relationships. She did want nice things, but if she didn't have them she didn't let that stop her from entertaining.' For the Townsends, hospitality was a kaleidoscope of possible arrangements.

POPSICLES AND PRESIDENTS

If Elaine had a skill for hosting, Cameron had a talent for picking up extra dinner guests. One April seventeen guests stayed the night, but when they tried to leave as scheduled the next morning, a tropical storm rolled in, and they came back to stay another day and night. Elaine had already begun to change the sheets when they came traipsing back into the house.

> Elaine lived with the reality that Cameron could bring someone home on a moment's notice, or interruptions to their plans for the day would surface… She handled interruptions well. Whether she was upset internally I don't know, but she didn't show any disturbance about it… She was convinced that God had called her to be the wife of Cameron Townsend, and she accepted all that that involved, including irregular hours, interruptions, unexpected moves, or trips to most any place in the world.

One February, R.G. Le Tourneau,[2] his wife, son, and the vice-president came to visit, as well as the president of Wheaton College, his son, and four others. 'Did you ever dream that your daughter would be someday entertaining Mr. Le Tourneau in her jungle home?' Elaine wrote her parents. 'I didn't! I have been looking over our house to see where we could put them all, along with five others… Talk about your expandable houses, this is it! I do enjoy my role of hostess however, so don't feel sorry for me. Do pray that the Lord will accomplish much for the future of missions through this trip.' In March, the president of Peru visited Pucallpa, and briefly stopped in Yarina during his stay.

'I realize that they are just people,' explained Elaine, and she told how the British ambassador walked into the kitchen while they were making cookies and joined right in on the fun. 'It certainly is true,' she wrote, 'that the higher the office… the easier it is to entertain them. It's the folks who think they are somebody that can give one a hard time. So I never feared those big men.'

Cameron designed visiting weeks, in which officials and educators were invited to experience life on the base. One week, several ambassadors, two ministers of state, various socialites, and miscellaneous media all came to stay. They had lunch with the teachers, took boat rides on the lake, visited an Indian village, gained first-hand experience of the SIL linguistics program, and shot balloons with blowgun darts. They stayed, of course, in the Townsends' home and in others on the base.

'IN THE JUNGLE?!'

The style of generous hospitality and the flair demonstrated by Elaine and others on the base gained much support for the work of the translators. Much of the opposition Wycliffe encountered in South America came through the staunchly Catholic national press. The owner of the leading newspaper in Lima, *El Commercio*, was said to be more Catholic than the pope, and it was with great reluctance that his daughter was persuaded to 'come out and see what the evangelicals were doing' in their remote outpost. A fashionable socialite, she was

---

2   A world-famous inventor of earth-moving machinery and Christian who founded Le Tourneau University in Texas.

Cameron and Elaine are decorated in Lima on July 25, 1963 by Peru's Minister of Foreign Affairs, Vice-Admiral Edgardo Llosa for distinguished service, grade of Comendador.

convinced that nothing really worthwhile could happen in the jungles. Uncle Cam's secretary, Cal Hibbard and his wife 'Corny,' invited her to be their guest… and plotted.

In anything-but-typical missionary style, the couple had their fine china and Czechoslovakian crystal glasses custom wrapped, along with white linen tablecloths, and packed the lot out to the humid, damp jungle in the middle of nowhere. 'Why we thought to take all that down with us I don't know,' said Cal. But bring it they did, and when news of the lady's arrival came, the china and crystal, must have felt, like Esther, that it existed for such a time. Corny, a born hostess if there ever was one, knew loads of etiquette and protocol, and under her supervision the Hibbard family prepared a splendid dinner. They set a table fit for a king.

Clad in a lovely evening gown, Elvira Miró Quesada flounced in, took one look around, and exclaimed, 'EN *LA SELVA*?!'[3]

'It not only shocked, but impressed her,' said Cal. 'She realized, *these people aren't the hoakies I thought they were.*' Upon her return to Lima, she informed the employees of her father's paper that anything regarding SIL would pass through her desk before publication. In effect, she became a gatekeeper who prevented any negative publication.[4]

LIFE AS CURIOSITIES

'I seem to be the official hostess for the many Indians who come to look us over,' Elaine remarked. 'Last night, a family of them came and stayed all night, spreading their blankets on the site for the hangar. They were here all morning as well because of the rain. I made a big pot of soup for them and gave them some bread and papaya. They went away very happy.'

The Indians soon recognized that they were treated with the same courtesy and attention as important diplomatic visitors. 'I remember Chief Tariri being so happy that he had a chance to sit in the same chair that the president of the country had sat in,' Elaine said.

Women loved to get away from home and visit from time to time… I showed them how to use an egg beater. Many of them hadn't seen a big mirror, only the tiny ones sold by merchants downriver, so it became the biggest attraction of a visit to take them by our full length mirror. They had never seen a full view of themselves and some just

---

3   '*In the jungle?!*'

4   A few months later, her father sent her on a trip around the world. 'He was probably worried about her 'cause she wasn't as Catholic as she used to be,' laughed Cal. The missionaries in Lima learned of her visit and informed the Philippine branch of Wycliffe. A party met her at the airport and escorted her to the group house, where she stayed for several days, shared meals with the team, 'and got to know us as people.' She loved it. The evening of her departure, a group drove her to the airport and said good-bye. She walked halfway out to the airplane, then turned around and came back: 'Would you pray for me?' No one could know for sure what occurred in her heart, but what was certain, the hospitality and fellowship of the Hibbards touched her deeply. 'She saw that we were just common ordinary people living simply. In Lima, she lived in a pretty artificial world. She was society gal number one.' From then on, she became an avid supporter of the cause of SIL, and was later influential in their work in the Philippines.

died laughing, while others got horrified and ran. Cockroach paper interested them, and 'garbage disposals' were always intriguing.

Elaine organized literacy nights once a week where Indians and missionaries gathered to visit and play games. This acted as an opportunity for missionaries to familiarize themselves with the local language and culture as well as for Indians to become comfortable around them. From her teaching experience in Chicago, Elaine contrived games which didn't require a shared language—like dropping peanuts from a nose into a jar, or carrying cotton balls across the room in a spoon. 'We also played [a memory game], and their memories were so good that they could go far, far beyond what I could.'

PECULIAR ORDINARY

One night, anticipating the arrival of around twenty Indians from different tribes, Elaine made Kool-Aid in her kerosene refrigerator. She was slightly surprised when the first lady took a sip and made a terrible face. The second did the same. They sat holding their glasses, with no one venturing a second taste. Elaine realized with dismay that she must have used the salt instead of the sugar, but when she tried the Kool-Aid, it was delicious. Finally, she asked one of the men what was wrong.

'We have such terrible, decayed teeth that this is just killing us,' he explained. 'One sip and it goes right to the cavities.'

So Elaine got out her big kettle and heated up the Kool-Aid. They all loved it!

Another comical incident occurred when a translator brought two natives to the base to do translation work. He warned them that the food might be different than what they normally ate, and sure enough, spaghetti was on the menu. During the meal, a few strange looks were exchanged, and as they left the house, the Townsend children snooped after them.

'Why did she feed us worms?' burst from one Indian as they left earshot of the house.

'We don't eat worms!' the second erupted, and with that, both doubled over beside the path, bestowing their dinner, spaghetti and all, into the jungle foliage.

FROM TEA TO FIREWORKS

'Elaine entertained anywhere she went,' said their friend, Peter. During one visit to Norman, Oklahoma, Elaine invited the entire group of new recruits to their temporary quarters, group by group. One woman wrote later of the significance of this effort:

> I know many felt somewhat in awe of Uncle Cam and you, so those informal gatherings were important to let us see you in a different context: as a family at home. You took seriously your responsibility to provide this kind of interaction. As I got older, I realized how much effort you had put into that kind of hospitality, the time it took to plan and invite the groups, as well to spend so many evenings that way.

After the move from Peru, Elaine wrote, 'Now instead of living in our lovely big home, we were in the third floor of our group house in Bogotá, Colombia.' At Yarinacocha a band of women had met the needs which exceeded Elaine's energy. Now Elaine lived among Colombian neighbors and a few already over-stretched co-workers. She found the culture of Colombia did not bubble with warmth and invitation. Nevertheless, she pressed on, and one woman said, 'I was always impressed with how quickly she could entertain folks from both ends of the Colombian social strata—anyone walking through her door could be assured of a cup of tea or coffee and something sweet to go with it. She had a lonely position as the director's wife and few invited her, so she invited others.'

Through many sorts of social gatherings, Elaine began to learn people's names, earn their trust, and forge relationships. 'Take the initiative,' she said.

> Don't wait for someone to invite you. I went around from door to door in a neighborhood in Bogotá telling the ladies I was so sorry that I had been there almost a whole year and had never gotten to know them. Would they enjoy coming to my house for coffee on Wednesday afternoons? Their reaction? 'Why, goodness! I've been here for eight years and I don't know anybody in this block...' Afterwards they have had me in their homes and invited other friends over. The last

Wednesday before I left they all came to my house again for a final farewell. They were so embarrassed that it took a foreigner to come to their country to get them together.

Just before I moved, there was a large demonstration of fireworks, and they were all looking out the windows, waving, and hollering to each other by their first names. I thought, *My goodness! what a different street this is from just a year ago!*

THE ART OF THE OPEN DOOR

Friendship through hospitality was a principle which grew deep roots and bore rich fruit on the jungle base of Yarinacocha. The Townsend home acted as a representation of the larger work of Wycliffe, and many caught a vision for the massive undertaking of linguistics and translation through observing the gospel's power to forge community in the middle of jungle. The homes of the base became its heartbeat, as warm fellowship broke down walls of culture and adorned the gospel in a way unique to each home.

19. A CHART FOR THEIR PILGRIMAGE

Finally, for discipline of children to be a blessing, the act itself must be full of Jesus and His gospel of grace… If you laugh it off, if you refuse to intervene, if you refuse to discipline, you are refusing an evangelistic opportunity. You are refusing a chance to proclaim the grace of Jesus to your family.

Toby Sumpter[1]

FRIDAYS AND ALL THE GLUE OF LIFE

When Elaine's children returned from school on Fridays, they smelled the incredible aroma of fresh baked bread. 'I remember the fun of being able to eat bread dough,' said Joy, 'and being so proud of Mom for not freaking out, despite the worms that we could see there with our own eyes!'

What would these stories be without unique, sometimes amusing touches? 'Thanks for being my hairstylist! Even in eighth grade you were rolling my hair at nights,' one daughter wrote in tribute. Reference was made to 'all the perms Mom so lovingly gave us at the folding table in the kitchen in Yarina—remember how Uncle Cal would wrinkle his nose at the stench?'

A greater flexibility of schedule was certainly one advantage of missionary life, and Elaine took advantage of this: 'We enjoy our time together with the children after supper each night. We have a good

---

1   Toby Sumpter, 'Blessings too Big', last accessed June 1, 2018, http://www.desir-inggod.org/ blog/posts/blessings-too-big

hour or more of playing, reading, singing, and praying. I think we all look forward to this time of the day.'

Elaine loved spending time with her children. She didn't parent perfectly, but there is no doubt that she did invest deeply. She made herself available. As the oldest said, 'We grew up feeling treasured.'

THE HONOR OF A CURTSEY

The afternoon meal concluded, and everyone prepared to leave. A good lunch had been had by all, including ten-year-old Grace. In fact, she had so enjoyed the luxuries of dining in a royal Peruvian dining room that she found it necessary to unbutton her skirt—just till they left, she promised herself.

She accomplished this surreptitiously enough under the table, but it was harder to hide when she stood up with everyone else and left the skirt behind. Her father continued his conversation with a Peruvian dignitary and kept right on walking, leaving his daughter to put herself together in peace.

On other occasions, however, the Townsend children were not left to themselves. It was in the middle of Spanish class, and everyone was getting out their books. Grace, this time thirteen, had become enamored of a Spanish swear word. She had discovered the expression entirely by her own initiative outside class, and although she had no idea what it meant, she adored the way it rolled off her tongue.

So on this particular day, in the middle of class, she decided to share this treasure of a tongue-rolling word, pronouncing it loudly for all to enjoy. In a very short time she found herself at home—after being fiercely glowered at by the teacher, then rushed off to the principle's office like a case of smallpox to the hospital.

When her parents learned that their oldest daughter had sworn during Spanish class they acted swiftly, requiring her to write an apology to the teacher and the principle and to vocalize an apology to the whole class.

Because Cameron and Elaine interacted with many people, the behavior of their children appeared particularly central. Manners themselves weren't the point; rather, mindset birthed manners.

Behavior presented a way to honor others and demonstrate respect. Wrong attitudes, quarrels, and rudeness soured and detracted from the mission which the whole family carried out together.

The Townsends also realized that manners were not genetic. They helped their children by not making excuses for them or giving them license because of their age. They saw their children as functioning— albeit developing—parts of society, and taught them to live by its standards and rules. Grace remembered well the lessons in formal Spanish greeting, accompanied by a curtsey. When official business became exceedingly dull during formal meal events, the Townsend children learned to occupy themselves quietly by counting the mistakes in a hand-embroidered tablecloth, or other spur-of-the-moment games.

However, interrupting, fighting, arguing, and disobeying were also realities, and Elaine generally carried out the discipline. One of Cam's punishments was banishment to a clothes' closet under the stairs— generally after misbehavior at the table—and this burned itself into the children's memories from the gall of embarrassment. After a second entrance was discovered, however, the effect began to wane.

THE SWEAT AND DIRT OF DIGGING ROOTS

As a parent, Elaine was like those around her, a flawed and fallen person on the pathway of sanctification. Although imperfectly, she adorned the gospel in the daily joy of living. One recalled, 'I always wanted to be like her, to follow her in what she did.' Observing this joy reinforced change toward the breaking of their *own way* so deeply entrenched in their growing souls.

In this era when most MK children were routinely consigned to boarding school, Cameron had wisely felt it imperative that whole families serve together. The school on the base resembled a co-op of sorts since many parents taught; these relationships became a flourishing and integral part of life at Yarinacocha.

Beautiful as it was, this tightly-knit community atmosphere possibly hindered Elaine's ability to discern the subtler heart needs of her children as they grew older. Letters confirm this did not signify an actual lack of love on Elaine's part, but an inability to connect with their hearts and to grow them gently into their own individual personalities and roles.

To her grandparents, Grace wrote once, 'How are things going in Chicago? This last past week we have been going to an American school in Lima. (It seems like every summer mommy gets these bright ideas.) Anyhow, in my first period class, my teacher thought I was a news reporter, and in my third period I was taken for a visiting teacher...' Grace was not alone. The Townsend children held few fond memories of those summer classes. Even Elaine's reference to her children as 'brave little soldiers,' during a two-month separation, might have belied their real loneliness and need.

Elaine struggled to discern the difference between heart rebellion in her children and misbehavior that simply inconvenienced or embarrassed her. It was not a simple path to cultivate hearts which stood in awe of the Lord more than it feared the consequences of sin, and there was always a balance to upholding personal holiness and demonstrating grace. Parents and children alike began to realize over the years that if the gospel didn't stand at the center of discipline, scars would form more readily than appetites for Christ.

Christian culture at the time generally valued upright moral behavior and cultivated appearances focused on accomplishment. This undermined an honest look at the realities of sin and the raw need for Christ's covering grace. The impossibility of good from human strength was perhaps believed but not always evidenced. One daughter of that era thoughtfully remarked, 'I would have loved to hear more about how God understands my weaknesses and even uses them for my good, the good of others, and for His glory. I grew up with more focus on my performance than acceptance of both my strengths and weaknesses as part of His plan.'

Pointing children to the gospel particularly stretched Elaine as a task-oriented parent. Neither Elaine's personality or experience lent her strength in these areas. The household in which she grew up was not focused on parental discipleship, although her parents set an example in prayer and trust. Both her mother and father fostered a rigorous, albeit affectionate, view of family life. After her conversion, during the seven years before her debut on the mission field, Elaine kept herself more than occupied with teaching, supervising, work at the downtown Mexican mission, Moody night school, SIL camp, and countless church activities. In addition, World War II was in full swing at the time, and this carried implications into the lives of every person.

All these things may have resulted in the relatively narrow exposure to the practice of motherhood with which she entered the field. Her mission work focused her intensely, and marriage to Cameron brought a whole new world her way. While her attention and creativity shone brightly through her children's younger years, a natural inclination toward daily responsibilities shortchanged their deeper needs for relational connection and nourishment as they grew older. As an adult, Elainadel expressed, 'She might have known me better than I realized, but she wasn't able to talk about matters of the heart very often. I have some precious things she wrote me that let me know she wanted to be an encourager to me and that she prayed faithfully for us... but talking about the things that were on my heart or hers did not happen nearly as often as I would have liked.'[2]

The Townsend children were among the 'least of these' to whom Cameron and Elaine were called to minister. Their need for love and care increased as the children grew older and developed into their own persons, and as seasons of change came. Moving to Colombia carried huge implications for the entire Townsend family, and parental attention less necessary in Peru now became critical, but Elaine frequently struggled to discern these changes. Later, in speaking of the move to Colombia, she admitted, 'I didn't realize how difficult this would be for the children. The three girls were teenagers and Bill was only ten. As we drove to the Pucallpa airport and they realized they were leaving their friends, many a tear was shed.'

---

2   Regarding their disagreement on a critical matter, Del remarked how everything changed after they talked. 'That instance is very precious to me because she wanted to know how I felt and it really helped her to understand me better. God has used that experience in deep ways in my journey.' She also recalled her mother exclaiming, 'I wish I could express myself like you!' Elaine seemed to sense a lack on her own part and to admire its presence in her daughter, but she nonetheless found herself unable to develop this skill.

SHUTTING THE GATES

Cameron and Elaine would inherit the privilege of dreaming with them into the next generation, and sending them on ahead as successors in the 'unfinished task', as Cameron liked to call it. In the meantime, the miracle of the everyday was not that everything was always right or proper, but that despite sin, the gospel still held true, the Spirit didn't let go of His unfinished artwork, and there was always hope in the love of a good Father. As an adult looking back on her upbringing, one of the Townsend children wrote,

> We were the kids that God chose to give to Cameron and Elaine. It's neat to think about the fact that God was placing us exactly where He wanted us to be. Some things were hard; some things were fun; some things were to our liking; some were not. But in it all, God was sovereign, and He still is. He was weaving our lives to bring glory to Him and blessing to us. Some of the hard things in our lives have been like a black thread to more sharply display beauty. And some hard things have been like a Refiner's fire to make each of us more like Him.

Many ministry children carry degrees of scars from years of their parents' fruitful, yet diverted work, and the Townsend children were no exception; yet the Savior who suffered made the sorest places redemptive. F.W. Boreham once wrote an essay in which he described early morning strolls with his dog, winding his way through beautiful meadows in his beloved England.[3] Repeatedly, he encountered the sign on a little farm—*Please shut the gate.* He opened the latch, walked through with his dog, then closed the gate and continued his stroll. The essence of the story illustrated the same need within lives. Gates prevent destruction from intruders; past hurts, experiences, and memories are intruders in their ability to steal joy and peace of mind from the present and the future. To pursue effective life and service, gates sometimes need to be shut. Paul himself wrote, 'Forgetting those things which are

---

3   F.W. Boreham, 'Please Shut the Gate', *A Packet of Surprises: The Best Essays and Sermons of F.W. Boreham* (Eureka, California: John Broadbanks Publishing, 2008), pp. 184-9.

behind, I press towards the mark for the prize of the high calling which is in Christ Jesus.'

There is no paint-by-number set, only this: that a parent's enthusiasm for holiness, for infusing their home with wonder at the reality of the gospel and for catching its massive, cosmic brilliance, cannot help but scatter seeds for a harvest of new generations convinced of Christ's worth and passionate for His glory. Ultimately, it is God who fills both parent and child. It is He who enables His love to translate in a remarkably personal, tangible way. This faithfulness points home.

'When he was home, he was our *daddy*'.

20. FAMILY AS GOSPEL APOLOGETIC

When I come to die, I am quite sure that I will not look back over my life and wish I had poured more time into the tangibly attractive distractions of the world. My greatest concern will be that I influenced my children for the kingdom of God with all my heart, soul, mind, and strength. … a family well raised will be a mighty weapon in the hand of Christ. It will reap fruit forever.

Catherine J. Stewart[1]

Perhaps Cameron's praying zeal for the several thousand unreached people groups carried him away on more than one occasion, leaving sleeping children scattered around at the end of family devotions. Nonetheless, their worshipping together created a family identity, as minds and hearts were filled, tended, and began to produce fruit. As soon as the children were able to read, they began to take part, and at the end of the Scripture reading, they shared a point or asked a question.

OUT OF THE MOUTH OF BABES

When Bishop Prevost from Pucallpa came for a meal and saw their family devotions, he was amazed at the attention and intelligent responses of the children. The evening closed in prayer that the Lord would help them each to apply the passage they had read.

A few days later, he invited Cameron and Elaine to attend a special service in the cathedral on January 6th, All Kings' Day. Given the hatred of many Catholics toward evangelicals in South America, this

1   Catherine J. Stewart, *Letters to Pastors' Wives*, p. 28.

was remarkable. Upon their arrival, Cameron and Elaine noticed a large table at the front of the church piled with stacks of New Testaments. 'You are probably wondering what all of these New Testaments are doing here this morning,' the bishop said at the close of his message. 'I urge each family to come and buy one. If we don't have enough here you can go to the evangelical bookstore as they have a good supply and they are much cheaper there. Get one and read it for yourself. And don't tell me you can't understand it, because I've seen little children who can understand it.'

Earlier he had asserted to the Townsends that the average people couldn't comprehend the Bible, and only the priest could interpret properly. Yet the power of the gospel at work in the lives of their children carried the weight of proof.

THE WORLD OF MINISTRY

'I loved it that you let us be part of your entertaining of visitors,' wrote one of Elaine's children. 'You included us in your work. That made me feel important.'

Peruvians traditionally drink their coffee sweet. First, sugar is liberally spooned into a cup, then a little coffee is poured over the heap, but *not* stirred. After mealtimes, Elaine assigned her children to clear the table. While eating, the children delivered a series of significant nods; afterwards, the fun began. A dozen place clearings combined with fertile imaginations soon produced creative results. As they cleared the places they closely compared each cup. The winner had correctly guessed during dinner which of the guests would leave the most sugar.

One afternoon, Elaine took the children in the jeep to visit an Indian teacher who had been flown to the base two weeks earlier with tuberculosis, in bed already for three months. They made popsicles and jello for him, and took along some clothes and a record player.

'WE ARE HERE TO SERVE'

Bringing the children along on such an errand likely cultivated a more joyful, invested heart at that stage in their development than, say, cleaning up after Indian babies who didn't wear diapers (which also happened). Seeing their parents minister to others bred compassion in the Townsend children, helping them to take part in the family calling and to understand the accompanying sacrifices. Organic growth toward service depended on the child's deepening walk with the Lord and it required the ordering of their loves. 'It's in reaching out to others that we will experience satisfaction (and exhaustion too!)' Joy commented later.

During Elaine's childhood and across her generation of peers, American culture created an expectation that every person contribute to the family with resources and giftedness. Productive work generally became the measure of a person. Elaine gladly gave both for her own parents.

When the missionary era came of age, much the same expectation existed in ministry: the allegiances to family simply carried over to the mission. To Elaine, it seemed only natural that her own children would contribute to the calling of the family. Good and admirable in many ways, this commitment produced a generation of hearty missionaries who generally lacked self-pity and who knew how to support themselves amid hard scenarios. A tremendous sense of urgency drove their work, and this propelled staggering accomplishments.

Nonetheless, this widespread challenge to balance linguistic, cultural, and mission advances with patterns of family life carried weighty implications in the Townsend home, particularly as Cameron's extensive travels began to tell more deeply.

Elaine and Cameron asked a great deal of their children. *We are here to serve* existed as a banner overarching their lives—something for which to aim, something noble for which to wish—and this mantra was spoken into a multitude of situations. One woman overheard a sibling squabble carrying on full tilt in the next room till Cameron walked in, rebuking them with the admonishment that their behavior cast dishonor on the mission.

THE COST OF LOYALTY

Certainly the investment of Elaine was particularly critical to their maturing in this respect. 'The key,' as one frequently-absent missionary pilot stated, '…is that the wife holds down the stability. If she is committed to the mission and to the reason for the husband being gone, that carries down to the kids.' Even more than her children, Elaine felt her husband's absence keenly, but she didn't express frustration. 'Mom was 150 per cent supportive of Daddy. I don't ever remember a controversy my folks had—ever. The key was that Mom had such respect for Daddy and his calling. I think the respect and being on board was why us kids were on board. We respected what they were doing.'

It was no small thing that one of their children remembered, 'Somehow they made us kids feel part of the ministry. It wasn't Mom and Dad's adventure, it was a family adventure.'

Cameron's prominent role wasn't often emphasized, and though the children grew up with an appreciation for his work, it was years before they grasped the magnitude of all he accomplished. As one of them said, 'He was always just Daddy to me, I had no idea he was so famous. It was only later in life that I realized.'

Bernie, a missionary to Peru mentored by Cameron (and later, president of Wycliffe), explained the tension: 'Where the rubber hits the road, you have your work, and your family, and you're in a hostile environment where surviving takes energy… And in the midst of the day people came by, an Indian chief dropped in with fifteen minutes' notice, or Uncle Cam invited half a dozen people to dinner. You just don't do that! But they did it every day.'[2]

The Townsend family, like none other, stood in the epicenter of the constant tension between the responsibilities of home and the many calls of ministry. 'It wasn't easy,' continued Bernie. 'There were sacrifices that had to be made, and no one sacrificed more than the Townsends did.'

Elaine created stability in the home so the children grew up in an ordered atmosphere despite their father running to and fro over the

2   'There's what I call the ministry of presence, and the ministry of sacrifice,' Bernie added. '*Presence* is you gotta be there, you gotta show up. *Ministry* is relational because ministry is about love and love is relational. You can't love in the abstract; love has to be worked out through presence, time, and sacrifice. Children must know their parents are not only there *with* them, but there *for* them; that they are their parents' chief priority and worth any time spent on them. And nothing gets done in the kingdom without *sacrifice*. So, you make choices.'

face of the earth. Life continued similarly with or without Cameron—they still did amazing things and spent regular time together. Elaine accomplished this in such a way that honored Cameron in the children's eyes, rather than pushing him to the side. 'I don't remember a Dad who was gone,' said one. 'I remember one who was home, because when he was home, he was *our* Daddy.'

She brought Cameron and her family into their lives from a distance by recording droll anecdotes in letters, preserving moments filled with their liveliness. As a little boy, Billy came to Elaine and asked 'Mother, how do you become president of this outfit? Are you born to it?'

Another time a group of boys got together on the base and began to brag about their fathers. 'My dad's a mechanic!'

'Mine is the radio operator!'

'Oh, that's nothing, my dad, he's a *pilot*!'

Billy couldn't think of anything to say, so finally he blurted out, 'Well, my dad's the *oldest*!'

OPPORTUNITIES

One summer when the Townsend children felt themselves a little shortchanged because they never had a 'tribe of their own,' Cameron and Elaine arranged for each to spend part of the season helping a missionary in another tribe. They looked back on those times as periods of growth, filled with life experiences and relationships they would never forget

As Elainadel and Billy traveled with their parents from Quíto, Ecuador once, the four stopped for a visit with the Auca Indians and Rachel Saint. 'I could hardly believe this was actually happening to me when I stepped off the plane,' Elaine said, 'and found myself in a spot that looked quite familiar (since I've seen a number of pictures of Auca land).'

> Even the people looked like old friends…Dayuma's mother proved ever so friendly. Two of Dabu's three wives were there—naked from the waist up… The men all had pants on but the boys twelve and under just had a string around their waist… Dayuma sent a lovely fishing net made by the Aucas to Elainadel and a fishing spear to Billy. I think

The Townsend family: (from left to right) Elainadel, Cameron, Billy, Grace,
Elaine and Joy (1962).

Elainadel and Billy have decided they prefer life at Yarinacocha, as there are so many more children there to play with. The big advantage here is the fishing and hunting, as far as Billy's concerned. We can certainly thank and praise the Lord for Rachel and her sticking at the job. There she was—the only American—with these former savages and even Dayuma not there. She wasn't a bit afraid—just happy to be able to give these folks God's Word…

The Townsends included their children in these and other fascinating parts of the ministry, giving them glimpses of the power of God in the lives of others, offering tastes of the glory of the gospel, and allowing them to feel a personal connection with other brothers and sisters from wildly different worlds.

DEVELOPING EARNESTNESS

As they grew older, drawn into the mission as into a illimitable secret, their excitement grew and they began to take their own initiative.[3]

Perhaps the most remarkable aspect of the Townsends' purposeful delight in the gospel and in all of life was the reality that the good news shone through the difficulties of their circumstances. Years later into adulthood, the children didn't remember the hardship as much as participating in the work of the gospel. Shelley, a missionary wife and mother, commented, 'He will give your children good gifts even among the hardships that they wouldn't have had otherwise.'

Elaine wrote, '… I was very touched yesterday morning when all three of the girls decided to turn all the money they have been saving for some time over to their Daddy to use for the Bolivian plane. The total wasn't very much—$24.00—but we are praying He will multiply this many times.'

'Grace was all excited this morning,' Elaine wrote another time, 'when Dean Sawdon phoned for her to come to the Sunday school teachers' meeting as they had a class for her. She had volunteered earlier in the week. She will have eight kindergarten children—age five. They met here at our house and she did a very fine job. I'm passing on to

---

3   One longtime missionary couple witnessed, 'Parents who are joyful in their calling will speak volumes to the children.'

her all the things I learned from Mom when she had the beginners' department at Grace Church. I think she'll make a good teacher.'

Although the missionaries were forbidden to teach English to the Indians, Joy became best mates with an Ocana girl who came to stay at the base and taught her to sing. Since Cameron and Elaine happened to be gone at the time, Joy convinced her to debut over the radio to them—likely it was the first time the Indian girl had ever seen such a novel contraption!

Elaine wrote, 'As I was helping Joy get her hair ready for school one day she turned her loving smile on me and said, "Please don't give me any gifts for Christmas this year Mommy."

'"Why not?" was my amazed answer.

'"Well, I want this Christmas to be the best one I've ever had and I've just been reading in the Bible that it is better to give than to receive, so I just want to give this year."

'"But Joy, I have all your presents bought already!" (I had to get them months ahead while we were in Lima).

'Joy was thoughtful for a minute, then said, "Well, just give me one present, Mommy, and give the rest to Grace and Elainadel."'

In Pasadena one Christmas, each girl got to choose a doll, but instead of choosing a white doll, Joy chose a brown one, explaining, 'Each time we go away [on furlough], I give my things away to the Indian kids, and I think an Indian girl would appreciate it much more if she got a little colored dolly.'

STRUGGLES AND FRUIT

On Sunday afternoons Elaine held a Bible study for native women in her home, but a steady stream of children broke up the attention of their mothers. The Townsend girls, ranged from about nine to twelve, began playing games with the children out in the yard. At some point, whether from Elaine or the girls themselves, came the idea to begin a junior Bible study. This developed to include a lesson, refreshments, games, and songs, managed by each sister in turn. Junior classes involved looking at pictures through viewers, singing, Scripture reading, and an explanation of the gospel, followed by more singing, prayer, and a handmade craft.

Elaine might have overestimated their preparedness to launch into this field. Memories from those Sunday afternoons were mixed, perhaps due to varying factors of age and ability. The situation was especially challenging for one daughter who didn't know Spanish well at the time and was terrified of teaching.

Yet even from this, God brought unexpected reward, 'During Christmas vacation,' Elaine wrote one year,

> Joy spent more time than usual preparing for her Sunday afternoon Bible class in Spanish. The Christian Peruvian girl we had helping in our home was watching Joy prepare, and she finally spoke up saying how much she admired Joy for her zeal. She told us how little she was doing for the Lord when she had some special training and Spanish was her language. She decided to see what she could do about starting a Bible class down the lake where there are many children who need to hear.

Joy shone most brightly in her individual interactions. On one occasion, as the family took a train to Chosica for Joy's health, they saw a little Peruvian girl around twelve years old, also with her family. Elaine wrote of the incident,

> Joy, as always, was eager to buy up every opportunity to tell others of her Lord, so she invited this bashful girl to sit by her. It wasn't long before we could hear Joy telling her all about God's love for her and explaining the way of salvation very carefully. The girl had to get off soon after that, but Joy was radiant, knowing she had told one more person of Him whom she loves...

Eventually, the little Sunday afternoon club grew to around fifteen or twenty children, and other girls on the base wanted to help. Much later, Elaine told Joy that she met a Peruvian lady who had came to believe the gospel through that Bible study, and whose children were also walking in the truth. Elsa, the grand-daughter of Doña Marta, also heard the call of Christ through Joy's teaching.

21. A WOMAN OF ONE THING

Fruitfulness may be a better measurement for success than productivity because it is based more in the evaluations of others as to the meaningful role we have played in their lives than in our own importance determined according to the amount of accomplishments we can list.

Karen Burton Mains[1]

Most likely, Elaine had a long list of important things to do on the day the police came to the door...

FOR THE AIRPLANES

Cameron's lifelong love of the ocean drew the family to the rural coastal villages of Peru during their rare vacation times. Once, while frolicking over sand dunes and heaps of ancient ruins, the children unearthed a skull so dilapidated that it looked practically Incan (which it probably *was*). In a temporary desertion of all sagacity, Elaine allowed them to take it home to the jungle, where they put it to grand use.

At the time, a girl from Elaine's home church in Chicago lived with the Townsends, and Elaine suddenly had an unaccountable relapse of her prankster self. When the unfortunate Faye retired to her room one night and pulled back the bedcovers, a crumbling and disreputable smile met her gaze. 'Of course she screamed like she was supposed to,' said Elaine, still unrepentant to the end of her life.

---

1   Karen Burton Mains, *Open Heart, Open Home: The Hospitable Way to Make Others Feel Welcome and Wanted*, (Westmont, Illinois: InterVarsity Press, 1976).

Having done its part towards the enlivening of the household, the skull earned its final rest, and Elaine instructed Joy to dispose of the relic. But rather than burying it, Joy dropped it down the garbage disposal which ran from the kitchen to a chute outside, where a garbage boy collected daily.

The next morning, while the children were at school, Pepe came with his wheelbarrow. As the trash tumbled out, he spied something carefully wrapped up, and what he found perfectly confirmed a rumor currently circulating in Pucallpa. It was true! The missionaries extracted oil from Indians to lubricate their airplanes!

That was how the police came to be at the door on that memorable afternoon when there was everything else to be done and Cameron was (of course) traveling. Persuading the policemen not to take her to jail turned out to be the most important thing Elaine accomplished that day.

JUNGLE RAINS AND BABY ELEPHANTS

Life as a mother to four children and wife to the director of a growing organization caused Elaine's responsibilities to resemble the parrots in the jungle which surrounded her home: diverse, multitudinous, and *very* colorful. Life happened. Even when Cal Hibbard joined Cameron as a skilled and able secretary, Elaine continued to help with mountains of ingoing and outgoing mail. A jungle base was in the making, and amidst the excitement of the Lord's work came the dust and grind of daily living. She wrote on one occasion that she'd been in bed with stomach trouble, the house was a mess, heavy rains had caused landslides which prevented any travel, the company was mysteriously multiplying, the maid hadn't come in several days, and the children needed fed.[2]

---

2   Just before a furlough to the States, Elaine wrote home, 'Cam got the bright idea of painting our house inside and out with diesel oil mixed with DDT to keep down the bugs. It is working beautifully, but has really been a mess to live in these past ten days. Just two more rooms to go, however.' Several days later, 'Just one more day here and then off to Lima. I am very happy to report that I am just about ready too, and the house is spick and span. We painted it inside and out with diesel oil, DDT and ant poison. We don't have an ant or a cockroach these days. Sort of hate to leave this clean spot!'

One letter gave a synopsis of their active lives just after Billy arrived to complete the Townsend family:

> You can be sure we don't have many dull moments with such live-wires as the Lord has given us. They do have lots of fun together, but they are also very human, so Mommy or Daddy have to step in quite often to settle their problems… The other day I found them getting into mischief in a new way… I had left [Billy] on our bed and when I returned, there they were, Grace on one side and Joy on the other, just getting ready to give him his first walking lesson—and that at six weeks!
>
> How the girls do enjoy having Mommy or Daddy take time to read and play with them before going to bed. The other night I was feeling especially peppy so we had lots of fun tussling on the bed, and to my surprise the girls begged me to tickle them. (Do you suppose they are normal??) Well, after several rounds of tickling I decided it was getting time for them to have their prayer time, then off to sleep. I wish you could have heard Grace pray and thank the Lord for giving her a Mommy who was willing to take time to tickle them! I never dreamed it meant so much to her.

And so, the days sped on. At a particularly low ebb she confessed to her husband, 'I'm feeling pretty worn out at this point… If you get back all worn out too, we really will be in a bad way. I feel like I've been hit over the head with a sledgehammer most of the time. I'm sure the Lord will help me find the solution, but I do need your prayers for more strength.'

BUT ONE THING IS NECESSARY

The daily pressure was immense. For Elaine, it became critical to evaluate her priorities, eliminate distractions, and focus on the ultimate scheme of things. Every decision carried ramifications, and each activity that didn't feed into her calling robbed from it. Prioritizing time became the balancing of consequences and gain. As Elisabeth Elliot put so well, '…It is perfectly plain to anyone who wants to do a difficult and worthwhile thing that he's got to deny himself a thousand unimportant and probably a few hundred important things in order to do the thing that matters most.'

In a letter written to prospective missionary candidates, Cameron described the focus required to succeed: '… we have found that often a person with a minimum of formal training but a maximum of drive and persistence, does a better job than the highly trained person with a degree but no ability to stick at his job in the face of setbacks and difficulties.'

Elaine worked intensely hard. Her most powerful asset in this purposing of priorities might possibly have been the fact that Mark Zuckerberg was not yet born, but she had also grown up with a strong work ethic. One person described her outlook with the words, *I've got this in my mind—let's get on with it!* She never quite relaxed, but still the quiet spirit of a noble woman shone amidst the bustle.

When back pain put her in traction for eight days, she called it God's way of getting her attention. If the pain did not lift, she faced surgery in the States. Meanwhile she was a semi-invalid, and commented that she felt a bit useless. Her daughter recalled those times, and her mother's admonition: 'Don't get too busy, then you can't hear the Lord.' As one missionary wife put it, 'Periods spent waiting on Him are not wasted— it's just time we feel like we can't account for to others, or give them the answers they want.'

Amid trials and interruptions, Elaine treated the Word as the only thing to speak truth, to heal hurt, to reveal wisdom, and to shed comfort—the only thing able to keep her *alive*. As she found herself in different seasons with various callings and priorities, she gave her time to the Lord for His use and sought out those things closest to His heart—people. Other things she had to let slide. Many times the house was not as tidy as she wished.

Rather than always making the house spotless and completing her lists before inviting a guest for tea, she invited them anyway and worked on something during tea time, like folding wash or going through mail. Participation from native women brought blessing for both. In Peru, as in many other overseas situations, it was simple and cheap to hire house help: a native woman who lived with the family and aided in the daily responsibilities of laundry, meals, and cleaning. Their maid Clara became an integral part of the family and was greatly influenced by her years in the Townsend home. Elaine took personal interest in her and the two shared devotional time each morning. When Christmas came and the children got beautiful Spanish Bibles engraved on the cover with their names, so did Clara.

THE IDENTITY OF INTERRUPTIONS

Elaine and her friends in their field didn't think about pursuing 'me time'. She found opportunities to refresh and reorient, but the key was that she came back energized to dive into her responsibilities. She took quiet moments to clear her mind and to break up the monotony of daily life. 'I've often been thankful for the piano lessons you enabled us to have even though you yourself weren't able to go very far in music,' she wrote her mother. 'How relaxing it is here in the jungle after a hard day's work to sit down and be able to play the good old hymns and lift my heart in praise to Him.'

Interruptions, like so many raiding warriors, came knocking every day, and Elaine was often tempted to see the people who came into her life as inconveniences. Once, in the midst of her exasperation, one of her daughters suggested, 'Mom, maybe the interruptions are your work!' The Lord used this simple sentence, and the lesson learned ran deep amid the fraying edges of a busy life. Cameron, also, encouraged her in this by his example: 'He could see that each person who came was sent by the Lord,' she said, 'so he had time for everybody.'

Toward the end of her life, Elaine wrote to a younger woman about guests, 'We tried never to let anyone stand at the door, but rather invited all into our home and tried to make them feel most welcome even when we thought we didn't have the time. It was hard at first to never have a schedule, but as I committed this area of my life to the Lord I became willing to have Him plan my day, and that took away much of the frustration...'

Her daughter Elainadel would later write,

The most important thing, true for all personality types and in all circumstances, is that *priorities* need to be in place before we can fulfill the assignments God has for each of us. Do you know the illustration of putting the large rocks in a jar first and then all the small ones will fit, but if you do it the other way the large ones won't?

When Christ is at the center and we spend time with Him in His Word, we begin to see things from His perspective. He will help us sort out what is important and what is not. When our bodies are in alignment and have the nourishment they need they can function the way they were designed. Spiritually, we cannot function the way God designed without putting Him first and letting Him use His Word to align our thinking and priorities. I see over and over how the evil one tempts us to get so busy doing good things that we forget the most important thing. I would say that often less is more when we put first things first.

Everything shifts when He is first. Troubles become blessings because they are opportunities for us to trust Him more; heartaches turn into intimate moments with the Lord as we pour our hearts out to Him; fear turns to peace as we focus on how much He loves us and He is in control of every detail of our lives. So the most important way that I can manage my schedule is to put my time with the Lord first and to keep Christ central in my thoughts all day.

JUST RAISE YOUR HAND

Of course, Elaine's time management sometimes went a little far. 'Elaine ate too fast—she did lots of things fast,' said Cal. 'I've been at meals where she finished eating long before her guests which, I'm told, is not polite for a hostess.'

At least during a short period, Elaine came up with a solution: 'I have a new system which is working quite well at meal times,' she wrote to Cam. 'You know what a fast eater I am and how slow the children eat. Well, I have decided to read some of the *Sugar Creek Gang* books to them when I finish. This is helping me to read more slowly and take more pains with enunciation as I've asked the children to raise their hands when I go too fast. So far it is working beautifully. Hope it keeps up.'

This practice carried to the evening reading times as well. 'I think our hands were permanently raised above our heads!' recalled Elainadel, laughing. 'We'd just lay in bed with our arms up.'

The time Elaine volunteered to help with the book-keeping of the base didn't go so well, and one accountant resolved that he would rather do his work alone than have Elaine's help. 'I gave her sheets of debits and credits to post to the journals involved,' he said. 'I appreciated her help and she worked fast. The one drawback was her lack of accuracy, which made it necessary to go back and correct all she had done.' The same skill which enabled Elaine to move through volumes of correspondence made accounting impossible. 'I was glad she never volunteered to help out again,' the book-keeper grinned, 'because I don't know how I would have handled it!'

WHAT IS THE QUESTION?

Elaine slowly learned that worrying wastes time, invisibly sapping energy and peace. When the incident of the skull sabotaged her day, she faced a choice:

You can imagine how I felt! Would the Lord let the work that we were doing suffer because of my dumb mistake? That morning instead of reading from Acts where we had been reading, I turned to James 1, and this was the comfort the Lord gave: 'Count it all joy, my brothers, when you meet trials of various kinds, for you know that the testing of your faith produces steadfastness. And let steadfastness have its full effect, that you may be perfect and complete, lacking in nothing.'

It was surely as though He Himself were at my side, assuring me that all would be well. Oh what rejoicing this brought to my heart! A few minutes before, the picture had looked awfully dark. I could picture myself in jail, as often the hearings are not just. I even had it figured out how I could prove I was innocent by having some specialist examine the age of the bones, since surely they would find them to be hundreds of years old.

Now, all that faded into the background as the Lord showed me that this very experience was to help me to know Him better and to be a more mature Christian. A soon as the children left for school I hastened to my room to read the portion again on my knees, that once again I might let Him assure me that all would be well.

In the end, it mattered not what visible tasks Elaine had accomplished if only God had done something through her. 'The question *What can I do?* is the wrong question,' one missionary friend claimed. 'The question is *What can* God *do?* If the only thing that gets done is what I can do, it's not going to be much. Let's not sit around and talk about what we can do, let's decide that we'll be available.'

Cameron, Elaine and friends, during the last days at Yarina (1960).

22. 'SHE BROUGHT MAKEUP TO THE JUNGLE'

The truly beautifully fierce woman has an otherworldly strength derived from a source beyond herself. She's plunged in fully to the forgiveness and love of Christ, and He holds her heart so completely that she's reached true contentment. … She is no 'halfhearted creature' but is drinking deeply of Him and experiencing infinite joy.

Kimberly Wagner[1]

To all accounts, Elaine seemed to keep a corner of pride in her heart for image and persona. Three-inch heels were not uncommon, and it was said that she began the ruination of her feet years before the airplane crash. She prized the attention of people, while her outgoing personality made her popular.

To her daughters she would later recount a story of greatly wounded pride. One evening, although she felt particularly sharp and attractive, her date didn't seem suitably impressed. At home, she gave herself a big smile in the mirror, only to discover the red peanut skin impishly clinging to her eyetooth. She was devastated.

When she heard God's call to the mission field, one of her first protests had been 'God, do you really want me to look like them?' referring to the common missionary image. But just as God firmly dealt blows to self in all other areas, He transformed this also into a thing of grace and beauty. He had turned her desire for attention outward in love for others, and He intended to transform this perspective of censure and pride into a useful tool.

---

1   Kimberly Wagner, *Fierce Women: The Power of a Soft Warrior*. Moody Publishers. Kindle Edition. (2012-08-24)

STEPPING OUT OF A SHOP WINDOW

Leaving for the mission field brought significant changes, though she arrived in Mexico bearing costume jewelry 'from here to kingdom come,' as Cal put it. In the first hot, dusty little Mexican town she called home, she ironed clothes by putting them under the mattress.

At the same time, one woman who knew her then commented, 'She was very down to earth and serious about important things. I never thought of her as being frivolous.' Culture at that time did dictate a certain standard for dress. Heels and hose were not uncommon in the jungle, though they may have been inopportune for two twenty-something friends of Elaine's when they stepped off the plane in a remote, savage village, into six-inch mud which claimed their heels.

In the aftermath of the plane crash, Elaine's deformed feet required orthopedic shoes—ugly, black affairs. All her life, as she suffered tremendously from pain in her feet and back, 'she kept everything inside,' one of her children observed. Few knew the half. In her elder years, Grace once found her mother crying in her bedroom, 'Just look at these things I have to wear! They make me feel so ugly!'

What started as a desire for fashion matured into a deeper understanding of beauty: a way to honor those around her, and an opportunity to adorn the gospel. This was not a claim that following Christ would bring nice clothes, but a realization that life in Christ was something full and joyous, and not best represented by frazzled hair and worn down heels. Elaine knew people judged much by appearance, and she took care to confirm and strengthen her witness in every way possible.

Elaine demonstrated through her clothes and her ready smile, and Corny Hibbard through her spiritedness and her beautiful table settings, that as Christians they were free to represent rich life in Christ in the most truthful, vibrant ways possible. Elaine encouraged other woman on the base to persevere in this undertaking: 'Wives and mothers, don't let down on your appearance even though you may have four children to get ready first.'

Memories of Elaine's classy appearance abound: 'She always looked like she had just stepped out of a shop window and she encouraged us to look a bit more like that, too.' 'She made it okay to look nice even though we were missionaries.' 'She brought elegance to the mission field.'

Elaine's notion of true beauty carried a sense of dignity rather than show, and this held consistent with her biblical witness.

KEEPING FIT

Resolution also propelled Elaine through various weight-loss programs (at times more humorous than otherwise). Weight trouble ran in her family, and in middle school her friends and Milly teased her. This remained a lifelong battle, and both she and Shirley perpetrated friendly competition, keeping one another accountable and cheering each other on: 'Glad to hear that you are losing, Shirley. Keep it up. It's a real thrill isn't it?' Despite the heat and humidity of the jungles she faithfully exercised and dieted, and this dedication lent her greater effectiveness in her daily responsibilities, for as she commented more than once, lack of exercise weighed down the days.

'Do you remember our daily 4:30 to 5:30 exercising classes at Yarinacocha?' Elaine wrote another woman. 'This is a must to keep in trim. So much of our work is deskwork that it is very important to take time for exercise. For that reason, we have volleyball time daily on each of our linguistic bases and most everyone shows up to play.'

One of the girls later wrote, 'Mom, you always looked so pretty, vivacious, and happy. I loved that about you! It was cool the way you put feather flowers in your hair, wore such spiffy clothes, and kept rolling on the floor in order to keep trim…' Cameron, also, doubtless appreciated her efforts, commenting '… the peppier and more beautiful she becomes.'

'Elaine dressed nicely, but not ostentatiously,' remembered Cal. 'She did have a few dresses which I viewed as rather "wild," but ladies can get away with stuff like that.'

Another said, 'She prepared me for hospitality, and emphasized the importance of one's own dress, since it speaks to the value of the other person…' Ultimately, Elaine saw fitness and beauty as a matter of honoring her God and of blessing her husband.

Lorrie, a missionary in Peru, recalled, 'Elaine was dignified. She always looked lovely, always prepared for anything and everything—like she was waiting for some special person.' Her children later bought housedresses for her to wear while working, but she would not wear them. She never started a day without fully preparing herself, clothes, makeup, and all; and she continued this habit till the day she died. Even her children were taught never to leave their room until they were dressed and ready for the day. She believed that one felt prepared in proportion to the role for which one dressed.

Unnecessary? Superfluous? Pretentious? No. The impression it left with all who knew her was summed up by one woman, 'It was a way she honored whoever she was with.' Even as Elaine exhibited outward beauty and set an example for others, this physical manifestation pointed to a deeper reality of the gentle and quiet spirit so precious in the sight of God.

SEASON 3

23. THE RUSSIAN FRONTIER

In world where success is the measure and justification of all things the figure of Him who was sentenced and crucified remains a stranger and is at best the object of pity. The world will allow itself to be subdued only by success… The figure of the Crucified invalidates all thought which takes success for its standard.

Dietrich Bonheoffer[1]

Elaine woke with a start. A glance at the clock showed the time was just after 3 a.m. But that wasn't what had sharply pulled her from sleep. *Someone was in their room.* Thoughts raced through her head—interrogation… arrest… imprisonment. This was not Mexico, from which they had recently come, or North Carolina, where they had established semi-permanent residence since moving from Colombia. This was the eastern side of the Iron Curtain—Russia—in a hotel directly across from the Kremlin.

'Only twice during our eleven trips to the U.S.S.R. did I ever experience fear,' Elaine wrote later. 'The first took place in the Hotel National on Red Square in downtown Moscow.'

They had returned to the room quite late after a symphony concert and had forgotten to lock the door. The intruder, it turned out, was a drunk who entered their room by mistake, and a hotel employee quickly came to remove him, but circumstances were nevertheless tense. This was a Soviet country in the midst of the Cold War. 'I had difficulty getting back to sleep that night as my imagination worked

---

1   Eric Metaxas, *Bonhoeffer: Pastor, Martyr, Prophet, Spy,* 363.

overtime and I could picture one of us being taken to some prison camp,' Elaine admitted.

A JUBILANT SCHEME OF LIFE

The summer before, Elaine and Cameron stayed in the luxurious home of some friends on the shores of the Catawba River just outside of Charlotte. Grace was married to Tom, and the two were living in Chicago; Joy and Elainadel were students at Colombia Bible College; and Bill was studying at Ben Lippen in Asheville. Elaine wrote, 'Our lives were filled to overflowing as our members looked to Cameron for advice, and our home always seemed to be grand central station for our many friends. We loved it.'

By the fall, Cameron and Elaine had traveled to South America, Mexico, the United States, and Central America, where Cameron used his latent farming skill on the mango trees. Surely, here was the perfect retirement plan for this aging but energetic couple who looked back on years of dedicated toil; the simple quieting of a life still occupied by selfless labors, and even—for the first time in decades—a little time for relaxation.

But to such an avid visionary as Cameron, this lifestyle was completely out of the question. 'For several days I had noticed that Cam seemed to be in another world,' Elaine recalled, 'Not eating very much, praying a great deal; obviously something special was on his heart.' One morning, as she carried a load of laundry from the guesthouse, Cameron called her aside: 'Sit down a minute honey, I want to tell you something. The Lord has put it upon my heart to take His life-giving Word to the U.S.S.R. There are over 100 languages who need His Word. If the Lord is leading me to go, and as the doors open, would you be willing to go with me?'

'What an earth-shaking question!' Elaine commented later, echoing any sane person's first thought. But to Cameron she said, 'If that's what God wants you to do, that's what I want you to do too, and if you're going to go, that's where I want to go.'

ENTRY

But things weren't all that simple. That night, the doubts rushed over her, and Satan exclaimed, 'You fool! Going to Russia?' Second thoughts abounded, and Elaine wondered what she had promised herself into. Her three youngest children were still in school and needing her, and all news about the U.S.S.R. was negative.

Fifteen years earlier, she and Cameron had encouraged new recruits in Norman, Oklahoma, to consider beginning work in the U.S.S.R. The group made a circle and prayed that the Lord would lay it on the heart of some to make advances in this area. No one volunteered, but the Townsends kept praying. Now here was Cameron claiming *they* should run out into this forbidding land themselves. It was no easy choice. The year before, Elaine had become concerned about Cameron's hectic pace, writing once,

> Good morning, sunshine!
>
> Before you phoned I had been thinking of how much I would like to see you take a month off upon your return… This morning when I asked the Lord to give me some special promises He certainly did. Isa. 40:29-31. So He took the anxiety away from my heart about you dear, knowing that He will renew your strength. I thought again of Ruth Graham's prayer—'Lord we don't need relaxation as much as we do refreshment.' How true! You sounded like a new man on the phone.

After a wakeful night, Elaine wrote another entry beside her Father's promise in Isaiah 41:10: 'Mexico 1943, Peru 1946, Colombia 1963, *Russia 1968*.' One more monumental transition remained to be bravely penned, but in every season the promise held true: *'Fear thou not, Elaine, for I am with thee, be not dismayed; For I am thy God; I will strengthen thee; yea, I will help thee; yea, I will uphold thee with the right hand of my righteousness… For I, the* LORD *thy God, will hold thy right hand saying unto thee, Fear not, I will help thee.'*

A PECULIAR SORT OF RETIREMENT

Eleven trips into the U.S.S.R. lay ahead of this intrepid couple. At that moment in history, Russia certainly seemed like front lines in the spiritual realm. A decade after the Red Scare, Russia remained closed, and its accompanying fearful stigma had hardly faded. 'Their going to Russia during the Cold War was an audacious thing to do,' commented Cal. Although the Townsends didn't undertake mass smuggling operations, and they traveled in less restricted areas, their visits nonetheless fell on the Eastern side.

Most assumed that Russia had the Scriptures, which was true; but as Elaine and Cameron explained to many audiences, 168 languages were spoken in this massive country, and over a hundred did not have readable Scriptures. Their goal was to enlist Russia's own skilled linguists to work alongside SIL in this endeavor. The Townsends set out to display God's warm heart for His people, to find the noble and the good in that frigid, unwelcoming land where atheism was the official religion. As Cameron told Elaine, '… it's going to be a great adventure with you and our Lord!'

At just past fifty, Elaine, with an almost elderly Cameron, found herself learning the difficult Russian language. She listened to Russian tapes while she drove an hour each way for classes at Queen's College.

'Elaine influenced my life long before I met her,' wrote one missionary. 'I was in Ghana trying to learn the language. I thought, *there is no way I can learn this French!* Then I realized that if Elaine could learn Russian at nearly sixty, I could do this.'

Elaine's mother, Lillie, stayed with them in Mexico City that fall. While they began Russian classes she, at 77, studied Spanish. For an hour and a half each day a tutor came, and they taped these lessons and studied for another four or five hours a day. 'It's lots of fun,' Elaine wrote. It seemed her indomitable sense of adventure was on the rise yet again!

Amid language studies, a group of recruits from Jungle Camp began to arrive, and Elaine invited them all over in groups of sixteen. After spending Christmas in the States with their children, the Townsends flew back in January to continue language study and to apply at the Soviet Embassy in Mexico for visas to the U.S.S.R.

'OUR FIRST *NO* BEHIND US'

'"No" was never a negative for Cameron,' Elaine often said. 'If the Lord was in it He would do it.' One day when Cameron was gone, she and her mother received a phone call: 'This is the Soviet Embassy. We have received word from Moscow that you can't come this year. Perhaps next.'

Elaine immediately shared the news with her mother, and both wondered how Cameron would take the disappointment. He returned home tired from a long day, and before he had time to take off his coat and Stetson hat, his wife broke the news. Neither expected his response: 'Praise the Lord, honey! This is wonderful! Now we have our first *no* behind us!'

'I think the average missionary would stop right there,' Elaine said, 'but not Cam.' He then proceeded to recall the seven no's which had stood between them in Colombia, and not a few in Indonesia. 'His faith never wavered as he pressed on with his plans, and in two weeks we were headed for the Soviet Union.'

When she received word that they had been accepted, only ten days lay before departure. She wrote to Cameron,

> It is now 12:30 Friday night and I have just located my passport and pictures. I can still hardly believe my ears about this trip. How faithful the Lord is, and greatly to be praised... Already I get a big lump in my throat when I think about leaving the children, so you'll have to pray much for this weak vessel; I don't have the strength on my own to say goodbye... Well, my beloved, life with you does get better and better and I am surely having to trust our Lord more and more.

Elaine used that entire first day to call eighty-two people. She and Cameron realized the challenges that lay ahead for them and the essential support of prayer in a formidable land. Three days before their flight, Elaine wrote friends,

> In closing, let me give you I Corinthians 16:9, 'for a great door and effectual is opened unto me, and there are many adversaries.' We are not unmindful of the adversaries but we are also conscious of the fact

Elaine and Cameron, off to the next frontier (1968).

that with God all things are possible, and that prayer does change things, so please uphold us daily. Looking forward to telling you of many more miracles in the days to come!

ADDRESS: HOTEL NATIONAL

Elaine later admitted that one of the most difficult things she faced during the first days in Russia was a telephone that never rang. She sat for hours at her 'portable' Hermes typewriter composing skeins of news. Once, when the ribbon ran out, she ventured into temperatures below seventeen degrees to find another. Unfortunately, she lost her way, and an older Russian man with a fur hat and earmuffs led her back to their hotel.

It was a fascinating historical and cultural landscape in which Cameron and Elaine found themselves. They had been invited by the Academy of Science in Moscow, and though they had to pay all other expenses, they were given expansive quarters in one of Russia's most historic buildings, the Hotel National. An older woman sat on each floor to monitor comings and goings, and after three days and nights she rotated out with another. During their stay, of course, Cameron and Elaine developed relationships with these ladies.

From their room Elaine wrote: 'The line for Lenin's tomb forms just outside our window. Saturday and Sunday it was three abreast and about four blocks long... At night, the two large, red lighted stars on the Kremlin towers shine right in our room. We couldn't be much closer.'

FORBIDDEN

Early on, the Townsends met Natashia, a young Russian who agreed to teach them Russian. They also made contacts with officials in preparation for survey trips into the small language groups of the Caucasus. One of their earliest friendships was with the Deshereev family: Yunus, an intellect and author of many linguistic books; Tamara, his gracious wife, who was also distinguished in the field of language; Julia, a student at the university; and Svetlana—recently married and the mother of two children.

'On each of our visits we were warmly received in their modest apartment and always fed a most delicious meal,' Elaine wrote her family in the States. 'It took us awhile to realize that the first course was just that, and not the entire meal! Knowing that they had spent hours waiting in line to get some of the delicacies they were serving us, I never felt I could leave even a mouthful, satisfied though I was.'

During one of their visits, Julia became rather forthright. 'Mrs. Townsend, do you know what the most popular book is among the students at Moscow University these days?'

'I have no idea Julia, what could it be?'

'The Bible.'

'The Bible?! How could it be when it is a forbidden book?'

'That's just it! That is why everyone wants to read it—to learn why it is forbidden.'

'Where in the world do they get it? I know you can't buy it in any stores.'

'Some of our grandmothers still have copies. We cut them apart and pass them around as fast as possible, always being sure the faculty don't hear about it.'

Elaine couldn't help thinking of the large building in Leningrad, once a church but now a museum for atheism. She read in their Spanish newspaper of a plea for atheists to work harder because despite all their efforts, including radio programs and compulsory classes at the university, the number of believers was growing. 'How good to know that the Word of God cannot be bound and that it will not return unto Him void but will accomplish His purpose,' she finished.

THE RADIO AND BALLET

But life in this corner of the world wasn't all work. 'Now for a bit of Moscow news,' she wrote family.

> We had a delightful time last night at the famous Bolshoi Theater where Dad took me to see Verdi's *Aida*. I can't find words to express the beautiful job they did…
>
> Although we got home late last night… I put the radio on for a few minutes while we were preparing for bed and what were they singing in Russian but 'And Then I Went And Spoiled It All By Saying Something Stupid Like "I Love You."' Of course that brought back memories of you kids singing that in the car on our way to and from Mexico.

The Mexican Ambassador and his family took them to see a stunning ballet performance, and the Academy of Science sent a chauffeur to take them to the Gorky settlement in Leningrad, where Lenin had died. Elaine marveled at the beauty of the newly-fallen snow and the magical feeling it created. Another evening they dined in the home of a scientist and his wife and sixteen-year-old daughter. Along with the rest of Leningrad, they had suffered through the starvation between 1941-3, when hundreds of thousands died. The Townsends gave them a Bible, and kept up a lively conversation till late, though the couple said Christianity was not for them.

CHRISTMAS AMONG ATHEISTS

As they improved in the language, relationships became easier. Cameron drew up a tentative contract, favorably received, and then he awaited a formal vote from the Academy. He also began to compose a New Year's letter that would be sent to 700 friends in South America.

In the square outside their window, workmen erected a three-story New Year's tree and as they began work on the lights, snow began to fall. As usual, Elaine set her hand to craft a home out of their surroundings, putting on Christmas music and decorating a suitcase on which to put a tiny tree. When the lady from their floor came in to see the Christmas decorations, along with the Indian weavings, a llama-fur rug, and family pictures, she exclaimed, 'This isn't a hotel room! This is a home!'

One night, Elaine lay awake thinking of past Christmases with her children, and her first Christmas as Mrs. Townsend in Pucallpa, expecting Grace. Cameron woke up, and when he heard she couldn't sleep, they began recounting the years together, 'praising the Lord for each one'.

That Christmas, for all they knew, Cameron and Elaine might have been the only celebrants in the isolated capital of that communist country. Yet Elaine wrote, 'As we look out from our hotel window across historic Red Square to the Kremlin and Lenin's mausoleum, we rejoice to know the truth of Psalm 31:21, *"Blessed be the LORD; for He hath showed me His marvelous kindness in a strong city."*'

Back in the States, Nixon had won his first term that November, and Apollo 8 launched three astronauts into space. From the surface of the moon, the first words of Genesis sounded to the globe whose gravity held it in place, and the first pictures beamed on thousands of televisions, including at least one in the Hotel National. Along with millions that Christmas Eve, Cameron and Elaine heard the words, '*From the crew of* Apollo 8, *we pause with good night, good luck and Merry Christmas and God bless all of you—all of you on the good earth.*'

Elaine and Cameron in the Red Square, Moscow (1968).

24. 'REJOICE WITH US!'

There is nothing thrilling about a laboring man's work, but it is the laboring man who makes the conceptions of the genius possible; and it is the laboring saint who makes the conceptions of his Master possible. You labor at prayer and results happen all the time from His standpoint. What an astonishment it will be to find, when the veil is lifted, the souls that have been reaped by you, simply because you had been in the habit of taking your orders from Jesus Christ.

Oswald Chambers[1]

In their search for entrance into Russia, someone had recommended that the Townsends approach the Latin American branch of the Academy of Science with their request to do linguistic research. When they arrived, Dr. Volski received them warmly, but skeptically. When they mentioned a film on their work in Mexico, however, he gathered 150 of his employees. 'Imagine Dr. Volski's surprise to find this film was all about translating the Bible into a language in Mexico, and the results!' said Elaine. The film vividly portrayed the joy of hundreds of people at receiving the Word. 'Poor Dr. Volski didn't know what to say when the film ended with a very moving scene of the two lady translators now going on to South America to translate God's Word for still another language. He quickly dismissed his employees and us as well.'

One Jewish linguist, however, stayed behind long enough to invite them to lunch. In her kitchen, while opening a can of sardines and

1   Oswald Chambers, *My Utmost for His Highest*, 2nd edition (Uhrichsville, Ohio: Barbour Publishing, 1963), Oct. 17.

cutting cheese, she asked the Townsends, 'I understand that Christians pray. Do you pray?'

'Oh yes, Estella, we wouldn't keep praying if God didn't hear and answer our prayers.'

When she asked to hear of their prayers, and ones that had been answered, the Townsends gladly obliged, but she soon stopped them: 'I want my husband and daughter to hear this. Could you come back tomorrow night for supper?'

The next evening, Michael and Marcia joined them. Later, they learned that Michael was not only a member of the Academy of Science, but a professor at Moscow University, and the author of over 200 articles and twelve books on biochemistry. Conversation gravitated to the work of the Lord and life after death. At one point, Marcia spoke up: 'Have you been to college, Mrs. Townsend?'

'Yes.'

'And you, Dr. Townsend?'

'Yes.'

'And you mean to tell me you still believe in those fairy tales you are reading about?'

When it came time to go, Cameron offered his Russian New Testament to the Professor, who wasn't about to act eager, but let him leave it.

SURVEYS BEGINNING

After three months in the jaws of the lion, so to speak, the Townsends set out on a language survey trip through the Caucasus Mountains of the U.S.S.R., along the borders of Turkey and Iran. Here lay the ancient home of civilizations founded before the coming of Christ, and also the 168 language groups which had thrown down their gauntlet in front of Cameron.

From early January till March of 1969, Cameron and Elaine traveled to five of the fifteen republics in the Caucasus area without escort—a rare venture at that point in Soviet history. As Elaine explained, 'All tourists in those days had to travel under the authority of *Intourist*. They told you where to stay, and gave permission and interpreters for our trips.' Their itinerary included Baku, the capital of Azerbaijan,

Cameron and Elaine visiting a school in Baku, Azerbaijan (1969).

Maxachkala, the capital of Dagestan, Tbilisi, the capital of Georgia, Erevan, the capital of Armenia, Suhumi, and Sochi on the Black Sea.

The country loomed mammoth—an almost entirely untapped mission field containing some of the most culturally and linguistically diverse regions of the globe. Of course, this only incited Cameron to action. The Townsends visited educators and linguists, focusing on the success of bilingual education in the various minority language groups

221

scattered across Russia. Among the vast range of Caucasus mountains, the Townsends heard a legend from locals: an angel had flown around the various regions of the world, dispensing languages; coming too close to these peaks had caused his bag to break, and spill hundreds of languages among the foothills.

A FRIGID LAND

Russia could hardly have differentiated herself more from South America. In October, Elaine wrote, 'Yesterday, Dad and I bought two fur hats, identical. They are both for men but so much warmer than the ones for ladies. It is the kind you can let down to cover your ears and tie under the chin. We look really cute.'

The temperatures only dropped. From Baku, on the Caspian Sea, Elaine wrote, 'We had quite a blizzard today and our hotel room is so cold that I am typing this to you in the bathroom with hot water filling the tub so that the steam can keep my fingers warm enough to type.'

That evening, the Townsends read Scripture with a new friend in the area who claimed to be atheist but read the Koran. The local museum displayed portions of the Koran and artifacts which dated back to centuries before Christ. 'We are more and more aware of the fact that history is in the making these days and that mighty miracles are just ahead,' she finished.

Sochi, later home to the 2014 Winter Olympic Games, was the last stop on their Caucasian tour. There, they found a ping-pong table for rent at thirty cents an hour, and they took advantage. Apparently, Cameron had improved since their courting days, for he beat her seven times out of nine. She beat two Russian men however, and what a sight it must have been— the wife of Wycliffe's founder squaring off against two Soviet gentlemen!

The isolated nature of these war-torn countries brought constant hurdles. That January found them fighting severe colds, but even finding eggs, milk, and fruit juice proved difficult. 'There is never enough to meet the demand,' Elaine wrote, 'and always you have to stand in line—a long one—and when you finally get to the front of the line you'll take a purple dress when you wanted a pink, for example, just to get one.'

Everywhere they went, the Townsends observed a strange contrast between long-held tradition and modern progress; between dire poverty and clean efficiency. 'Although most Soviets don't believe there is any life after death, yet in downtown Moscow you see huge banners across the street reading "Lenin Lives Forever!"' Elaine observed.

One evening they had dinner in the home of a renowned linguist, whose daughter, Mary, had just come in from work on one of the farms. It was September, and Elaine asked, curious, if school had not started yet.

'Yes,' came the reply, 'but the country is so far behind on harvesting potatoes that the universities have been closed until we get the potatoes in.' She told Elaine it was the best part of her summer. At first, however, she didn't understand the rules, and tried to sit down when she got tired. Someone quickly informed her that if she did that she would have to stay and peel potatoes for several hours, after ten hours of digging them.

When Elaine showed dismay at this, Mary assured her, 'Oh, no, we are governed by our own young people. We made the rules and we didn't think that was too bad.'

In general, Cameron and Elaine found themselves impressed with the methods of the various linguists they met—most had grammars, dictionaries, poetry, and, of course, works by Lenin and Marx, though they lacked the Bible. Cameron was interviewed on several occasions for radio, TV, and newspapers, and numerous friendships began.

A BETTER CHOICE

Upon their return to the hotel in Moscow, Elaine phoned Estella, the Jewish linguist. She came over immediately—just radiant. 'You know that Book you left with us, Uncle Cam? My husband has read it all the way through. I have also, and two of our neighbors. We're happy now, and pray to God every day. Could you get us some more copies?' All in the course of six weeks.

A few years later, Marcia married and had a little boy. Her father, Dr. Michael, asked Cameron to dedicate his grandson to God. 'Cam took him in his arms and asked God to make him another Samuel,'

Elaine wrote. Estella also informed them that Marcia read the New Testament as she nursed.

This new field of work fast absorbed all other pursuits, and the opening of Russia's shuttered country became the height of their aspirations. All energy poured into this endeavor, and if they weren't actually on Soviet soil, their thoughts turned toward the orchestration of the next trip.

BACK AGAIN

Six months after returning from their first encounter with the United Soviet Socialist Republic, the Townsends were back. Each of their ten future expeditions into this land wove its own exotic tale. The second trip was no less ambitious than the first, as Cameron intended to gather further information on integrated bilingual education toward the publication of a book.

This was also the first of three trips on which Bill, then sixteen, accompanied them. Without a doubt, their new venture carried implications for those closest to them. Of their first trip Elaine said later, 'Billy was just a fifteen-year-old at Ben Lippen, and it wasn't easy for him. When you're fifteen and all your family is away from you, and your Mom and Dad are in Russia—that [is] very hard, *very* hard—I had no idea how hard.' Now in his junior year of high school, Bill planned to carry on correspondence courses along the way. Likely he was the only person mailing assignments from an address in the U.S.S.R.!

On the last trip they had taken eight New Testaments and everything had gone fine, so this time they took thirty. When customs officials found four, he asked if they had more. 'What do you plan to do with these?'

The Townsends responded that they would give them to anyone who was interested, but this didn't impress the Russian officials. They let the Townsends take only one. They simply asked friends to mail more, and distributed those.

In October 1969, about a week after their arrival, they left for a linguistically rich section of Dagestan, and an area where ordinary tourists were forbidden to travel. They planned to rent a car or a helicopter for travel to more remote villages.

ARRESTED

Then, just to remind them of the precarious travel in a communist country, which hitherto had seemed reasonably safe, Bill was arrested. In Baku, a group of linguists held a banquet for the Townsends, and Bill wandered around town, taking a few pictures.

'He was a little injudicious,' Elaine remarked. 'He ended up at the market place and when he saw the villagers washing their feet in a water trough he thought that would make a good picture. The police were not of the same mind. They took him into the small police booth, took the film out of his camera, and gave him a good lecture which he didn't understand.' For three hours, Bill didn't know how long it would be till he was released, or if he even *would* be. Meanwhile back at the hotel, the long, drawn out banquet was over and still no Bill returned. Elaine's anxiety grew, and she began to cry.

At this point, the authorities became frustrated by Bill's lack of comprehension, and came to the hotel for the Townsends' interpreter. Still the Townsends were none the wiser until she returned, bringing Bill. 'He should have known better,' Elaine said in retrospect, 'but it was so unusual and strange that he thought he would get a picture of it.'[2] Fortunately, no serious charges were brought.

CHURCH SCENE

In this land of strangers and religious doubt, both the Word and the fellowship of other believers became doubly prized: 'The promises are exceedingly real and precious to us. We make quite a trio as we lift up our hearts in praise with one of the mighty hymns each day.' Through days of strenuous travel and intense interaction, they found strength in recalling the faithfulness of their great and powerful God, who by His right arm had opened the way into this vast and formidable country.

---

2   It was presumed that the scene Bill witnessed in some way contradicted the picture of prosperity and sophistication that the Soviets desired to portray to the world at the time.

Everywhere they went, they sought out brothers and sisters. Elaine described the Baptist church in Moscow:

> When you looked down into the auditorium you could see how packed it was. There was one man standing in the middle aisle with an old-fashioned ink bottle and pen and every time a Scripture was read he would write it down. We were very much impressed that when it came time to pray, all the people knelt so that the aisles were crowded, and there was much weeping before the Lord.

FROM RUSSIA, ON

Though they continually made light of it, travels into the U.S.S.R. were no small achievement. After their departure from Russia, Elaine wrote, 'We didn't realize how much tenseness Billy felt and neither did he until we got to India. The first night he sat on the bed and exclaimed—"Oh, isn't it good to have this wonderful free feeling?" You don't realize until you are out… that you didn't act normal because you were on your best behavior all the time.'

After that month in Russia, the Townsends set off to encourage workers on SIL bases in five other countries. November saw them in New Delhi, India. The contrast was intense: in Moscow it had been snowing, in India, it was warm; Moscow was bleak, India was filled with flowers; Moscow suffered a shortage of everything, while in India they could find most things easily; in Moscow, school was mandatory, in India, illiteracy was rampant. Elaine wrote of an incident burned into her memory: 'At one of the stop signs this morning, a boy about seven came up to the car with a small baby girl, perhaps nine months old. The baby was dying and had legs about the size of my thumb… I am told that the average income is $60.00 dollars *a year* per each member of the family.'

Elaine's response when asked about the Taj Mahal, reflected her and Cameron's perspective on life: 'You can't help but be impressed. It took twenty-one years to build and cost millions of dollars in memory of this man's wife… but Cam is not one for tourist sights. He would far rather go out where the people are, and that is what I prefer too.'

From India, the Townsends traveled to Nepal, the Philippines, Papua New Guinea, Australia, and New Zealand. On November 11th, thirty-six years to the day since Cameron entered Mexico, they received word that officials would once again grant entrance to American linguists. From a little valley in Kathmandu Elaine wrote, 'In the near distance we can see the beautiful Himalayan mountains, Mt. Everest...' Cows had the run of the streets, and Elaine noted that the punishment for hitting one of these sacred animals was much greater than for hitting a man.

Elaine described Cameron closing a plane dedication ceremony, praying God's protection over the plane, pilot and passengers in the years to come. 'The sun was going down behind the beautiful snow-capped Himalayas painting them gold, then purple and blue and finally back to a breathtaking white. I have never seen anything so beautiful!'

In Ukarumpa, New Guinea, the Townsends were invited into the homes of the base so that they could get to know all 308 members. Each served their best, and Elaine bemoaned her resulting waistline.

Before they returned, the Townsends hoped to stop in Vietnam; but hostilities with the U.S.S.R. prevented this. Russian officials would frown on a Vietnamese stamp, and could even forbid them further entrance into Russia.

TIME IN BETWEEN

Two months after their return from the second exploit of their 'retirement,' having traveled for sixteen out of the past nineteen months and visited fifteen countries, Cameron developed heart trouble; but he continued to rise early for prayer. 'He remembers so many people every day around the world and he couldn't get it all in if he didn't wake up so early,' his wife said. 'What a full life he has had,' she reflected, 'and all of this traveling certainly seems to agree with him.' But adventures of the magnitude that Cameron's zeal prescribed couldn't help but take its toll. Twenty years younger, it took Elaine a full six weeks to recover.

The months between winter of 1969 and spring of 1972 marked the longest period between trips to Russia. During this time, Joy married David Tuggy, and shortly afterward they became SIL members; Elainadel married Bob Garippa; Cameron was hospitalized for atrial fibrillation; the former Mexican President and close friend of Cameron's, General

Lázaro Cárdenas, died and Cameron traveled to Mexico for his funeral; Cam and Elaine celebrated their twenty-fifth wedding anniversary with friends; Cameron celebrated his seventy-fifth birthday, and resigned his post of General Director of WBT; they both traveled to Mexico in May; and in September to Washington D.C., New Jersey, New York, Chicago, and Wisconsin.

Cameron wrote a book on the languages of the Caucasus: *They Found a Common Tongue*. Elaine continued her hospitality and pursued Russian classes. Moving into their newly completed home, which Elaine had designed, they put it straight to use by sleeping seventeen one night and holding a gathering for sixty guests.

OFF AGAIN

As she prepared for a third trip into the U.S.S.R., Elaine found herself particularly encouraged by the promises of her Father: 'If the Lord gave me a thousand dollars it couldn't have blessed my soul as much as these precious promises did.'

They arrived in April of 1972, and for seven weeks they visited various cities in the Caucasus. In May, they visited a famous health resort. One of their Russian friends, observing the superhuman pace they routinely set, had arranged for their stay; and Elaine's descriptions of this place are slightly humorous, both from the detail she includes and her childish wonder at all the luxury so unfamiliar to both of them. She and Cameron soon had their individual routines of rest, bathing, exercise, mineral water, and massages. Teeth had come out of the upper plates in Cameron's mouth on several occasions ('very embarrassing,' as Elaine put it), and he was also able to get these repaired.

Here too, people captured the Townsends' focus. When they heard they would be sitting with the same couple for three weeks, they prayed the Lord would guide the assignment. As usual, the time the Townsends spent at that health resort held eternal implications for those they met:

> Today I had a little talk with one of the doctors here about the fact that I love God and am a believer. I told her about our Russian friends in Ashford, and how we spent Easter, when they greet each other with

'Christ arose!' and the answer is 'He truly arose!' She showed great interest so I let her borrow my Russian Bible.

In a letter late that May, Elaine casually commented, 'Last night Cam sent a telegram to President Nixon—or rather a night letter, as it was quite long, telling about the [Russian] school.' As it happened, President Richard Nixon himself was in Russia then, and for the first time in history, the Grand Palace of the Kremlin carried the flying stars and stripes. Nixon had arrived on the 22nd of May to confer with Soviet leaders, including Brezhnev.

A SECOND HONEYMOON

Elaine also wrote about the fun she and Cameron seemed to be having, 'We are both feeling ever so much better and didn't realize just how much we needed a break. I even felt up to playing ping-pong last night and beat my Russian partner.' On June 3rd, from Sujumi on the Black Sea, Elaine wrote to friends, 'We are both feeling well, enjoying each other on this, another honeymoon, and thrilled with the trip.'

In Armenia, they received news that their first grandchild had been born—Christopher. They visited Yerevan, a city dating back 2,750 years: 'From here you can see the snow-capped peaks of Mount Ararat, where Noah's Ark came to rest.'

Cameron celebrated his seventy-sixth birthday back in Moscow, and Elaine wrote to family, 'He gets better all the time! We praise the Lord for the added strength provided for both of us.' Altogether on that trip, the Townsends entered twenty-nine homes—more than all the British embassy members combined.

That July, the Townsends returned to the States via London. In August, they traveled to Mexico, stopping by Tetelcingo to meet their first grandchild; Cameron danced a little jig when he held him in his arms.

25. THE GOD WHO ACTS

This I saw, that when a soul loves God with a supreme love, God's interests and his become one. It is no matter when nor where nor how Christ should send me, nor what trials He should exercise me with, if I may be prepared for His work and will.

David Brainerd[1]

Early in May of 1972, Harper & Row published Cameron's book on the tremendous success of bilingual education in the Caucasus, *They Found a Common Language*. For about two weeks it was available, then every copy disappeared. The late McCarthy era seemed not entirely dead. Cameron had written in favor of Russia's school system, and America did not want it on her shelves. As a result, this book on which Cameron had spent hundreds of valuable hours never gained wide recognition. But Cameron and Elaine were soon to find God's greater purpose working out through this misfortune.

MYSTERIOUS WORKINGS

In April, a month before the book's release, Harper & Row had sent the Townsends advance copies which they took to Russia with them and gave to various linguists and dignitaries who showed great interest. While still in Russia in June of 1972, the Townsends received remarkable news. The World Congress on Socio-Linguistics invited Cameron to give a presentation on his book in Turkmenia. Attendance at this international event would open at least one other major door to future Wycliffe work.

1   David Brainerd, Public Domain.

Cameron's lecture was well received, and he was soon scheduled to speak a second time at the conference. While all the other delegates read their speeches with haste, Cameron decided to give an ad-lib report. 'I wish you could have heard him,' Elaine wrote their friends. 'He spoke for twenty-five minutes and held his audience spellbound.' A delegate from Pakistan, in a rare move, asked for the floor, and expressed gratitude to Cameron for his report and the work of Wycliffe. He also invited SIL to work in Pakistan.

In Tashkent, Cameron and Elaine visited an illegal church. The outside looked like a big garage, and they weren't sure they were at the right place till a lovely Russian girl stepped up to the taxi and said to them, 'Yes, this is the house you are looking for.'

At the end of the service, Cameron said a few words, closing with Romans 1:16. When they all stood to sing 'God Be With You Till We Meet Again' in Russian, to the waving of scarfs and handkerchiefs, Elaine thought back to her friends at the North Side Gospel Center circling around her as she left for the field in 1943—almost thirty years ago, and of the Mexican believers from the Mission in Chicago as they gathered at the train station to see her off. She could see the Aztec believers in Mexico singing it as she and Cameron moved from Tetelcingo to Peru shortly after their marriage; and their beloved co-workers in Peru weeping as their family left to begin work in Colombia in 1963. And now, 'all of these dear Russian believers are also looking forward to that day when we shall meet at Jesus' feet. How precious indeed!'

In October, Cameron and Elaine returned to Moscow, where they paid their promised call to the ambassador of Pakistan. He told a group of distinguished guests that he had read Cameron's book through twice, quoted from it several times, and asked them to consider working in his country. Things moved quickly on this front, and six days after returning home to Waxhaw, the Townsends received a call from the Pakistani Ambassador in Washington D.C., saying he had just heard from the President, who had issued an official request for them to come.

EXPANSIVE

Meanwhile, the doors of Russia continued to swing open as new relationships were forged and old ones strengthened on every visit. Surprisingly, in a country so hostile to the Word, that Book rarely failed to break ice and endear them to the Soviet citizens. Once, while Cameron read, a doctor leaned over to Elaine, whispering, 'How different it is to hear the Bible read with sincerity, and not critically.'

When Elaine phoned to say goodbye to a journalist friend, the woman exclaimed, 'Oh, how I hate to see you go; you are the best friends I have had in this world. Please don't forget to pray for me and my daughter.'

During their last week in Moscow, twenty-two people came to visit in their hotel room, including a newspaper reporter writing an article on Cam for the popular magazine, *Soviet Life*, and a radio announcer for *Radio Moscow* who taped an hour interview; professors from Lithuania and Ethiopia, students, and linguists. They received expensive bouquets of flowers and other gifts.

After traveling 60,000 miles that year, visiting the four republics of Turkmenia, Tajikistan, Uzbekistan and Kazakhstan, Cameron wrote at the end of a partnership letter, 'I trust that this report will correct any idea that may exist that my resignation last year as General Director was tantamount to retirement. How could we retire when God gives energy and there are still 2,000 tribes without God's Word?' One can almost hear his tone—at seventy-six he remained completely incredulous that anyone would think him capable of such a thing!

And so they charged on.

AN AUDIENCE

In February of 1973, the Townsends made their shortest visit to the U.S.S.R.—just five days. But first they took a stint in Islamabad, Pakistan, where they conferred with President Zulfikar Ali Bhutto. Unfortunately, on the heels of their arrival in Pakistan, Elaine caught an intense cold and almost stayed back. At the last minute she changed her mind, and both she and Cameron were ushered into the office of the President, between two rows of tall, handsome soldiers standing at attention. For twenty minutes, President Bhutto listened attentively to Cameron, promised to give land to Wycliffe, and expressed interest in talking further.

After the audience, the Townsends were taken to the site of a university under construction. 'Islamabad is the new Capitol less than ten years old and is still very much in the process of being built,' Elaine explained. She found it remarkable that the head of the university was a woman, in a country where the women remained so hidden behind their veils. Many of the educators they met had attended Harvard, Berkeley, Oxford or elsewhere abroad. When they returned to the hotel, Elaine collapsed into bed for the next two and a half days.

A QUESTIONABLE PLAN

Already another trip had entered the works, and this one would prove itself epic. Cameron believed they could more effectively survey the Russian dialects if they traveled with a car and house trailer. Elaine wondered how reasonable such a proposition was, particularly since there was no car and no house trailer as yet; and even if there were, the distance from their Waxhaw home to the Caucasus charted in at around six thousand miles—most of them open sea.

For fear of a dull moment, the Townsends traveled to Mexico that May, along with Elaine's mother. Soon after, both the car (a '68 Chrysler) and the trailer had materialized. A private mechanic would also accompany these vehicles, in the form of Bill. As Elaine so aptly put it: 'Who would have thought… But it happened.' Elaine herself loved driving, and since Cameron was not fond, she began to practice driving, parking, and backing up with the trailer.

The next job was to find a ship. The Russian steamer, *Mikhail Lermontov*, was scheduled to leave the New York port on June 12th, arriving in Leningrad two weeks later. Elaine made sure to pack Scrabble.

With the departure date just six days away, visas had not yet arrived, so Cameron caught a plane to Washington to expedite the process if possible. That left Elaine and Bill to board the ship alone. Everyone at the JAARS base circled them and prayed, then off they went! On the way, they stopped by the home of famed photographer Cornell Capa, who lived on 5th Avenue.[2] 'I had the pleasure of being behind the wheel,' recalled Elaine, 'which meant I had to drive in downtown New York pulling our twenty-six-foot house trailer—and during the noon rush hour traffic at that. Quite an experience!'

On board ship, the trailer quickly became an attraction. The captain, as well as many passengers toured it, and it featured in two documentary films and two newspaper interviews. Elaine commented that it was the first house trailer to make such a journey into the U.S.S.R. Cameron had painted 'FRIENDSHIP' in Russian along the side, and this was noted with great favor.

TROUBLE

Upon disembarking, the Townsends received troubling news. Their travel agency had not cleared their arrival with Intourist, which meant they had to leave the country at once and wait in Finland to receive permission to enter. They also learned that tourists to Moscow in the summertime were not allowed to stay any more than four days. Immediately, they went to the Lord in prayer. They were allowed to continue on to Moscow, but only on condition that they report to Intourist immediately upon arrival. There, they learned that not only would they be allowed to stay, but they would be given an extension of two weeks. Increasingly, they became conscious of God's hand, guiding them in all their endeavors.

The amount of driving over the next weeks was intense, but Cameron had been right—it would make their travels exceedingly more efficient (especially with the price of gas at a whopping thirty-four cents). They spent sweet time in the Word each day, and Elaine gave Bill lessons in Russian, as she herself studied. 'We are reminded that "faithful is He who has called us, who will also do it,"' she wrote to home, and quoted her verse for the year: '"In everything give thanks." When we do this we experience the joy of the Lord which is our strength. Keep praying!' she reminded their supporters.

---

2   Cornell, who held Cameron in genuine love and admiration, wanted to see them off. He had helped Bill purchase a camera for the trip. Cornell remained one of the people Elaine most wanted to see come to the Lord.

Years later, Heather, her grand-daughter, remembered Elaine telling stories of gas stations with huge lines of people waiting for their ration; but the crowds parted for Cameron and Elaine: 'The people would always let Grandma and Grandpa go to the head of the line when they learned that they were Americans. She said the Russians would tell them, "You are Americans. You helped us in the war!" And this at the height of the Cold War!'

Elaine's niece recalled a more chilling story:

> She talked about a long train ride that they took... to see the more remote places. She described the stark but beautiful cabin they were in and how an austere man came through and darkened all the windows with a stern warning to them both to not so much as peek out of them until they reached their destination. As a child it impacted me of the darkness of the place at that time.

Upon arrival in Tbilisi one evening, they couldn't find their scheduled place. Elaine asked a policeman, who guided them to a gas station where he gave them fifteen free liters, then through all the red lights in town, to their motel.

SAFELY THROUGH

Over five weeks, they drove 3,700 miles on roads left in great disrepair. The steep mountain scenery was breathtaking, with snowcapped mountains in the distance and herds of sheep and goats along the slopes. They forded streams with the trailer, just hoping it wouldn't get stuck. Elaine compared it to a drive from Chicago to Mexico City over washboard the entire way. A year and a half before, doctors had prohibited Cameron from driving the four hours from Charlotte to Atlanta, and now here they were! Intourist changed their schedule at least once, requiring them to return to Moscow early, driving more than ten hours a day for five days. Through it all, Elaine wrote, 'We marvel at the extra strength the Lord is giving us.'

True to style, Elaine took every opportunity of showing hospitality in their makeshift home. 'We were delighted to have around 300 Soviet Citizens take the tour of our cozy home on wheels. It was quite a vehicle for making friends.' No matter how important or how humble, each guest found themselves graciously welcomed and served with whatever came to hand. Neither tight quarters nor lack of resources counted for much since Elaine spiced up every situation with her keen interest in each individual. 'It was good to be able to serve dinner to several of our friends in Moscow,' Elaine wrote. '… the largest number at one sitting was eight—a bit crowded to be sure!' The Chrysler also made a hit: 'even the women were interested in seeing the engine!'

A NEED TO MATCH

The Townsends decided to cut their travels in half, as the abundance of tourists made campsites scarce. 'I wish I could report that the doors have been flung wide open but such is not the case,' Elaine wrote home. The question then surfaced: what to do with the car and camper? It made sense to leave both in the country for further use, but upon entering they had signed a statement promising to remove them by September. The Academy of Science arranged with officials in Leningrad to extend their permit and to find a guarded lot on the bank of the Moscow River.

And so, leaving their vehicles to weather the brutal Russian winter— not their brightest idea, as it turned out—Cameron, Elaine, and Billy set their faces toward home.

That September, Elaine wrote from Waxhaw, 'In many ways, the trip was like a glorious dream and yet there were times when we needed to match Ephesians 6:12 with Romans 8:38-9.'[3]

Incorrigibly, they began plotting:

> … Now we are making plans for next summer. We've marched around the walls six times and trust they will be coming down soon. What lies ahead? Our marvelous Lord is the same yesterday, today, and forever.

---

3   Ephesians 6:12: 'For we do not wrestle against flesh and blood, but against the rulers, against the authorities, against the cosmic powers over this present darkness, against the spiritual forces of evil in the heavenly places.' Romans 8:38-9: 'For I am sure that neither death nor life, nor angels nor rulers, nor things present nor things to come, nor powers… will be able to separate us from the love of God in Christ Jesus our Lord.'

Whatever has been accomplished through us thus far was His doing. The use of weak instruments is one of His specialties.

A different wall came down before their next trip to Russia, however. In May of 1974, Joy and David Tuggy sent word that the first draft of the Aztec New Testament had been completed. As Cameron set his face toward yet a new land, God granted him the satisfaction of seeing fruit ripen from his labor years earlier. 'How wonderful that together we can serve our living Lord!' Elaine wrote to their children.

26. AND YET HE LEADS ON

See that God's aim in providing for you has been your transformation, not your ease... God's goal is to make you like Jesus, and that he will do. [The] cross is the most vivid demonstration of God's love for us, and every little good we've seen has flowed from that glorious fountain. It did yesterday, and it will tomorrow.

Jonathan Parnell[1]

Deposited once again in Leningrad by the steamship S.S. *Lermontov*, Cameron, Elaine, and Bill made their way south by train that June to retrieve their car and house trailer from the parking lot in Moscow. Getting there proved more of an adventure than anyone wanted.

AUDACITY REWARDED

On the way, Bill suggested, 'Let's pray that this time they won't open any of our baggage.' Elaine was skeptical. Customs had opened their baggage on all eight visits. It was the same drill every time: they found a Bible in Cameron's coat pocket and inquired if they had any more. Well, this time Bill wanted to ask that they wouldn't even look, so Elaine mumbled a half-hearted prayer and went to sleep.

Arriving in Leningrad along with 700 other passengers, they saw a crowd of customs officials thoroughly checking all bags. They moved through the line with their six new trailer tires, a battery, and plenty of baggage. *Here it comes*, Elaine thought. Suddenly, a young man

---

1 Jonathan Parnell, 'Seven Details to see in your Past'. Last accessed July 1, 2018. https://www.desiringgod.org/articles/seven-details-to-see-in-your-past

approached Cameron. 'Dr. Townsend, you here again? Welcome to the U.S.S.R.!'

Cameron looked at him, then nudged Elaine, asking frantically, 'Who is he? *Who is he?*' After a few seconds, Elaine remembered him as a campsite guard they had met the year before, plus a new beard. The Townsends had invited him and his wife into their trailer for coffee and given him some portions of Scripture.

'Now, if you'll just wait a few minutes, I'll take care of you,' he said. Not one bag was opened.

THINGS GET COLORFUL

They soon arrived at the train station, where they stored their baggage till the train left that evening. This settled, they rested in a hotel room and returned to the train station around ten, two hours before their train was due to depart. The Intourist office reassured them, 'Oh, you've got plenty of time, lots of time, just sit down and watch a TV program.' The Townsends had nineteen pieces of baggage to move out of storage to the platform, but every time Cameron approached the counter, he was repeatedly told that there was no rush, and to have a seat. They did, but 'rather anxiously'.

All of a sudden it was ten minutes to twelve, and they heard the train warming up, and Cameron asked, 'Don't you think we should start doing something now?'

'Oh, you wanted to get on *that* train, didn't you?' At this point the railway assistant realized he had let too much time go by, and the baggage man ran to get a cart, while three others helped load the bags. Bill called Elaine to come carry the handbags, but she struggled to keep the pace.

'Oh, I wish you could have seen us!' she wrote later.

It was panic… We were in the first car on a long, long, train. So Cameron started running and a fellow with some of the bags; everybody took something and started running. I was about three or four cars behind the fellows with all of the documents in my purse. All of a sudden the train started pulling out! What a terrible feeling. I saw there was no hope… So I started to slow down. But Billy grabbed me—'No, mother, keep running; keep running.' It was agony.

Looking up I saw that Cam had jumped on the train and was begging the conductor to stop the train—impossible! The fellows on the platform began throwing baggage on as fast as possible—the train still moving—and I kept puffing as I ran and prayed. Fortunately those fellows were very fast now; no doubt they realized it was their carelessness that had put us in this predicament. By now I almost gave up as the train was going faster than I could possibly run.

At this point the conductor softened and stopped the train for a very few minutes, all the time shouting *'Quickly! Quickly!'* I jumped on (can't you see me?), the train again began to move, and the Russian fellows continued to run, throwing baggage to Cam, who relayed it to Bill and down the corridor to me. We had very little room to work in!

Those fellows could very easily have just kept the rest of it because they knew they'd never see us again, but they kept on throwing and everything got on. Oh! We were just trembling. It was such a narrow experience. You see, Cameron was on the train but I had all the money and the passports, so if he went on that train he would have been stuck. It could have been just so terrible.

Once they regained their breath, they began to look for their compartment—the last one at the end of the car. They walked in, happy to finally settle in, when an undressed man jumped up from the lower berth.

'Sir, I think you must be in the wrong cabin!' Elaine exclaimed.

He assured them he was not, and produced a ticket. 'He had come all the way from Bulgaria, and sure enough, he was supposed to be there too,' Elaine said. 'So we had this man and all of our baggage… Bill and Cam somehow squeezed in and we were all on board.' Sleep was scarce that night. The end of their car joined to the next, so every noise was amplified.

The next morning they arrived in Leningrad, meeting a man sent by Intourist. The tires were on another train and would not arrive for several hours, so they went to move the car and trailer to their campsite. Elaine's optimistic 'We were happy to see they were both in good condition' soon showed itself to be premature. Bill started the car, shortly afterwards 'something burned out,' and three days went by while a mechanic from the American Embassy labored with all his restorative powers.

TROUBLE... AGAIN

Soon, the hours of garage repair began to add up. The Townsends logged six hours in a garage waiting for a part to be welded, then drove till the early hours of the morning. Soon, something else went wrong, and another five hours ensued. To make matters worse, heavy truck traffic had destroyed the roads, which often lacked middle dividing lines, and many slow vehicles inhibited their progress. 'I'm sure the Lord is teaching us much in the way of patience these days,' Elaine commented.

From a garage in the historic Ukrainian town of Rostov on July 4th, she wrote:

> At this point in our journey we are having to leave [the trailer] behind as twice now one of the springs has broken due to the rugged driving over these bumpy roads. We'll be gone three weeks to Sochi, Sukhumi, Tbilisi, Orjanikidze, Pistigorsk, then back to Rostov. We trust this can be arranged with Intourist, but they almost refuse to make any changes. In fact they have refused so far, but our confidence is in Him.

Then, an adventure occurred which Elaine would call her favorite story of their time in the U.S.S.R.

They were making their way south, visiting schools and universities. Traveling with a dirty car was prohibited, and while Cameron and Bill were conducting the daily washing, a handsome Orthodox priest walked up to them. His black clothes and large cross and chain appeared striking, and he told them in broken English that he needed a ride to Sochi, where his car was being repaired. The Chrysler also stood in need of more repairs, and the Townsends were eager to accommodate this new friend.

That evening, as Cameron, Elaine, and Bill sat at supper, Father Victor Federenko came knocking with another request: 'I hate to bother you folks especially at mealtime, but I wonder if you would have room for my wife and little girl tomorrow?'

Conversation was lively during the thirty-mile drive to Sochi in the morning. A long line of cars waited for service, but when someone noticed their U.S. plates, they were moved to the front. The repairs took about six hours, during which time Victor and Cameron continued their conversation in the front, while Eugenia and Olga, their six-year-old daughter, and Elaine visited, read Scripture in Russian, and sang. Elaine taught Olga the 100th Psalm, much to the disgust of the mechanic who was working under the dashboard and could hear every word. At one point, he came around to the window: 'You surely don't believe those fairy tales you are reading, do you?'

They assured him they did, and the more he ridiculed them the louder they read and sang—a Russian mechanic attending a compulsory Bible study which featured lengthy readings from a forbidden book.

The next day was Cameron's birthday, and their new friends arrived early to join the celebration, bringing the gift of a Russian icon book. Eugenia also offered Elaine her ring in exchange for her Bible, and would not be refused.

When the Federenkos learned that the Townsends' return from their two-week trip would take them through their own hometown of Kropotkin, they urged them to drop by for the weekend. Unfortunately, this would be impossible, given the restrictions exerted by Intourist: 'You stop where they tell you, and if you miss a night there is a big fine.'

Eugenia wasn't discouraged. 'That's okay. We'll pray that you can stop, and we're going to be prepared for you.' Elaine was far less confident.

PROVIDENTIAL BREAKDOWN

On their journey back to Moscow after the language survey, Elaine took the wheel. Just as they passed the village limits of Kropotkin, a red warning light flashed on the dashboard. Elaine didn't pay much attention, but the more mechanically-sensitive Bill, riding shotgun at the moment, said, 'Mother, that could be serious. Hadn't we better stop?'

Till that point, they hadn't seen a soul, but at that moment, a crowd appeared from nowhere, surrounded the car, and began pummeling its occupants with questions. A few minutes later, a patrolman appeared on the scene, and a dozen people gave him their versions all at once. He barked back that this was *his* job and *he* would take care of it, and everyone dispersed quietly. Turning to Elaine, he growled (in Russian, of course), 'Well lady, what do you propose to do?'

'I don't know, officer. What do you suggest?' she replied brightly. For a few minutes he pondered the predicament. They had no time to reach the garage in the next town before it closed, and since it was Saturday afternoon no one could service the car till Monday. Suddenly he turned back to her, 'Do you by any chance know anyone in this village?'

Yes, they did know a certain priest and his family. 'I'll tell you what I'll do,' he said, 'I'll take you to his home and see if he'll do me the favor of putting you up for the weekend.'

It was an impossibility.

'At this point, our hearts began to skip a beat as we saw God's hand planning our steps,' Elaine said.

Father Federenko was doubtless surprised to see his friends under police escort, but he and his family were ready for their arrival, and the Townsends were ushered into the patio, where they found a meal prepared under a beautiful grape arbor. Eugenia had invited a group of ladies from her church to help her earlier that day.

That night the Townsends visited the Federenkos' church, where they found nearly three hundred worshippers, almost all women; but no chairs. When Elaine expressed hesitation because of her bad feet, the priest offered her a chair behind a screen; 'but don't let anyone see you sitting down,' he cautioned. Elaine wrote,

> During parts of the service Eugenia sang from the Psalms for about fifteen minutes… and [when] the priest prepared to sprinkle holy water, everyone got as close as they could to the altar where the big Bible was. If you didn't get this holy water you might as well have not been there.

The service lasted almost three hours… our hearts ached for these dear people who seemed so sincere in their worship, yet were being fed so little.

The next evening a heavily-bearded young man joined them for dinner, and Father Federenko introduced his brother, who was studying to become a priest. 'Could you help him?' he asked. Elaine gave him her last Russian Bible.

On Monday, the Townsends piled in the car, and the red warning light did not come on. Elaine thought of the three groups of people praying for them around the clock back in the States: 'We were reminded of the promise in the Psalms where God says, *"The steps of a good man are ordered by the Lord,"* and at that point we added that He also orders our *stops*, even when a Soviet policeman is used to carry them out.'

ON TO MOSCOW

A few days later, a car skidded into the Townsends' Chrysler, destroying the front headlight and damaging the fender. No one was hurt, but it further delayed them two days, for no one was allowed to drive with a damaged fender.

In Orjanikidze, the smallest autonomous republic of the U.S.S.R., Bill met Armen, the son of some friends. Together they walked around taking pictures of town scenes: a market selling sheep for sacrifices, sheep blood being put on the forehead of a nineteen-year-old son, a little girl being blessed by a priest, snow-capped mountains, a gypsy camp along the road, a mountain village of collective farmers, and cows covering the road.

While they were in the Ukraine, a professor from the university in Kejachkale rode ten hours each way on the train to visit them, loaded with gifts of books and homemade food. As a child, he had memorized large portions of the Koran, but he was rather wary of the Bible.

Elaine also wrote, 'Just got our shortwave radio up and are saddened with all of the news about Watergate. The Russians of course listen to the *Voice of America*, and one of our friends told us how tired they were of hearing about Watergate.'

The weather began to turn cold as they returned to the trailer and set their faces toward Moscow. There, they visited the Baptist church again, where people crowded in the aisles, on the stairs, and behind the altar, despite the three services. This congregation had begun fifteen churches since Cameron and Elaine had visited the year before.

HOMEWARD

In a gesture of friendship, Cameron offered the car and trailer to the Academy of Science. One can't help a certain dubiousness, due to the amount of grief these items had cost the Townsends on their recent travels; but the Academy was greatly honored, and planned to make a plaque with pictures of Cameron and Elaine, and a statement of friendship between Russia and America. They gave the Townsends a room at the Academy of Science Hotel and purchased their tickets to Leningrad. 'I gave Dr. K. and another official a ride in the Chrysler, they were tickled pink,' Elaine wrote. Doubtless the officials weren't the only tickled ones!!

Upon their return, Cameron wrote an article for the October issue of the *Christian Herald* to dispel suspicions regarding their work in a communist country. He spoke of the warm hospitality they had received, the energy and drive of the citizens, the creativity of the schools, and the order and diligence that prevailed everywhere. Many spoke a second language before they were ten.

Cameron and Elaine had joined an all-black church, with the goal of serving wherever the Lord could use them most. Particularly in North Carolina during the seventies, this was a step outside social convention. From the first visit, entering late, this became apparent. Everyone turned to gaze at them, and the pastor stopped talking. 'I don't know who you are,' he said at last, 'but you're the first white people to ever step over that threshold.' For the next years, the Townsends faithfully served this body of believers, and Cameron occasionally preached.

Cameron's seventy-ninth birthday saw the completion of the Cakchiquel New Testament, and Elaine wrote that 2,400 copies had been sold in just eight days: 'As far as I know, this has never happened before in the history of the church. Do pray with us that the good seed

A growing family (September 1973): (back row to front row, left to right) Robert and Elainadel Garippa, David and Joy Tuggy, Bill Townsend, Grace and Tom Goreth, Elaine, Christopher Tuggy, Cameron.

sown might bear much fruit. What a thrill to think about the joys that await them as they too find our Savior and best Friend.'

IMMERSION

The next year, Elaine faced a particularly formidable challenge as she attended a nine-week Russian immersion course in Vermont, prior to their return to the U.S.S.R. in October. She signed a pledge that she would not utter a word of English except over the phone and at the store, and wrote that she was thrilled for such a remarkable opportunity.

At the camp, Elaine made a home of her dorm room, created song sheets for a Russian Bible study she held on Friday nights in her room, and reviewed her homework by typing out the lessons and drills on her new Russian typewriter. She wrote of one man's illustration: 'He said to imagine ourselves as paint brushes in the hand of Rembrandt, and then to imagine a conversation in which the paint brush looks at the picture and says "My! Didn't I make some wonderful strokes when I painted the sky?" Yes, how foolish, and yet how often we are tempted to think that the success lies within us. May I only give Him all the glory always.'

There she was—nearly sixty and enduring the rigors of speaking a difficult foreign language with an inscrutable alphabet, away from home, family, and friends. She wrote,

> We are working under great pressure. So much so that one of the students tried to take his life the second week of school. Another developed ulcers, was in the hospital for four days, and finally had to go home. The director found that so many students were at the breaking point midway, that he declared a long weekend. And the Lord has made this a special blessing for me as my teacher and I are enjoying three wonderful days at Schroon Lake Word of Life Camp… Some new friends in Middlebury offered me the use of their car for the weekend and it has been a treat to drive again. I feel like a bird out of a cage. We go back to studies tomorrow and I'll appreciate your continued prayer support.

'I was amazed that she was willing to go…' said Cal. 'They only let her talk to Cam once a week because they didn't want her thinking English, they wanted her thinking Russian. And that was no fun, let's face it!'—'especially,' her daughter added, 'for a woman who loved to talk!'
Elaine took advantage of every minute during this time, leaning in to her Father for strength. 'I have had more time to spend with the Lord here now that I am not responsible for keeping up a home, entertaining, etc.,' she wrote. 'This has been the greatest preparation of all for the spiritual battle and victories that lie just ahead.'

Eleven days before the end of the camp, she wrote, 'Here comes the last letter for this summer. And what a wonderful summer it has been! Lots of fellowship worked in with much, much hard work.' After three several-hour exams, Elaine's rigor came to an end. From then on, the Townsends traveled in Russia without an interpreter.

27. JUST AS HE PROMISED

In some strange way, when we are about His business, He makes the eternity, about which we know so very little, work in our favor.

Karen Burton Mains[1]

Not long before their departure in the fall of 1975, Elaine's mother entered the hospital. 'Isn't it wonderful, Elaine,' she said over the phone when her daughter called to say goodbye, 'that I am here in the hospital and will have two weeks to pray for you in Moscow?'

IF IT WEREN'T TRUE

After Paris, Switzerland, and Germany, the Townsends entered Russia for the eighth time. But this visit, for which they had such high hopes, seemed destined to crumble at their feet. With more prayer support than ever before, copies of Cam's latest book, *The USSR As We Saw It*, and the gift of the house trailer paving the way for deeper friendship with the Academy of Science, 'our hearts were so... so sure things were going to go just great this time.'

Upon their arrival at the Academy, they learned that the main person with whom they had interacted since their initial entrance in 1968 had retired and that one of the young officials least inclined to favor SIL had been appointed to take his place. When they sat down, he pulled out a manila folder 'in a very austere manner.'

'I wonder if you know what was in the paper this week?' he asked, and began to read troubling news about SIL's situation in Colombia,

---

1   Karen Burton Mains, *Open Heart, Open Home.*

finishing with the caustic remark, 'So now we know that you are a part of the C.I.A., Dr. Townsend.'

Cameron began a defense, but the official stopped him mid-sentence—'How could you possibly *not* be? You tell us you have 3,500 members. Who would support a work like this? It has got to be supported by the government.'

As much as they tried to deny his accusations, he kept asserting that the paper wouldn't publish such things it if weren't true. Such claims had also been broadcast on *Radio Moscow* and *Radio Cuba*.

As it turned out, Wycliffe was being removed from Colombia, and faulty information had been sent to all the embassies. Cameron had brought copies of his new book, and the response was represented by one young man who asked them 'How many copies did you have printed?'

'Something like 5,000.'

'Oh, so you really are making money on that book, aren't you?' Elaine noted that it had in fact cost them a great deal to print the book, but the most discouraging thing was the rampant skepticism they encountered.

ENCOUNTERS

Despite these bleak beginnings, God brought fruit even from this visit. Elaine wrote home on November 19th, 'We had a wonderful ten days in Moscow. Our very first night there we were invited to have dinner with the head of the English Department of the University on Lenin Hills. Our visit lasted three hours and most of that time was spent talking about our Lord Jesus.'

They visited the Colombian, Pakistani, American, Peruvian, Mexican, and Australian Embassies, as well as the Academy of Science, and various homes. The Ambassador from Colombia invited them for dinner, and showed understanding. The next day they flew to Tashkent, then to Pakistan, where the Ambassador received them warmly.

In Kabul, Afghanistan, an unusual encounter took place. Entering the lobby of their hotel, Cameron spied a paper which told of a linguistics seminar that week. Three years earlier, in Ashkhabad, he had met a linguist who was now the director of a prominent university. When they phoned him, he promptly invited them to attend.

As the Townsends left the conference, a young man approached them. 'Aren't you Uncle Cam Townsend?'

'Yes.'

'Would you come downstairs with me a minute? I want to talk with you.'

'He got us away so nobody could hear,' Elaine said. Then he told his story. He was from the Netherlands, but had taken an SIL course in England, and married a girl from Finland who had also taken the course. Currently, they were both at the Kabul University studying and seeking to open doors for translation with their fellow students. Cameron and Elaine invited him and his wife, along with two others, to their hotel that night, where they prayed and encouraged one another.

> They were so excited because they had been praying for a long time that Wycliffe would try again to get into Afghanistan. In fact, just that week they had held a special prayer time pleading, 'Lord, put it on the heart of some member of Wycliffe to try again.' And here he spotted Cameron at that meeting—one this man hadn't even planned to attend due to his late recovery from hepatitis the month before.

BETTER ALL THE TIME

Cameron and Elaine spent Thanksgiving Day in the airport waiting for their flight to India. Hostile relations between the two countries proved problematic for their travels, and because of a mistake with their visas, it seemed they would have to stay in Afghanistan for several months. At the last minute, however, they were allowed to fly to New Delhi, where they had an audience with Indira Gandhi, the prime minister.

She expressed no interest in bilingual education for India, but after their audience Elaine wrote, 'I brought in some roses to her, and [...] as I approached her beautiful oval desk in this palace, she stepped up and came towards me, "Oh, you look as pretty as a flower garden yourself!"'

They began to talk about the linguistic situation in India: sixteen official languages and over sixteen hundred dialects. She brushed off Cameron's proposal, and the ambassador there advised that they proceed slowly. India, too, had heard the rumor that SIL was part of the C.I.A., and their relationship with the United States wasn't the most cordial at the time.

That January of 1976, Elaine wrote to friends, 'As we begin another year, isn't it great to know we are on the winning side and that the things that are impossible with men are possible with God?'

Two weeks later, Cameron and Elaine flew to Bogotá to seek resolution on the damaging rumors halting SIL's work. Elaine wrote with relief, 'How we praise the Lord for His undertaking in this crisis situation!'

On his eightieth birthday, Cameron received forty-seven phone calls and 100 birthday cards or telegrams, including a telegram from President Ford. The mayor of Waxhaw declared July 9th William Cameron Townsend Day, and 300 attended his celebration.

In a speech at the dedication of Wycliffe's Mexico-Cárdenas museum, Senator Carl Curtis from Nebraska stated, 'Townsend and Wycliffe Bible Translators have done more for the countries where they have served than the sum total of all the [U.S.] government or foreign aid which has been extended to those nations.'

Elaine expressed the heart of their vision in a letter that month when she wrote '… Our first New Testament was completed in 1951 and I just learned that now in 1977, seventy-one New Testaments are completed. Imagine the joy of the people speaking these languages as they can now come to know of the Savior who brings forgiveness, new life, and a hope beyond the grave!'

As Elaine anticipated their next departure she commented, 'If I didn't know the Lord would give me strength for my day I know I could never make it.' Earlier that year she wrote, 'How good it is to know that He is on the throne and as we commit our ways unto Him, He gives peace, quietness of heart, and the assurance that "greater is He that is in us than he that is in the world."'

FIRST LIGHT

The Townsends' ninth trip to the United Soviet Socialist Republic saw the first light through a cracking door. Underway on the *Lermontov* for the fourth time, Elaine wrote to her son, Bill:

> The first letter I am writing on this ship goes to you…Tonight is the captain's cocktail. We plan to give him a copy of our book. The ocean has been too rough today to enjoy hiking. Too many folks have heaved and it hasn't been cleaned up yet. Dad has spent most of the day in bed getting caught up on rest.
>
> … I asked for a table for six thinking it would be more interesting: Voila—a Russian lady … born in the States, moved to the U.S.S.R. when she was thirteen. She is looking forward to getting back to her family in Leningrad after a two-month visit to the States.
>
> David Schvailz—a Russian Jew from Lithuania.[2] He is a dentist. Since today is Jewish New Year he has been fasting all day.
>
> Olga…the other member of our table…was hand picked by the Lord…Her husband died two years ago. She is a court secretary and is working presently on the Son of Sam case.[3] Olga is Russian Orthodox…Every morning from now on Olga will be coming to our cabin for Bible studies…I know you'll be praying for her salvation.

A little less than a month later, Cameron wrote from Baku with stunning news—translations of I John had been promised officially in several languages.

DEEPER IN HIM

In August of 1978, on the eve of another departure to Russia, Cameron underwent gall bladder surgery. Just two weeks later—with the doctor's blessing (and his observation that Cameron would rest more aboard ship than otherwise) he and Elaine set sail.

From Hotel Roccia in Moscow, Elaine wrote, 'The temperature is in the 40s and no heat in the city as yet. We trust we will be able to keep well. Dad has his overcoat on in the room and is still cold.'

---

2   Under Nazi rule, 70,000 Lithuanian Jews were escorted out to the forest—never to return.

3   A bizarre serial killer whose apprehension in New York involved 200 detectives.

Three days later the weather continued miserably, but 'His promises are exceedingly precious.'

In October, the two celebrated the sixty-first anniversary of Cameron entering Guatemala, and the ten-year mark of their own entrance into Russia. Then, they hadn't known a soul; now they had many friends, and three translations were shortly promised by officials from the Academy of Science.

In the advent of the new year, she wrote,

> May I share with you my verse for 1979? Colossians 2:7 *'Let your roots grow down into Him. See that you go on growing in the Lord, and become strong and vigorous in the truth you were taught. Let your lives overflow with joy and thanksgiving for all He has done.'* Let's pray these goals for each other and then be able to look back over the days, weeks, and months, and see how He has enabled us to grow deeper in Him, to be stronger and more vigorous, more joyful and thankful.

Over the course of their four-week stay the Townsends visited four republics, then traveled to Germany, for SIL/WBT board meetings. In Washington D.C., they kept an appointment with Ambassador Dobrynin of the Soviet Union.[4] Later, Elaine related what Ambassador Dobrynin told them: 'I was raised in a Christian home and I am one of you; a secret believer. My grandmother had a copy of the Scriptures.'

GORKY ST, MOSCOW

On October 3, 1979, Cameron and Elaine landed again in Moscow. For Cameron, this was the last time he would set foot on Soviet soil. During the next three weeks the couple traveled to Azerbaijan, Georgia, Armenia, Uzbekistan, and Russia, visiting linguists, scientists, and educators. By now, they had observed the socialist education system

---

4 'Dobrynin... his name is associated with a whole epoch in Russian and global foreign policy... There can be no overestimating Anatoly Dobrynin's personal contribution to resolving the Cuban missile crisis and normalizing Soviet-American relations... His outstanding abilities as a negotiator and analyst earned him the respect of both colleagues and opponents, and his goodwill, deep knowledge and wealth of life experience won him the respect and liking of everyone around him.' (Presidential Press and Information Office. http://eng.kremlin.ru/news/17#sel=2:1,4:38 8 April 2010. Accessed July 24, 2014).

over the course of a decade, and they openly recognized helpful aspects, including incredible linguistic abilities from a young age (fifth graders worked in three languages).[5]

While Cam and Elaine received criticism for their positive review of the U.S.S.R., their continued focus stood as an acknowledgment that in eternity the state of men's souls would admit no political ideology. They saw the Russian people as created souls, not as working units determined by man's vain imaginings, and they realized that each man and woman whom they met desperately needed the Life-giving Word. Cameron told of one scene reflecting beautifully the simple and driving passion propelling them on each of their eleven rigorous trips:

> At the Baptist church in Tashkent ... a lady asked us for a Russian Bible. Fortunately we had one, and of course we let her have it. Her joy knew no bounds! After the luncheon she sought us out to say goodbye, at the same time placing an envelope in our hands...we found forty-six dollars in rubles. To her, the Bible was worth all of that; its simple binding didn't matter—it was God's Word in her own language!

After several weeks of travel across the U.S.S.R., Cameron and Elaine arrived once again at Hotel Intourist on Gorky St., Moscow. Elaine's last lines on Russian soil ran, '... Many, many thanks for upholding us these five weeks. It has been far better than we dreamed, just as He promised.'

---

5   One of their most memorable times was spent visiting a kindergarten where 'The teachers were excellent, and the children were well behaved and showed great interest.' It might be that the Townsends missed a deeper insight into the widespread impact of an education system which socialist leaders openly declared to be so integral to the advancement of their agenda. Elaine may not have understood the full ramifications of the strong ideological alliance this created, presented as she was with the best and the brightest Russia had to offer.

Cameron and Elaine with a tea cosy from their travels in Russia, in their home in Waxhaw, North Carolina.

SEASON 4

28. WOUNDS OF LOVE

… not only can we trust the hand that kindles it, but we have the assurance that the fires are lighted not to consume, but to refine; and that when the refining process is completed (no sooner—no later) He brings His people forth as gold. When they think Him least near, He is often nearest. 'When my spirit was overwhelmed, then thou knewest my path.'

L.B. Cowman[1]

The next two years held a trip to Washington D.C. for Cameron's eighth National Prayer Breakfast, and interviews with three ambassadors; the dedication of the Nahuatl (Aztec) New Testament which David and Joy Tuggy had just finished in Mexico; the dedication of a goodwill airplane in California; speaking engagements in Chicago and California (after which the Mayor of Los Angeles declared October 18th 'Cameron Townsend Day'). Then, board meetings back home in Waxhaw, speaking engagements in Atlanta, a flight to Mexico for the eighth Inter-American Indian Congress, visits to ambassadors from Papua New Guinea, Indonesia, Mexico, and Cameroon, a month of rest in Bradenton, FL, Cameron's eighty-fifth birthday, attended by 500 guests; and, two weeks later, the diagnosis of leukemia.

---

1   L.B. Cowman, *Streams in the Desert* (Los Angeles, California: Cowman Publications, 1925), p. 91.

VERY MUCH MORE

As if they had not heard properly, the Townsends flew to Lima three months later for SIL's 35th anniversary celebration, then on to Bogotá; and from there, to Mexico. 'We have been studying Ephesians together and have been greatly blessed,' Elaine wrote. 'How wonderful to meditate on the last part of chapter 3 and His power that is able to do exceedingly abundant above all that we could ever ask or think. I know you and we can think of a lot to ask for but He wants to do so very much more…'

After a Christmas at home in Waxhaw, Cameron was hospitalized in January of 1982 for acute leukemia and anemia. The doctor gave him less than six months to live, and prescribed platelet transfusions every two weeks. On February 3rd he was able to return home and during that month, dozens of friends came to visit this aging pioneer.

FOR LOVE

Elaine had been warned years earlier by people who thought twenty years an unwise difference in age. When the two met, 'they were both young and vibrant and challenging the world,' their daughter commented, 'but people asked her, "What will happen later? What will it be like when Cameron Townsend is ill and bed-ridden and you have to take care of him?"'

Without missing a beat, Elaine had responded, 'Well, some people do it for money—why can't I do it for love?'

'You know, she didn't see it as an obstacle,' her daughter said. 'That was a real strong characteristic of their marriage.'

But Elaine, too, was human, and her patience sometimes wore thin with Cameron's growing limitations. As the hardships grew, Elaine kept everything inside, causing Elainadel to write later,

> We didn't talk about things like that, and I would have benefited from knowing how she saw those things as her weakness and as opportunities to lean more into His grace. I'm sure she cried out for His help in those and other areas and I think it would have helped both of us if we could have talked about them. Part of it was her generation, and I'm sure part of it stemmed from being in leadership and having to be careful about

what she shared, but I wish I had been able to process things with her that would have helped us both to grow in godliness and in closeness.

Many people who spent time around the two during Cameron's last years observed Elaine's persevering respect and care for her husband. 'We both have a lovely memory of Elaine always putting Uncle Cam in the foreground when he would be content to have her tell the Wycliffe stories,' one couple said. 'Often, in a social setting she would say, "Cam, tell them about the time…" and he, in his own inimitable style, would begin to relate a story of God's help, intervention, supply, or direction that would bless us all.'

'She kept Uncle Cam's mind primed like the old hand pump,' described Peter Brouillette. 'She'd pour in that little thought and get him started, then out would come these marvelous things… That, to me, was wisdom, because she was not only blessing the people with the stories, but she was blessing him by keeping him fresh and keeping him going.'

'It wasn't a burden,' one woman recalled, observing Elaine's detailed care of her husband; 'just two people loving each other and doing what needed to be done.'

Then too, Cameron and Elaine only continued to exhibit shocking amounts of flair. 'Uncle Cam *invented* mischief!' as Peter stated it. 'They sat here at our dining room table, and that's where I saw it—that banter back and forth… And let me tell you, *it was not one-sided!* Elaine could hold her own in any sort of verbal sparring, and it was fun to watch.' He continued with a story:

> If you wanted to make Uncle Cam happy, for dessert you would serve him cherry pie. Well, he was making his way through cherry pie at our house one night when Elaine had just turned sixty-five. He was the world's *slowest* eater, so everyone else had long since finished and we were sitting at the table talking, when he leaned over and said in a confidential tone, 'You know, Peter, Elaine just had another birthday. She's much older now. So we're going to have to leave pretty soon so she can get her rest.'

Their devotion to each other was until his last breath, and the love between those two people was something incredible—but it was for real. And that mischief stayed—I mean he was eighty-five, and, *'Elaine needs more rest'!?'* That was the closest he ever came to putting somebody off.

… the rest of us who knew Aunt Elaine knew that Uncle Cam had found a good wife because we also obtained the favor of the Lord because of her presence, her actions, her words; and a little bit of her mischief. I remember sitting at tea one day and she had made a tart that was absolutely awesome… she was still passing them out, and I said, 'Oh that looks *wonderful!* I can hardly wait! The only thing I see wrong is that they're just too small!'

'Oh, here, have another one,' she said. 'Cameron's trying to quit.' So I got two and everybody else got one and Uncle Cam didn't get any! Like I said, he wasn't the only one.

GOING TO COUNT

Elaine's letters over these months reveal her Father's comfort to the hearts of His children. Promises came to mind during sleepless nights, and the Word grew ever more precious. After his stay in the hospital, Cameron received blood transfusions twice a week, and Elaine wrote,

> These are very difficult days and at the same time very blessed as we wait upon Him day by day. The Lord is teaching me many things these days—like what is going to count for eternity. God's great faithfulness and His many promises have been so very precious. I Peter 5:7 reminds me to cast all my care upon Him, because He cares for me. Along with that, I like to think of Psalm 55:22: 'Cast your burden upon the Lord and He shall sustain you.' I am finding this oh so true!

Often, Cameron was heard saying, 'God is *so* good to me!' He told one friend he felt he had one foot in heaven. 'How good he felt when the doctor told him he would soon be there,' Elaine said, adding, 'Despite his illness he hoped that one more trip to the U.S.S.R. would still be possible.' That inveterate man!

INTO THE PRESENCE

On April 4th, Cameron and Elaine celebrated their wedding anniversary and took the time to look back over the goodness of the Lord. A stream of company visited, and they also invited a group to see a videotape of the Golden Jubilee Celebration the previous May.[2]

Returning from some travel, Cameron suffered a relapse and entered the hospital. Those who visited commented on Cameron's 'sweet, loving spirit.'

When Cameron left the hospital for the last time on April 23rd, it was in a far different state than he entered. At six o'clock in the evening, Cal said, 'he quietly slipped out of his weary body and into the presence of Jesus Christ, whom he loved and served.'

SERVE... FINISH... TRANSLATE

Nearly a thousand people from all over the country gathered in Charlotte to bid farewell to Uncle Cam as his body was laid to rest between his beloved México-Cárdenas Museum and the Museum of the Alphabet at the JAARS Center. The time of sharing which followed the graveside service lasted three hours. His gravestone read: 'By love serve one another, finish the task, translate the Scriptures into every language.'

Another entry appeared in her Bible beside the promise of Isaiah 41:10 which had held so true through past turbulent decades— 'Mexico, 1943; Peru, 1946; Colombia, 1963; Russia, 1968; *Widowhood, 1982.*'

---

2   With Billy Graham giving the keynote address, 6,000 people gathered in Ana-
     heim to celebrate the fiftieth anniversary of Uncle Cam's Cakchiquel New Testa-
     ment translation. Cameron was also honored in a 'This is Your Life' presentation.

Elaine during her last visit to Russia (2000).

29. CONTINUING PURSUIT

The most that Christians have in this life is only a foretaste of their future glory. The most outstanding believer is only a child compared with what he shall be in heaven. This is why the greatest degrees of holiness believers reach in this world do not quench their desires after more. On the contrary, they become more eager to press forwards.

Jonathan Edwards[1]

While waiting for a flight to Miami, two Wycliffe missionaries caught sight of Misael Pastrana, the former Colombian president, in the Bogotá airport surrounded by six tall bodyguards, and they introduced themselves. Misael immediately responded with a question: 'How is the widow of Uncle Cam?' Doubtless, many others wondered the same thing.

THE AFTERWARDS

In the weeks after Cameron's death, Elaine grieved deeply as one who had loved deeply. 'You know,' she said, 'when you live with a man so closely, you don't realize what a great guy he is until he's gone; then you wonder, did I really live with him for thirty-six years? What a privilege! What a *privilege!*' But the mission still lived on after Cam's death, and to the day of her own passing, Elaine held it dear. It was this passion, born out of love for her Father, which propelled her through dark paths of testing.

---

1   Jonathan Edwards, *The Experience that Counts*, (Grand Rapids, Michigan: Evangelical Press, 1991), p. 108.

When Cameron died, Elaine's life slowed to a painful pace. She had written of how the silence of the phone on her first trip to Russia was excruciating—but this period threatened to become for her a silence of life. In the four decades since she had set out for Mexico she hadn't looked back, and she had poured out all her resources of energy and talent to augment Cameron in his burgeoning visions. 'If ever there was a First Lady of Bible translation, she was it,' said Jim Akovenko (then president of JAARS).

Now, for all practical purposes, she played an insignificant part in the mission. Residence in the U.S. might have seemed a welcome respite for some, but for this outgoing missionary veteran it felt more like a relegation. Every day of her life had been filled to the brim with high activity. Now, no one truly *needed* her. Several close friends stepped in with an attempt to fill the void as her years grew longer and her strength grew dimmer, but God alone knew His purposes for this season of her life.

LOOKING FORWARD

Months earlier, Elaine's mother had come from Wisconsin to live with her and Cameron, who 'made our home a bit of heaven so much so that my dear mother loved spending time with us.' As she entered singleness once again, Elaine poured the love of her smarting heart into this ninety-year-old woman, and their companionship grew. Virginia Snoddy, a longtime friend of Elaine's, remarked, 'Elaine was so gracious with her mother, and her mother was a sweet, dear lady, very quiet.'

Reading Philippians 3, Elaine wrote in her journal, 'Forgetting the past and looking forward to what lies ahead, I strain to reach the end of the race and receive the prize for which God is calling us up to heaven, because of what Jesus did for us. May I not live in the past but expectantly look to the Lord for the future that He has planned for my life. I know it will be good for He has promised.' Fortified by the healing of Christ's presence, she pressed on. In the midst of discouragement and loneliness, she spoke truth to herself, and amid coming hardship this practice deepened. 'The power of the Word and her relationship with the Lord just came out of her,' said Sue Akovenko.

Many people saw the outgoing side of Elaine that never stopped giving, but few glimpsed the sometimes hurting woman who fought to live life joyfully and to press on through straightened days. She told one friend, Carol, 'I just can't stop crying. Pray for me that I'll be able to get a hold of myself. I just cry all day long.' But she was determined in her gratitude. One verse shared by a friend particularly ministered to her soul: *'Lord, when doubts fill my mind, and my heart is in turmoil, quiet me and give me renewed hope and cheer'* (Ps. 94:19 TLB).

'It was so powerful in her life, and that made it come alive to me!' another friend, Shirley, said. 'I loved her appreciation for the Word. You didn't have to be in her presence but a few minutes and she was leaning forward in an intimate, relational way, saying "Now tell me, what is your favorite Scripture verse?"… It made an indelible impression.'

A GREEN NOTEBOOK

That year after Cameron died, Elaine began writing in a simple, green journal. She documented the paths of her heart, His loving kindness shed all around.

These pages reveal the grip of a desperate heart which refused to let go of promises till it received a blessing.

> Lord, teach me to never be anxious, but to share with you my heart; and thank you so much for your peace as I share with you. Oh, how I thank you for peace of heart and peace of mind! With your peace you have given me your sweet, loving comfort. Even as it says in II Thessalonians 3:5, you are bringing me into an even deeper understanding of the love of God and of the patience that comes from you.

TO KEEP ME ALIVE

'What drove Uncle Cam?' her interviewer asked. 'What drives you?'

'What the Word has done for our own lives and how we couldn't live without it,' Elaine replied without hesitation.

> We want to share it with others, and the Lord has given me many opportunities now. Most of my work is with the fellow Christians who live at Waxhaw, but in Hebrews 6:10 it says, 'God is not unmindful to

forget your work and labor of love that you labor and do ministry.' So He's promised a reward for doing that. But I long to be where the fish are; I am very, very happy about every chance I get to be with people who are not Christians.

People ask, 'Can't we travel with you?' because I'm getting older— well, I'm not getting older, I am older! They want to carry my baggage, but I really prefer to go by myself so I can make contacts with people who don't know the Lord. It's been wonderful, wonderful, wonderful to keep me alive.

When you meditate on His love, and what He's done for us, it changes your life, doesn't it?

30. 'SUCH AN INTERESTING PERSON'

Our love to God will be found to be a delusion, except as its truth is proved in standing the test of daily life with our fellow-men… humility toward men will be the only sufficient proof that our humility before God is real… and there is no love without humility as its root.

Andrew Murray[1]

The Tillets had already explored a number of mission organizations, several of which expressed distress at their large number of children. They trailed along a passel of seven, all sixteen and under, that Monday morning as they toured the JAARS base. At lunchtime, their chattering, lively bunch crowded around a cafeteria table, doubtless turning a few heads. All around them, people were eating, but they knew no one. Suddenly, a woman at the next table said to Kevin, the husband, 'I hear you're going to come serve with us!'

'Well, no ma'am,' he replied. 'I'm in the Navy, and I don't get out for another year, but we're praying and asking the Lord what would be next.'

The woman looked around. 'Are all these children yours?' Their hearts fell. *Oh great, here it comes.* 'Yes ma'am, we've been blessed with seven.'

'I love big families!' she immediately returned. 'Won't you come serve with us?' And with that, Elaine nearly won them over on the spot.

---

1   Andrew Murray, *Humility* (New Kensington, Pennsylvania: Whitaker House, 1982), pp. 43-44.

Upon Kevin's release from the military, the Tillet family trained in Georgia, then returned for another visit to the JAARS center in Georgia. 'She remembered all the kids' first and middle names and had all their birthdays memorized,' said Gale. 'I don't even keep all *my* kids' birthdays straight, and I *had* them!! She was incredible for remembering people and things about them that were significant to her. That was why it was so hard to get her to talk about her story, she always wanted to hear *yours*.'

SHIRLEY

Perhaps the most striking influence on Elaine was her sister, Shirley. Despite the arthritis which crippled her intensely as she grew older, she reached out tirelessly to those around her. 'What a full life she had!' exclaimed Elaine. Shirley's own condition, and her passion to help others likely influenced Elaine's early focus on mentally handicapped children in Chicago.

In more ways than one, Shirley exerted a shaping influence, and Elaine called her 'one of my greatest causes for thanksgiving.' Joy in hearing the true gospel for the first time doubtless bound them more closely than any other earthly tie, and when Elaine left for the mission field, letters indicate that Shirley was her closest companion—the one who understood her best and who perhaps most believed in the crazy venture. Every Sunday she wrote, and she prayed faithfully. Affectionately termed 'pal,' Shirley became a source of great encouragement amidst all the rigors and unknowns of an expatriate life.

When God brought Cameron into Elaine's life, Shirley traveled to Mexico for their wedding and worked hard to learn Spanish so she could communicate with people. 'She loved people so much and she just had to be able to talk to them,' said Elaine.

Short and dark-haired, with beautiful, brown, sparkly eyes, Shirley kept a smile for everybody and had no fear in telling them about her Lord. She wrote to missionaries the world over, attended Wycliffe's yearly missionary conference whenever able, and traveled to Mexico several times. She also partnered in founding the Christian League for the Handicapped. She sent countless numbers of her father's tracts to soldiers overseas, and wrote to encourage many of them. Because her limbs were nearly immobilized, even writing a letter posed a monumental endeavor; but this ministry grew till she corresponded with more than two hundred soldiers. Yet her biggest realm of influence was among the Chinese and Japanese. Not much remains about the nature of this ministry, but at her death it become evident that hundreds had found encouragement—and many, Christ—through her witness.

She saw many doctors, and finally had an operation on her feet that put both her legs in casts and caused her great agony. But it was her tongue that choked her—it fell back while she was sleeping and cut off her air supply. Elaine received word over the radio while she was in Lima. She was by herself at the time, and she vividly remembered for years afterward having to bear the hard news back to the base to children who had a great affection for their aunt.

Chicago didn't have a funeral parlor large enough to hold everyone who came for her service. They lined up for blocks to see her the day she was laid out—more than a thousand people. The undertaker wanted to know, who *was* this young lady? He declared he had never tended a mayor with so many friends.

NOT JUST HAPPENSTANCE

Elaine learned well from her sister, and after her death, dozens of people remembered the warmth of her presence as it entered their lives. 'Elaine never tried to impress or appear to be anything else but herself,' said one woman. 'She had a quiet integrity that you knew was there, with nothing hidden or disguised. She loved to hear details and had an incredible ability for formulating questions to bring out what people wanted to say, leaving them feeling heard and cared about.'

'I remember the first time I walked up the road with you toward the dining room,' said one MK from Colombia. 'You turned to me and said, "Tell me all about yourself in thirty seconds!" I was more impressed with your interest in me than with the time element; but I was later amused by that.'

Even at that age she still allowed herself to be fascinated by the unique human beings around her, and believed, with Lewis, that 'there are no *ordinary* people'; that '[she had] never talked to a mere mortal.'[2] She sought out the places where God was at work; and to those who weren't saved, she showed the love of Christ by pouring out the exuberant tale of the gospel. In the deepest sense, Elaine was outward-focused. 'It sometimes came across as stubborn,' one person said, 'but I think it was a discipline she had, not to talk about herself and to be concentrated on others.'

Doris, a missionary translator, remembered how Elaine walked along the trail on the base at Yarina, and lifted the spirits of everyone she met on the way to the post office or store by her cheery smile and greeting by name, and often a question 'as if he or she were the most interesting person she had met that day.' With Elaine it was never just a curt 'Hi.' She believed that every time you met someone it was a divine appointment.

CULTIVATING CURIOSITY

Elaine cultivated in herself a curiosity about every person she met. On meeting Lloyd Goss, a new recruit, and hearing him speak of his wife, Elaine responded with animation, 'Oh, she sounds like *such an interesting person*—I'd love to meet her!' With her magnificent skill for asking questions, she drew people out and made them feel comfortable around her. Every individual had his or her own story, so she began a ministry of listening.

Witnessing how older people were often set aside, or young people ignored, she freely gave her time, her ear, and her prayers, determining to shine the light of the gospel by making people feel welcome. If she noticed someone in a corner, she considered it her job to approach them, then she called people over to come meet 'her new friend'. She visited older people for games of Scrabble, and cultivated friendships with many young people. Drawings from one child with Down's Syndrome were displayed around her kitchen and dining room, and young visitors always felt her genuine interest in their activities. 'She made you feel that your being there was not just happenstance but for

---

2   C.S. Lewis, *Weight of Glory*, 2nd edition (New York City, New York: Harper-Collins, 1980) p. 91.

a *reason*, and you had something to share that was of importance to her,' said Shirley.

Ready to chat with anyone at the drop of a hat, Elaine's capacity to retain hundreds of people's names years after meeting them was noted universally by those who knew her. It was her stunner, and while Cameron was alive he made great use of it, often whispering in her ear to ask people's names. Nevertheless, it didn't come naturally, as many assumed, and she put time into reviewing. 'She didn't pick and choose, but valued every person,' said Adele, who had worked alongside her during her earliest days in Mexico. 'She had a wonderful gift for that and never wanted anyone to feel on the outside. She was like that from the beginning: it was just Elaine.'

WHAT SHE PLEASED

Someone once asked a receptionist at the JAARS office what *exactly* Elaine Townsend did, and they received the reply: 'Mrs. Townsend does whatever she pleases.' Elaine hosted her own particular table in the JAARS dining room; absolutely anyone was welcome, and the more the merrier. 'Whatever Elaine included in her introduction of you, that was what she wanted you to talk about, and if you were smart you caught on.' said Peter. 'She was leading you to share with others what they needed to know about the organization, and the ultimate goal was what God could do in their lives. It was fascinating to watch her.'

Three times a week, during one period, she hosted luncheons for recruits, pilots, aircraft mechanics, radio men, maintenance men, and all their wives. She also invited groups of young women into her home, then drew them out in a purposeful way, asking their name, a little about them, how they came to Wycliffe, something God was doing in their lives, and lastly, a verse they were memorizing. Women left these gatherings feeling cared for and invested in the ministry, a small part of its heartbeat. One woman, Rebecca recalled how Elaine instructed each woman to get to know the woman to her right, then introduce them to the rest of the room: 'So you had to be really creative and ask the right questions!'

The collective atmosphere of fellowship and belonging that this hospitality created could hardly be measured. To be not only a part of the larger mission of Wycliffe, but also invited personally to the home of the founder's wife and welcomed warmly as a sister, impacted many new missionaries soon to leave with their families for a daunting field.

Strange as it may seem, Elaine carried out hospitality in the homes of others. Once, before Cameron died, Grace recalled coming in to see her mother preparing to take dinner to someone's home. 'Honey, people are intimidated to invite Cameron Townsend into their home,' explained Elaine, 'but we've decided that it's important for us to get to know these people.' Instead of sitting at home pitying themselves, they called and invited themselves over to homes, offering to bring dinner.

As her health declined, Elaine freely accepted the help of others in tackling whatever overstretched her. 'I *loved* her house. It was bright, cheery, comfortable, peaceful. It felt like home. She had small artifacts from various countries on the shelves in the living room that were always fun to dust and to rearrange,' wrote one woman who often came to help her. Though she was often particular, Elaine knew well the art of delegating, and she presented everything in a way that made people feel that it was *their* idea, and an honor to do it.

'She had a way of acknowledging any kindness done to her,' said one. But she made sure that even the young teenage girls who came to clean or do odd jobs for her sat down at some point for a cup of tea. Then she would lean across, look them in the eye, and ask for their favorite Bible verse, or speak a word of encouragement. 'It was almost like she did not want to waste a single conversation—it should be valuable,' recalled another woman.

A sense of humor didn't fail in good purpose. While living in the South, the Townsends held a prayer meeting where an old man found Elaine pulling his beard instead of shaking his hand upon his departure. Her sense of hilarity endeared her to him and his family faithfully supported the Townsends for years.

CALVARY LOVE

In Colombia, Elaine had once taken a group of missionary wives into town, and knowing they would be shocked by the poverty and filth around them, she sought an opportunity to reorient their perspective. Walking along in the middle of a slum, she caught sight of a row of flowers planted outside one of the houses. When a woman emerged from the doorway, Elaine exclaimed, 'Any woman who loves flowers is a friend of mine!' quickly easing any awkwardness. One of her children later wrote,

> I think one of the gifts my Mom and Dad both gave us kids was being comfortable with everyone, regardless of age or situation. We didn't feel any difference. If you were the garbage collector or the president of a country—there was no distinction of class. Also, because Dad was fifty when I was born, there was no distinction between younger people and older people. Both my parents were like that—they valued the individual. It wasn't something we were taught, it was just osmosis, something we all watched.

One of Elaine's first letters from the mission field had included a quote by Amy Carmichael, 'If I belittle those whom I am called to serve, talk of their weak points in contrast, perhaps, with what I think of as my strong points; if I adopt a superior attitude, forgetting "Who made thee to differ? And what hast thou that thou hast not received?" Then I know nothing of Calvary love.'

Elaine lacked the close friendships she might have desired, since her position restricted open sharing and close connection. Because of Cameron's stature and the prominence of Wycliffe she often felt she could not get truly close to anyone or share the challenges of the ministry, and at times she felt quite alone. Of course, there were many 'friends,' but few true friends who held real through the decades and accompanying trials.

After Cameron died, even this diminished. Seated among a gathering of chattering ladies once, she remained quiet, and afterwards her daughter asked why she didn't join in—'They didn't ask,' was the reply.

Near the end of Elaine's life a falling out occurred between her and a close friend—a rift which failed to heal. She prayed and strove toward restoration but fellowship was never renewed. Only her Father saw the deep grief her heart weathered during this time, and even those near her remained ignorant of this wound.

Elaine felt the isolation deeply but she never turned to self-pity, though depression occasionally influenced her outlook. She poured her longings into greater energy in serving others, and they drove her to deepen her dependence on her Lord and her desire for His presence. And this was the way of the cross—to love, not necessarily to be loved back. Nothing was guaranteed except that hurt would come. But so would the crown.

31. 'NOT JUST SOMEHOW, BUT TRIUMPHANTLY'

I don't think older Christians can ever fully know what an important role they play in the affirmation of younger believers. When you're just a youth, it means so much to have someone who's farther along the road say to you, 'I see something in you, and I want you to be encouraged in it.'

Ravi Zacharias[1]

Back in the 1990s, drivers coming down a certain stretch of road near Waxhaw, North Carolina, would have seen an older woman walking from her home to the JAARS headquarters. And she likely would have refused a ride—she had work to do! People could have set their clocks by this routine, but what most did not know was how many people she lifted up before the throne during those walks; how they themselves were prayed for as they sped past and waved at Elaine Townsend.

HER YESTERDAYS

At the end of her life, Elaine gazed back at past mercies to renew belief in future grace—the grace which had first captured her energies and her love. She ran her aching heart back to the character of this God for solace, remembering His character. In her journal, she listed past events: some hard, some joyful, but each one attributed to the care of Him who loved her and purposed to refine her into His likeness. The words welled up to fill a worn heart: 'How I thank you Lord Jesus for the day You showed me that salvation is not by works but by believing in Your work.'

---

1   Ravi Zacharias, *Walking from East to West*, p. 149.

When asked once what stood out to her as the biggest cause for gratitude in her life, Elaine laughed.

> Most thankful for? The night I said *Yes!* I'll never forget—my arm was all just goose pimples and I wasn't going to leave that bathroom until I knew what He wanted me to do…You never know what will happen when you say, 'Yes, Lord! Where you lead me, I will follow'; but I've never, ever heard a missionary say, 'Oh, I wish I hadn't followed the Lord. I made a big mistake.' To the contrary! No matter now sick they are and no matter what they've gone through, they're happy, happy, happy. And that's what we crave, isn't it? Joy, hope, and peace.

Ten years before her mother's death, Elaine had written her, '… it was encouraging news that life begins at eighty! It does get better and better as we walk together with Him, claiming His wonderful promises day by day.' Now Elaine herself approached eighty, and the golden skins of heady-scented fruit began to appear under the leaves of her tree.

When asked what they saw of Elaine's relationship with the Lord, one close friend replied, 'That is actually a *bad* question. "Would it ever be possible to see Elaine Townsend and *not* see her relationship with the Lord?" would be more realistic. Because she lived it—it oozed out of her and she couldn't help it. She was the cup that was full to the brim and running over and all the time.'

Katie, the Tillets' daughter, who ministered to Elaine as she aged, explained, 'Elaine fundamentally identified herself as Christ's. She seemed to divide her life into two portions: "pre-Christ" and "with Christ." All that seemed to matter to her, as she looked back over her life and gave us glimpses into her memory, was that Christ had redeemed her and marked her as His own. This was demonstrated in how she lived, right up until her final illness… What mattered was the reality of her relationship with Christ and its eternal significance.'
In the margin next to Isaiah 41:10, Elaine wrote, *'All this way the Lord has led me. To Him be the glory.'*

A WELLSPRING

From the resources of prayer and time in the Word she brought forth deep springs of counsel. 'She was a lady Solomon—a woman of wisdom,' Shirley said of her. She had ready responses to what others shared: an insight into Scripture, a lesson God was teaching her. She rarely expressed her own struggles, though they were apparent to a few. 'It wasn't that she dwelt on it,' said Shirley, 'but she dwelt on the fact that even in the midst of it God was there, bringing peace and comfort.' Walking with Christ gave her the fragrance to touch others' lives.

Having something worth saying wasn't an accident, or a personality trait. No, it came from diligent application of the Word, in the Spirit. 'She never hesitated to share personal things from her own life to encourage me as a young mother,' one woman remembered.

Her grand-daughter, Heather, wrote,

Grandma's desire to keep growing and her humility in sharing ways that God was convicting her made quite an impression on me. Whether having an 'attitude of gratitude' or something else, it was her heart's desire to finish well and to be sensitive to God's continuing work in her own life. She loved to encourage others in the same way. As a bride, she encouraged me to ask guests to share their testimonies and so to learn from and to encourage them.

Katie recalled visiting Elaine on days she knew were a particular struggle, yet coming away feeling that she herself was the one blessed. In her last season of life, Elaine developed a special love for young women just beginning the rest of their lives. Esther, a young African woman from Cameroon, once came to visit Elaine, only to be told at the door that she was not taking visitors that evening. Elaine came up behind the person and said, 'Oh, I'll see *her!*' Esther recalled later:

Her presence was overwhelmingly a blessing, I wanted to be in her close proximity. Ten or fifteen minutes felt like forever with God's presence. She was dying graciously but she was the one who lifted me up, reminding me of God's limitless power—that we serve a God who is amazingly awesome… and we can't put Him in a box. Nothing stopped her from oozing God…

She always made you feel like you were so important, because she would stop everything for you. She would visit with you like she was praying and ushering in the presence of God with you. She didn't say that much. She looked you in the eyes: 'How are you doing? How is it with you?' When you really love someone you are compelled to battle with them, walk with them, move them…

Even the maintenance men coming to her nursing-home apartment did not escape untouched. Three men more comfortable with a hammer and a screwdriver were unabashedly asked to say a verse for Elaine… well, that was fine. Then she asked to hear a hymn. One recalled, 'I'm not sure if she was more satisfied with our singing or with the fact that she was successful in *getting* us to sing!'

NOT JUST SOMEHOW

Elaine saw the life of faith as an exciting one: prayers would be answered, and that which was bad turned into good for His purposes. 'He *knows us,*' she said. 'He's the best, the *good* Shepherd; "No good thing will He withhold from those who walk uprightly". When afflictions come, it's not because He's punishing, but because He loves. If you can remember that, it helps a whole lot.'

Amid her own sleepless nights, she looked for every opportunity to share the promises that had sustained her. Just before the stroke that encumbered her speech, she recalled the promise that He who had begun a work in her would complete it, and the verse, *'Cast not away your confidence which has great recompense of reward.'*

Elaine sought out missionary women and young recruits, giving them timely advice. When asked what she would say to young people, Elaine replied without hesitation,

Trust the Lord to take care of you… I've been with people who've gone to the top and they're not happy. I've been with Indians who have nothing but Christ, and they're so very happy. Get your perspective right and *He* will guide you; He's certainly faithful. Listen carefully to what He's telling you, but take the next step, and the next step.

...The joy of the Lord certainly is our strength. We want to be enthusiastic Christians, don't we? *Not just somehow, but triumphantly.*

CHILDREN'S CHILDREN

By the time of her passing, Elaine had seen twenty-one of her grandchildren, and fourteen great grandchildren, ranged from babies to young adults. She took particular joy in teaching them verses and in learning alongside them.

'She made everything fun,' said one, and several expressed a deep desire to be like Grandma Elaine. She taught them how to whistle from the theme song in Andy Griffith, and there were rumors of tap dancing in 'the chair that moved up and down.' Always one to take risks, she even taught a very young grand-daughter to do her makeup. Following Cameron's habit, she made sure that Scripture was read and discussed during every mealtime. People with a birthday on any particular day could be sure of prayer.

One grand-daughter, Heidi, recalled getting off the bus every day and marching straight to 'Grandma's breakfast nook' where tea was inevitably prepared in Elaine's exquisite blue-painted teacups. It was during this time that Cameron died, and Heidi wrote, 'I remember the day well, as, after jubilantly getting off the bus, I was shocked to discover that our sacred tea time had been disrupted. There were strangers in the kitchen and Grandma was crying. I remember thinking, "Grandpa is with Jesus, now and I don't see how that justifies disrupting my Grandma time!"'

Her oldest grandson, Chris, who passed through a difficult period of life, warmly remembered her: 'She showed a genuine love for me— for who I *was*. She showed that love to everyone and looked past the outward appearance.'

'NOT HALF BAD'

Elaine never stopped stepping into the unknown, and she didn't hesitate to drive with fifteen-year-old grand-daughter, Faith, who had just received her permit. Not that driving with Elaine herself was a safe endeavor, when it came down to it. There was the time she careened at un-grandma-like speeds down a street headed straight for a garbage truck until someone pointed it out to her. Swerving, she narrowly missed it, but adamantly insisted it had no right to be there, and later admitted that it hadn't occurred to her to slow down or move since she knew she was in the right lane. 'Hers was like the driving of Jehu!' recalled onlookers at the base.

Another day, while running an errand with her mother, Del noticed a group of children crossing the road. Elaine, however, drew rapidly nearer, and finally Del alerted Elaine, who responded, 'Oh, thank you so much for telling me! I didn't see them!' Del suggested that it might be time for Elaine to give up driving, but this only made her indignant: 'Oh, no, no, no! I never come by here at this time of day!' she retorted.

Elainadel remembered one trip to the States from Mexico when her mother had reached 100 miles per hour, 'but she later felt convicted of breaking the law and asked God to forgive her.' When it finally became necessary for Elaine to stop driving, her car sat in the driveway for a time, and she confided to a friend, 'It is such a great temptation to get in that car and drive. I just can't have it here.'

'Mom loved speed and numbers,' said one daughter. 'Getting the dishes clean when you washed them was irrelevant. Getting them done fast *was!*'

Her grand-daughter Heather agreed. 'Details were never her strong suit. Editing notes was a waste of precious time. What mattered was getting the job done. We always knew our cards were truly typed by her because of all the typos.' Even letters to important dignitaries sometimes lacked the proper decorum of perfection, but when her children bought her a special typewriter which could erase letters, they found the whiteout tape never wore out: Elaine kept herself in too much of a hurry to utilize it properly. She looked at everything from the standpoint of productivity. 'I can type almost as fast as I can talk, so I'd hate to slow me down with a secretary!' she commented once.

'Grandma loved being communications central for her family,' said another of her grandchildren. 'In the days when long-distance phone calls were an extra expense, she faithfully called us in Mexico on a weekly basis, learned how we were doing, and shared any news she had gathered from the rest of the family over the week.'

One person put it aptly—'Even though her tent was folding, she was still Elaine.'

MILE A MINUTE

Always one to count, Elaine faithfully logged three to five miles a day between her house and the JAARS center. She walked rain or shine, often taking the uphill track for an extra challenge. When she approached eighty, Jim Akovenko became afraid she would fall, and put in 'Elaine's sidewalk' for her to go to lunch. Once, someone picked her up at the furthest terminal of the Atlanta airport and she insisted on walking the entire way to the car rather than taking the train, so she could get her exercise for the day.

'Then somebody gave Mom an electrical wheelchair and *oh my goodness!*' exclaimed Grace. 'We all had a heart attack because Mom was very dangerous behind the wheel—I mean very dangerous. We thought, *Who's she going to kill between the house and JAARS?!* Fortunately, she could never get the hang of the steering mechanism so she never used it; then we had the opportunity to give it to a lady who needed it really badly.'

Once safely arrived at the cafeteria, 'she had no qualms at all about reaching down in her purse for her bib,' said one friend, then quickly corrected herself—'*excuse* me! *Garment protector!* Yes, it had a name, and she made sure we called it that!'

After lunch, Elaine left the dining hall and walked home for her nap. 'We all knew what hours we could call Mom, and boy, you did not call her at naptime!' said Grace. 'But then we didn't have a choice—she took the phone off the hook.'

Throughout her life, Elaine remained direct and to the point. Once asked about something she had learned about herself, she responded, 'I learned that I wish I could talk slower. But it's impossible!'

Uncle Cal told about a time he drove Elaine somewhere in his car, as he often did: 'She was talking—she talked fast, and I mean *fast*. Others will agree that Elaine talked so fast that anyone with a hearing problem (or a non-English speaker) would have big problems. This was also a time when my hearing was giving me trouble, so as we drove along I had to ask her to repeat several times.' Tempers frayed, but Elaine continued to rattle off quickly, as was her manner. Again, Cal asked her to repeat.

'You need to get a hearing aid!' she snapped back, and he retorted, 'Elaine! It's not my fault—you just talk too fast!!'

'All right then, you do the talking!!' she returned, and silence ruled for the remainder of the drive.

'I later apologized,' said Cal. 'She continued talking at her normal, fast speed and we returned to normal terms. It's true that she and I locked horns several times,' admitted this dedicated friend of several decades, 'but we always straightened it out just fine.'

On another occasion, one of the Townsend girls felt the need to apologize to Uncle Cal for her mother's uncanny vigor, but he affectionately reassured her: 'Even at her worst your mother is not half bad!'

32. 'A GRAND RECRUITER AND A GRAND FRIEND'

'I did not choose. It was God's choice for me.' How can a man 'choose' a 'calling'? If a man is called *he* does not choose. It is the One who calls who does the choosing... It is God's right to choose. It is simply ours to ascertain and obey. For next in its eternal moment to the salvation of a soul is the guidance of the life of a child of God. And God claims both as His supreme prerogative.

Mrs. Cowman on Charles Cowman[1]

A friend recently wrote me saying that a particular language community didn't have a word for 'love.' The team working there eventually discovered that when visitors arrived in the village, the local community would host them by extending the folds of their tents, making them bigger, thereby making room to fit the visitors inside the tents. Upon further research, the team discovered that this community's concept for love is best expressed by this word picture: extending the heart to someone else... literally making it big enough to fit them in.

Extending the heart to welcome someone expresses very well what Elaine Townsend does when she meets someone. When she's first introduced to you, she'll almost always say, 'Tell me something about yourself so that I can remember you.' And she does! This has become more important as her eyesight has failed. The next time she 'sees' you, she'll ask about what you told her. No one extends their heart better, or more freely, than Elaine does. She does it in her home, at her table

---

1   Lettie B. Cowman, *Charles E. Cowman: Missionary – Warrior,* 93.

at JAARS over lunch, with visiting dignitaries, and now… from the retirement home.

KEEPER OF THE FLAME

Another epoch of Elaine's life had begun, but her zeal in encouraging others and in the spread of the gospel countermanded any softening of her vision. 'She was focused like a laser beam, reaching the unreached,' said Shirley. 'She didn't want to be at ease in Zion, so to speak; she wanted to keep on getting the Word out, and all the time she was encouraging believers, nurturing them, spurring them on to good works for the Lord.'

Right before his death, Elaine had asked Cameron what he thought she should do after he had gone, and he encouraged her to continue staying in touch with people the world over. One of her most apt descriptors termed her 'the tireless keeper of the flame for her late husband's vision, championing the cause of those who speak minority languages, sharing her beloved husband Cam's dream of seeing the Bible translated into every language, no matter how small the number of speakers.'

Instead of turning inward like so many aging people, she saw each encounter as a distinct appointment from her Father: an opportunity to demonstrate *His* sacrificial love. In her hallway she mounted three large corkboards with dozens of photos—all the people for whom she prayed. Even as she downshifted, she knew how much could still be accomplished by prayer, fellowship and letters.

Many would have considered Elaine's zeal a bit ambitious for her age, but she held a different perspective. 'She wanted to keep people engaged and enjoying each other and their service together,' recalled one woman. 'She was always one for adventure!'

For years before his death, Elaine had driven Cameron to the airport on the JAARS base for his flights, but she herself had never flown from that field. Finally, at age eighty-four, helped by Jim Akovenko, she climbed up the steps to the airplane for her first flight out of Townsend Field. Similarly, the second Bible dedication she ever attended, after sixty-two years of work with Wycliffe, was the Gullah translation for the southern blacks of the U.S.[2]

In this way, her days filled with worthwhile activities, and on a card in her journal she wrote out goals for future ministry, which included training new members, encouraging MKs at college in the States, recruiting new workers, making government contacts with women, ministering to singles and widows, and spending time with younger children encouraging them to memorize the Word. At the head of this list, in a sort of summary, she wrote, 'to be an encourager of the brethren' (Heb. 10:25).

RECRUITER

Elaine, of course, assumed that everyone else saw so-called 'retirement' as the biggest opportunity of a lifetime; she quickly enlisted Marlene and her husband, a retired couple with a sailing hobby, to sail to the Solomon Islands and serve there with their boat. It was absolutely the most exciting thing to her; she told them all about the story of the plane crash and the beginning of JAARS, and soon she was calling this couple 'the pioneers.' Elaine wasn't too far wrong—boats were the next avenue of development to reach much of the 10/40 window.

Tom Hopkins had served for thirty years in the Air Force and found himself stationed at the Pentagon when Wycliffe dedicated the 200th translation of the New Testament in the Senate Office Building. After the ceremony, Elaine came right up to him: 'Tom, I understand you're retiring from the Air Force tomorrow.'

'Yes Ma'am.'

'Well, *Monday morning* you report for work with Wycliffe Bible Translators!'

One didn't say no to Elaine. Tom gave her a snappy salute and drove to the Wycliffe office in Falls Church, Virginia. 'She was so single-minded she would recruit anyone from anything!' said his wife, Ann. 'She was like Uncle Cam.'

'We often felt like she saw something in each of us that was worth cultivating or "fanning into flame,"' another added.

---

2   The first was the Tetelcingo NT in January of 1980.

WORLD TRAVELING AGAIN

Along with a traveling companion, Elaine set out once again on her third trip around the world. For three months, she and Peggy Richards visited Wycliffe bases to encourage field workers. 'She was a wonderful traveler!' said Peggy. 'She'd find something fun to do everywhere.'

Jim and Sue Akovenko, who also traveled with Elaine, told the story of one visit to a remote village in Indonesia where Elaine decided she would go for a walk. 'There was a balance, I learned later,' said Jim, 'between pushing and giving up: in dialogue with her, you were always in a competition. But for some reason I let her go on a walk by herself.' For a long time Elaine did not return. A policeman finally found her where she had fallen and helped her back. 'It was all okay in her mind,' recalled Jim. 'She was always ready to explore, to be a pioneer wherever she was.'

She gathered with 350 Peruvians in Lima, to celebrate fifty years since she and Cameron had entered the country. 'When I walked into my former kitchen, a lovely Peruvian gave me a warm embrace… She was so happy to tell me that when she was just twelve years old I had led her to the Lord there in my home. She is now the mother of six and all of the children are following the Lord as well. You can be sure that made my day.'

But for Elaine, the most deeply affecting part of the visit took place out in a remote area near the Yarina base. After Elaine's absence of more than thirty years, and now at more than a hundred years old, she sat perched on board slats in the middle of the jungle next to a radio given her by one of the missionaries: Doña Marta still lived.

Elaine recounted the reunion with her precious friend: 'She had a gauze strip across her nose—it was all eaten away—but this hadn't dampened her joy in the Lord. She almost died a few weeks ago but He raised her up.' The two women reminisced about Marta's salvation, and she told Elaine that she had prayed for her every day. They recited her favorite passages, and recalled the hymns they used to sing together; she told Elaine she most loved 'Are You Weary, Are You Heavy Laden, Tell it to Jesus'. 'Then we offered our final prayer together before she enters the joy of the Lord. You can be sure I was moved to tears...' Elaine wrote.

Back in Waxhaw, Elaine was hosting a women's luncheon when the phone rang. After a hundred and five years of life, Doña Marta had passed into her reward.

THE NEW RUSSIA

In 2000, Wycliffe Russia prepared to dedicate a new office in St Petersburg. Jim and Sue offered themselves as her traveling companions; and at eighty-five, Elaine returned to that land where she had traveled and witnessed over a span of eleven years.

For nine days, several Russian members of Wycliffe drove them around to churches, schools, and other familiar places. Unfortunately, Slava's English wasn't as good as Bolevi's, so Elaine became the schoolmaster, taking every opportunity to instruct him. 'She was *tough!*' remembered Jim. 'Of course, with five other English speakers in the car, Slava was on the spot, but he was fine, and he went through the drills with her—or, rather, *she* was making *him* drill—she was in charge of the lesson.'

Elaine once asked their chauffeur how women her age managed the high steps on every vehicle. 'Oh, they never even try!' came the response. 'They either walk or stay home.'

During their travels, Elaine spoke at a new Christian university, schools, and to the large Baptist congregation in a town whose fellowship she remembered so well. One of their stops included a hotel where she and Cameron had lived. 'Oh, it's so different. I hardly recognize the place!' she exclaimed. That night, Elaine cried herself to sleep, remembering her time with Cameron.

FACING THE MEN

April 1st dawned: the big day. As she struggled with her presentation, Elaine felt the Lord leading her to abandon the speaking notes she had prepared. What He laid on her heart that day, as she stood before the newly-formed board of Wycliffe Russia, was the vibrant tale of God's faithfulness in direction and provision for Wycliffe during its infancy.

What Elaine didn't know was how closely the Depression era straits faced by her husband and his friends mirrored the situation of the Russian missionaries before her. They had become discouraged by adverse circumstances that handicapped their branch, and her message carried tremendous impact. 'She had no idea, going into the scenario, what the picture was—none of us did,' said Jim. 'But she was very intuitive about interacting at a leadership level because she had been at the leadership level herself. So much of the development of Wycliffe happened around the dining room table as she discussed plans with Cameron.'

So she faced a group of Russian men in a country where women were the babushkas that carried the firewood, and few would have taken that initiative—to face a challenge and stand to witness of God's faithfulness. She radiated a confidence that what she said was the most important thing they needed to hear, and exhorted them in an authoritative way rather than merely sympathizing and offering prayer. 'She came in and wowed them,' said Jim. 'They were encouraged to press forward. And the Lord *did* provide.'

FOREMOST ENQUIRER

In 1992, after several surgeries, Elaine was forced to give up extensive trips. 'Which is not to say she has taken to a rocking chair,' ran one JAARS newsletter.

But even as traveling doors closed, Elaine remained active, and kept up on news. 'It is a joy to see how the Lord is working in our midst,' she said. She stayed current with all changes in Wycliffe, and loved nothing more than learning tidbits of news which even Jim, the president of JAARS, had not yet heard, exclaiming, *'I gotcha!'* 'She wanted to be in the know,' said Jim, 'and I'm sure she spent a lot of time praying about things.'

Elaine faithfully attended board meetings, and if anything needed clarification, she raised her hand at the end and explained or gave more history, proportional to what was needed. When people gave reports on their work, Elaine inquired further. It became a kind of a joke in the community, and some drew a good-natured comparison to Helen

Thomas (the premier reporter in the White House press room to whom everyone deferred in honor to her tenure, and who always came with the first enquiry).

'I knew Elaine would have the first question,' said Jim, 'so I would finish, then look at Elaine. She was a lady of questions. I'd always say to her, "the thing that has stumped me all these years is that there's always one question in every encounter I have with you that I can't answer. You think of something I haven't thought of and I have to find the answer and get back to you." She had a discerning mind that went beyond the mundane.' Slowly, people began to understand what an integral role she had played in the development of Wycliffe all along.

'I SAID YES!'

People asked Elaine if she didn't get tired sometimes. 'Of course I do!' she responded. 'But I'd get tired sitting in a rocking chair too, so I might as well be out doing what the Lord has asked me to do! I said *yes* to the Lord, and I have no regrets! At eighty-seven, life is still exciting, and I look forward to every day. I enjoy my work so much. I love to write letters. I love to telephone. I love to travel. I love to talk with people. I love to entertain. It doesn't seem like work anymore. It's just pure joy.'

'Elaine lived for that God,' said one of her friends. '… if she told a story, the Hero was God: "This is what *He* did! The plane went down, and my feet are crippled… still. But my baby didn't die, and because of that we have our own airplanes now."'

To younger men and women, Elaine said, 'It's about a commitment, so don't just say, "Well, I'll go and try it for six months." Go, and be willing to stay! Make it a life project. We did that fifty years ago, and a lot of us are still going strong. I was talking to some of our old timers like Ben Elson, and they said that none of them are doing today what they started out to do. So if people come in thinking "I'm going to only do this specific thing," they're not very useable. We certainly have to be available for anything the Lord wants us to do.'

Once, Elaine was asked if she had any regrets. In her winning, transparent style she answered, 'No. Isn't that wonderful? It would be awful to come this close to death and regret what you've done. No, I don't have any regrets… Well, I could have been more cheerful!'

'I think of that verse in Timothy,' she continued, 'where Paul says, "It is required of a steward that a man be found faithful"—not successful, not popular, but *faithful*. I shared that one time when I was speaking over in Indonesia, and a printer there was about to quit, but he told his wife, "Well, if I can't be successful, I can be faithful." Today, he's gone on to be a printer in other countries. You never know how the Lord is going to use one little sentence of what you're sharing. *"Faithful is He who calls you, who also will do it."* [3]

---

3   Philippians 1:6.

33. GLIMPSES OF THE PORT

If none of God's saints were poor and tried, we should not know half so well the consolations of divine grace... God's grace is illustrated and magnified in the poverty and trials of believers.... If then, yours be a much tried path, rejoice in it, because you will the better show forth the all-sufficient grace of God.

Charles Spurgeon[1]

The latter years of Elaine's life held great trial—the last blows of the Refiner, as it were. Elaine was described as 'a vivid person who could always speak articulately' but everything changed after a severe stroke. 'She was bound: bound in a body that didn't respond,' said Shirley.

SIGHT REMOVED

Of all the hardships Elaine faced, perhaps the hardest for her to bear was losing her sight. 'That's when I started seeing a change in Mom,' said Grace. 'The Word was her life, and to not be able to read it crushed her. She got the Bible on tape, but she struggled with that. It was studying the Word that was so important to Mom; not just hearing the Word, but *studying* it. Even when she was completely bedridden in the hospital she asked people to read Scripture to her—she hungered for the Word to her last days on earth. And that's when I saw Mom lose spirit. It was hard to see this vibrant lady start drowning. She had so much to give everyone, but she couldn't talk. The theme of her later life was *giving up*: giving up her gifts, her dreams.'

---

1   Charles Spurgeon, *Morning and Evening*, March 4.

Many observed changes in her disposition around this time, commenting that she did not seem like the same woman they had known in past years. Some saw the change as significant enough to suggest age-related chemical change in her brain, though heavy sorrows also came to cloud her heart, among them, separation from one of her closest friends. 'She carried it with grace and with a humble heart—a *very* humble heart; a crushed heart, but there again, she said *"Here I am. God, I'm Yours."* Her offering of sacrifice in praise was the fragrance of Christ. And I saw that in her,' testified one friend.

The constriction of her emotions, which perhaps began merely as self-discipline, often grew in the darkening days. She seemed to be shut in by circumstances, stifled by pain and hurt. Elaine herself admitted, 'Discouragement—it comes…' Yet she held on, trusting the Father's hand which orchestrated every event, knowing her frame. He alone knew the troubles that stormed her heart, and He was not insensible.

PLENTY OF CHAIRS

Through her pain, she still retained a bit of her original spark. 'Mom was a speed demon!' said Grace. 'At the grocery store, she took off in her wheelchair and we'd just cover our eyes. When we attended the dedication of the Orlando building, Mom and an old-time friend, Bill Bright, happened to be at opposite sides of the building in their wheelchairs. She whispered emphatically to me that she wanted to talk with him after the ceremony was over. "Grace," she kept saying, "Grace, be ready! Be ready, Grace!" Barely had the closing *"Amen"* left the speaker's mouth and we were off, with Mom clearing space out ahead of us with her cane. We got to Bill Bright all right and they had a nice little chat.'

Elainadel told how Elaine worked hard to walk after her stroke, and faithfully exercised till she left earth: 'I'd walk into the nursing home and she'd be raising her arms and legs on the side she was able… They did take away her privileges of driving an electric scooter after one episode—the very first time she drove it. She was so excited that she could drive again, but she ran into the wall and marked it up.'

Several of those who cared for Elaine attempted to spare her from the pernicious influence of sugar, but when one of her children came to visit, she beckoned them over, 'Please, go find me a Milky Way!'

'Where are they, Mom?'

'They're under my underwear,' she replied in a whisper.

ALL THE WORLD

After a second stroke, an aura of peace and joy returned once again. The Refiner was also her Father, and as the days darkened, He granted His daughter a deeper longing for heaven. She yearned for His presence, writing, 'Thank you, Jesus, that my homeland is in heaven where You are; I'm looking forward to Your return—oh, so much!'

Elaine spoke to the staying power of the gospel:

> I've learned that because of affliction you get to see 'It's good for me that I've been afflicted that I might learn Your statutes.' So don't refuse the affliction. Don't think *Poor me. Why is He doing this to me?* But thank Him that He sees you're so valuable that He's going to teach you another lesson. I'm sure I haven't learned all the lessons by any means, but I want to be learning. And where I live there's such a wonderful opportunity to share with fellow believers.

To this perpetual hostess, any visitor presented the opportunity to provide hospitality in whatever way she was able, if only a bright smile and a warm greeting from her hospital bed. 'Praise the Lord for wheelchairs, and for friends to push them!' Elaine said once. As her sight faded, and with it her ability to recognize the hundreds of people whose names she knew, a remarkable voice recognition took its place. Sue remembered, 'Her center vision was bad, so if people approached from her side she could see them and knew their name, but if they came face on, she relied on voice recognition. She could remember so many people's names just from the tone of their voice!'

Sue readied Elaine for church and accompanied her each Sunday. She recalled, 'She needed three things before she was ready to go: she had to have her offering, her Bible (even though she couldn't read), and her hair fixed. What a lady! She loved to look nice and be up with the styles—she wanted to present. She was very winsome, very today. Not that this clouded her focus, but it supplemented and augmented it.'

Witnessing became a great concern to Elaine when she entered a nursing home. 'She saw it as a challenge to live in a Christian community—because then, how do you get out of it to reach the lost?' She sent emails after she had her stroke, saying she was in a nursing home and she was so excited because she was going to witness to people there.

As a sort of symbol of her life, God brought nurses of four different nationalities to minster to her needs. A friend, Peter, who had previously traveled to Ghana came to visit, and while he stood by Elaine's bed, a Ghanaian nurse walked through the door. Peter asked, 'I wonder if you would recognize this?' and began a song, stamping his feet as he did so.

The face of that nurse lit up in a heartbeat, his face came alive, and he joined Peter in singing 'God, in Christ Jesus, is *stamping* on the head of the Enemy.'

When they finished, the nurse exclaimed, 'I have not heard my language since I left Africa!' As he described this moment later, Peter said, 'I knew this was between the man from Ghana and Aunt Elaine—I just happened to get to see it. And that told me, not how much Elaine Townsend loved Him, *but how much God loved Elaine Townsend.'*

She passed to glory a few days later, on July 14, 2007, but that song was one of the last things she witnessed on earth. Those who observed saw the joy on her face as she realized anew the victory already won and the glory that awaited.

34. AFTER THE LAST MISSION

He who is with us now to call us, will be ever present with us, in all whereto He calleth us. And in His purpose and love, every degree of grace and glory, lies wrapped up in His next call. All eternity of bliss and the love of God will, through His grace…accompanying, following, lie in one strong, earnest, undivided, giving of thy whole self to God, to do in thee, through thee, with thee, His gracious, loving will.

Edward Pusey[1]

What encapsulates a story like Elaine's—wild and improbable because *true?* In the wake of her life lie hundreds, if not thousands of lives changed—to the corners of the globe. Yet, incongruous to our minds, the catalyst of such widespread change was her simple, faithful obedience. The extraordinary span of her life was measured not in awards received or in countries visited, nor even in the sheer number of people taught or guests housed. All these she could have gained in the way of the world. But the grace of the cross awakened freedom like light showered forth in a room—enlivening, illuminating color, depth, and meaning which radically altered the course and effect of her life.

She enacted much change, yet it came through mundane living, challenging relationships, inconvenient hospitality, physical struggle—a daily doing of the next thing. This, she believed, was what God had called her to. Her legacy is embedded deeply in the lives of people, and the result has remained for generations.

---

1   Edward Pusey, Public Domain

The testimony of Nard, an Isnag man from the Philippines, stands as one representative among a host:

> Aunt Elaine Townsend was well known around the world, and even to the deepest jungles, as she and Uncle Cam took His Word to the ends of the earth. That's the reason I am here—a ripple effect, fruit of their labor like it says in 2 Corinthians 3:3, 'You show that you are a letter from Christ, the result of our ministry, written not with ink but with the Spirit of the living God, not on tablets of stone but on tablets of human hearts.'
>
> I also think of 2 Corinthians 2:15 when I think of Aunt Elaine: That's what she lived for—the Word of God! She was an aroma of Christ to all those she met: dignitaries, high officials and those lowly forgotten people of the world like me. Aunt Elaine was our encourager… We have lost a prayer warrior, but we are rejoicing because she is free indeed with awesome victory! This marks the end of an era…

NEVER THE SAME

One thing stood out in bold relief to Elaine at the end of her life, 'When you volunteer to go on the mission field you have no idea how far it will reach.'

'I think it goes back to the Word and to her realization of what He had accomplished on her behalf,' commented a friend. 'She was, as the Scriptures call it, "working out her salvation"; not earning it, but *working it out,* letting it live out through her, reaching out. At the core of everything, she never got over the fact that she was saved by grace.'

When asked what had inspired her passion for missions, she responded, 'Seeing what the love of God has done compels me, and realizing that few people know. For years I thought He was just a Judge marking my good days and bad days and maybe I had enough good days to make heaven but it's not that way—He *loves* us! He loves *us!'*

'In fact,' she said, 'nothing in my life can I take credit for.' Christ had become her shining righteousness.

'God is *awesome* to make just one of Elaine's mold,' said Nard, 'and He, through His grace, will bring up another one.' Elaine had said no to her own way, only to find herself on a journey of growing in grace, in holiness, and in resemblance to Christ—in whose glorious likeness she would one day awake. There was no limit to what God would choose do when He was taken at His Word, when His child believed that *His* ways were good.

And jungle rain came to pound on the tin roof in a downpour like the sound of thunder—a torrent of grace drowning out all else beside: grace to a new generation, grace to carry through and hold out and strain upward toward the goal for the prize of the call of God in Christ Jesus.

BIBLIOGRAPHY

Andrew, 2010: Andrew, Brother. *God's Smuggler.* Chosen Books, mass market edition (Grand Rapids, 2010).

Benge, 2000: Benge, Janet and Geoffe. *Cameron Townsend.* YWAM Publishing (Seattle, WA, 2001).

Bonhoeffer, 1954: Bonhoeffer, Dietrich. *Life Together.* HarperCollins (New York, 1954).

Boreham, 2008: Boreham, F.W. *A Packet of Surprises.* John Broadbanks Publishing, second edition (Eureka, CA, 2008).

Burroughs, 2000: Burroughs, Jeremiah. *The Rare Jewel of Christian Contentment.* Banner of Truth Trust, second edition, sixth reprint (Carlisle, PN, 2000).

Byrd, 2013: Byrd, Aimee. *Housewife Theologian.* P&R Publishing (Phillipsburg, NJ, 2013).

Challies, 2013: Challies, Tim. *Prayerlessness is Selfishness.* Challies.com, online publication, accessed January 18, 2017 (published online May 13, 2013).

Chambers, 1963: Chambers, Oswald. *My Utmost for His Highest.* Barbour Publishing, second edition (Uhrichsville, OH, 1963).

Chesterton, 2011: Chesterton, G.K. *In Defense of Sanity.* Ignatius Press (Chicago, IL, 2011).

Cowman, 1925: Cowman, L.E. *Streams in the Desert.* Cowman Publications, twenty-ninth printing (Los Angeles, CA, 1925).

Cowman, 1928: Cowman, Lettie B. *Charles E Cowman: Missionary, Warrior.* The Oriental Missionary Society (Los Angeles, 1928).

Dallimore, 1970: Dallimore, Arnold. *George Whitefield*, Vol. 1. Banner of Truth Trust (Carlisle, PN, 1970).

Edwards, 1991: Edwards, Jonathan. *The Experience that Counts.* Evangelical Press (Grand Rapids, 1991).

Elliot, 1989: Elliot, Elisabeth. *Trusting God in a Twisted World.* Fleming Revel Company (Old Tappan, NJ, 1989).

Flavel, 1963: Flavel, John. *The Mystery of Providence.* Banner of Truth Trust (Carlisle, PN, 1963).

Hefley, 1981: Hefley, James & Marti. *Uncle Cam.* Mott Media, second edition (Milford, MI, 1981).

Hibbard, 2010: Hibbard, Calvin T. *Significant Events in the Life of William Cameron Townsend and the Organizations He Founded.* Wycliffe, unpublished archive, second revision (Waxhaw, NC, 2010).

Howard, 2006: Howard, Thomas. *Narnia and Beyond.* Ignatius Press, second edition (San Francisco, 2006).

Lewis, 1966: Lewis, C.S. *Letters of C.S. Lewis.* Harcort Brace Jovanovich (New York, 1966).

Lewis, 1980: Lewis, C.S. *Weight of Glory.* HarperCollins, second revision (New York, 1980).

Lightbody, 2007: Lightbody, Arthur. Publication released on the death of Elaine Townsend, Wycliffe informal publication (Waxhaw, NC, 2007).

Lucas, 2013: Lucas, Sean Michael. *Contentment in Christ, Tabletalk Magazine.* Ligonier Ministries (Sanford, FL, Oct. 2013).

Mains, 1997: Mains, Karen Burton. *Open Heart, Open Home.* InterVarsity Press, second revision (Downers Grove, IL, 1997).

Mathis, 2012: Mathis, David. *Hospitality and the Great Commission.* Desiring God, online publication, accessed January 18, 2017 (published online October 2, 2012).

Mathis, 2016: Mathis, David. *Joy Is Not Optional.* DesiringGod, online publication, accessed September 18, 2018 (published online February 3, 2016).

Metaxas, 2010: Metaxas, Eric. *Bonhoeffer.* Thomas Nelson (Nashville, 2010).

Murray, 1982: Murray, Andrew. *Humility.* Whitaker House (Kensington, PA, 1982).

Parnell, 2014: Parnell, Jonathan. *Seven Details to See in Your Past.* Desiring God, online publication, accessed January 18, 2017 (published online January 7, 2014).

Piper, 1995: Piper, John. *A Challenge to Women.* Desiring God, online publication, accessed January 18, 2017 (published online January 1, 1995).

Piper, 2008: Piper, John. *Risk is Right.* Crossway (Wheaton, IL, 2008).

Piper, 2008: Piper, John. *The Ultimate Meaning of True Womanhood.* Message at the True Womanhood Conference, accessed through Desiring God online (Chicago, IL, 2008).

Rockness, 2003: Rockness, Miriam Huffman. *A Passion for the Impossible.* Discovery House Publishers, second edition (Grand Rapids, 2003).

Sayers, 2004: Sayers, Dorothy. *Letters to a Diminished Church.* Thomas Nelson (Nashville, 2004).

Schaeffer, 1975: Schaeffer, Edith. *What is a Family?* Raven's Ridge Books (Grand Rapids, 1975).

Segal, 2013: Segal, Marshall. *Single, Satisfied, and Sent.* Desiring God, online publication, accessed January 18, 2017 (published online March 13, 2013).

Spurgeon, 2003: Spurgeon, Charles. *Morning and Evening.* Crossway (Wheaton, IL, 2003).

Stewart, 2013: Stewart, Catherine J. ed. *Letters to Pastors' Wives.* P&R Publishing (Phillipsburg, NJ, 2013).

Sumpter, 2014: Sumpter, Toby. *Blessings Too Big.* Desiring God, online publication, accessed January 18, 2017 (published online February 1, 2014).

Taylor, 1955: Taylor, Howard. *Hudson Taylor's Spiritual Secret.* Moody Press (Chicago, IL, 1955).

Wagner: 2012: Wagner, Kimberly. *Fierce Women.* Moody Publishers, Kindle Edition (2012).

Wilkins, 2002. Wilkins, Steve. *Face to Face.* Canon Press (Moscow, ID, 2002).

Zacharias, 2005: Zacharias, Ravi. *Walking from East to West.* Zondervan (Grand Rapids, MI, 2010).

Christian Focus Publications

Our mission statement –

STAYING FAITHFUL

In dependence upon God we seek to impact the world through literature faithful to His infallible Word, the Bible. Our aim is to ensure that the Lord Jesus Christ is presented as the only hope to obtain forgiveness of sin, live a useful life and look forward to heaven with Him.

Our Books are published in four imprints:

CHRISTIAN FOCUS

popular works including biographies, commentaries, basic doctrine and Christian living.

CHRISTIAN HERITAGE

books representing some of the best material from the rich heritage of the church.

MENTOR

books written at a level suitable for Bible College and seminary students, pastors, and other serious readers. The imprint includes commentaries, doctrinal studies, examination of current issues and church history.

CF4•K

children's books for quality Bible teaching and for all age groups: Sunday school curriculum, puzzle and activity books; personal and family devotional titles, biographies and inspirational stories – Because you are never too young to know Jesus!

Christian Focus Publications Ltd,
Geanies House, Fearn, Ross-shire,
IV20 1TW, Scotland, United Kingdom.
www.christianfocus.com